For LANDLORD'S, TENAN
SOLICITORS BARRI
anyone intereste
law relating to Dil<

CW01501647

The Dilapidations Handbook

- An invaluable reference book giving practical guidance

- Summaries of 201 cases on 377 pages indexed both alphabetically <u>AND</u> by subject

- Reports dealing with many repairing covenants

- Appendix of relevant statutes

- Sample Schedule of Dilapidations and section 146 notice

- How to prepare for a Court hearing

No. 11 IN THE NEED TO KNOW SERIES

The Dilapidations Handbook

Written by

Victor H Vegoda FRICS IRRV FBEng PEng MEWI

Edited by

Richard Clegg BA Cantab of Grays Inn, Barrister

Number 11
in the "Need to Know" Series

Copies of Acts of Parliament and Explanatory notes reproduced by the kind permission of Her Majesty's Stationery Office

Grateful thanks to Estates Gazette and to The Incorporated Council of Law Reporting for England and Wales for permission to reproduce their law reports

Published in February 2002

ISBN 1 898383 70 7

Table of Contents

WARNING

Be warned that neither the writer, editor, publishers nor anyone associated with this book will accept responsibility for problems arising from its use – even if we are wrong[1].

Other Titles in the "Need to Know" Series:-

Practical Ways to Recover Your Debts
A Practical Guide to Residential Surveys
Schedules of Dilapidations
Heave Demolition and Reconstruction
Draft Your Own Terms of Engagement
Condam
– Draft Your Own Safety Plan
Landlord & Tenant Covenants Act, 1995
An Introduction to the Party Wall etc Act 1996
Contract (Rights of Third Parties) Act 1999
Liability of the Negligent Surveyor

Coming shortly:

Right of Access to Neighbouring Land Act, 1994

---

[1] Especially if we are wrong.

CHAPTER 1

START HERE

This book is intended as an introduction to dilapidations for landlords, tenants and those concerned with the land. If it explains something you already know, please forgive me. It is the policy of 'The Need to Know' series to try not to leave any interested reader behind.

I do hope that this book will give you a grounding but please extend your knowledge by consulting other works where appropriate.

Unless you are a litigant, in which case you have my deep sympathy, dilapidations is a fascinating and rewarding area in which to work. It taxes your brain, your stamina and occasionally your patience.

There are sections aimed at landlords: tenants: and at surveyors. If you are a landlord, please read the section for tenants because you might find something useful and conversely tenants should read the landlord's section. Surveyors should read everything, particularly the small print.

I have included a sample notice; a sample schedule and a comments on the schedule and arguments for and against. Negotiated settlements are desirable but not always possible.

Also included are extracts from statutes for easy reference, and summaries of many of the landmark cases, indexed both by name and subject. These are present to give a grounding and to help you find cases which may be similar to the particular circumstances of the matter with which you are dealing.

However, if you have a dispute resting on the facts of a particular case, you are strongly advised to obtain a full report or transcript and to read and understand it. Above all, don't be your own lawyer. A man who acts for himself has a fool for a client. Lawyers are gifted at making distinctions between cases and no case is exactly like the one before. Take advice where warranted. Be warned that neither the writer, editor, publishers nor anyone associated with this book will accept responsibility for problems arising from its use – even if we are wrong[2].

Jurisdiction

This book deals with dilapidations law as practised in England and Wales. It does not attempt to cover the law as practised in Scotland or Northern Ireland.

Read the Lease

The starting point when dealing with any Schedule of Dilapidations is the lease and any subsequent licences or agreements. It or they will establish the obligations placed upon the landlord and tenant. A Schedule of Dilapidations is a list of breaches of covenant and the importance of reading the lease and summarising the relevant covenants cannot be over emphasised.

---

[2] Especially if we are wrong.

CHAPTER 2

FOR THE LANDLORD

Factors dictating lessees obligations

You want to let your empty building. Regardless of the condition the building is in, you will wish to maximise the rent you receive and ensure that the repairing and insuring covenants imposed on the tenant are as comprehensive as possible. What you achieve will be dictated by the market; the demand for premises like yours and the available supply.

If there is a glut, you may have to accept a lower rent or assume some of the repairing obligations. Your tenant may insist upon a schedule of condition and covenants which do not require him to hand back the premises in a better condition than when he took them. If he is the only tenant in sight and there are acres of empty space from which to choose, you may have no option but to accept these terms. You may be delighted to get any rent, just to avoid the burden of the rates which an occupying tenant will assume

What is a Schedule of Dilapidations?

My dictionary defines a "Schedule", among other things as "a list of tasks to be performed, especially within a set period". "Dilapidation" is defined as "the state of disrepair of premises due to neglect" and "the extent of repairs necessary to such premises". Put the two together and you have "a list of tasks necessary to bring premises into a state of repair".

It is important to note that the essential purpose of a schedule is to identify the <u>defects</u>, not the remedial work required, (which involves questions of legal standard of repair), although the schedule can of course, identify both.

Liability to make good the wants of repairs will depend upon the wording of the lease. In most cases, it is the tenant who takes on liability for repairs, particularly where the premises are self contained. However, there are cases where the landlord is liable. Such cases usually, though not always, concern buildings in multiple occupation. Just as a landlord may give notice to a tenant of a breach of covenant, so may a tenant serve a Schedule of Dilapidations on his landlord, if he fails to repair. In the Appeal court case of Wallace –v- Manchester City Council[3], the tenant was awarded damages for "discomfort and inconvenience" by a County Court judge and the decision was upheld upon appeal. In Hallise –v- Petmoor Developments Ltd.[4] the landlord was also held liable for repairs.

Lack of clarity and particularity in a schedule of dilapidations has resulted in the court deciding the schedule was bad. However the inclusion of items which are not properly the tenant's liability (or the landlord's in appropriate cases) does not in itself render the schedule bad. Those parts for which the lease does not provide will be unenforceable.

Using a Schedule as a lever

Some landlords use schedules of dilapidations as levers in rent review negotiations in order to turn the rack another notch. They offer to waive the schedule for the present, if the tenant agrees the enhanced rent. Tenants may succumb to this blackmail and thus put off the evil hour. They often do not care if the premises they occupy fall into ruin as long as they can trade, and some landlords are equally untroubled by lack of repair, just as long as they receive

---

[3] Wallace –v- Manchester City Council [1998] EGCS 114
[4] Hallise –v- Petmoor Developments Ltd. ChD The Times 7th November 2000

their rent. This is not the case with the large landed estates who normally strenuously enforce repairing covenants.

I have a friend who used to buy fag end leases and sublet in suites at a profit rent. He would bodge the dilapidations whilst he still had possession because it is difficult for a landlord to argue about the quality of work a tenant has carried out.

One of his buildings had roof spread and he jacked up the roof with car jacks. He then plastered over the loft access and painted the ceiling to remove all traces of the opening. So far as I am aware, the roof and car jacks are still there. The roof looked sound the last time I drove past[5].

Landlord cannot guess at repairs

The landlord cannot guess at repairs. He has to make clear what must be done and if he cannot inspect, he will be unable to see and list a defect. He can use general terms like "Leave all roofs weather tight" but if he cannot inspect and there are no signs of penetration, how will he know whether or not the roofs are in repair?

Difficulty with access

Tenants often have alarms wires or security grilles on windows making it impossible to lean out to look. If there is no other access as is sometimes the case, the landlord's surveyor may find himself in difficulties I have never mastered levitation. I have used a cherry picker on occasion, which is an acceptable substitute. Fork lift trucks can also be useful for gaining access though doubts have been expressed about their safety and the legality of this means of access.

---

[5] Despite the fact that this took place about 40 years ago. They don't make them like they used to.

I once used a fork lift truck to lift a factory drain cover. The truck lifted off its back wheels and then fell back as the 25mm wide forged "T" drain key was torn apart. Fortunately no one was in the way. They would have been killed.

Schedule of Condition

If you are forced to accept a schedule of condition whereby the tenant does not have to hand back your premises in better condition than when he took them, try to be as precise as possible in the drafting. If there are 59 damaged bricks on the east elevations and he hands it back with 211 damaged bricks, it may be cheaper for him to rebuild the wall than to cut out and replace 152 newly damaged bricks, even if he can identify which they are. Take photographs. Mark the areas of disrepair on an accurate plan with positions and quantities of damage.

If the roof is in poor condition and the tenant has taken the premises subject to a schedule of condition, the roof will not stop deteriorating and remain frozen in the condition it was when first let. It will probably suffer further deterioration and may even leak. If water is coming in and the landlord has not covenanted to do external repairs, regardless of the schedule of condition, the tenant will have to repair the roof. He may be able to patch it for a time but he cannot put it into exactly the condition in which it was described on the schedule of condition. If it was in disrepair but not leaking at the outset and is now leaking close to the end of the lease, the tenant will have to repair it.

Full Repairing and insuring leases

Full repairing and insuring leases are the standard form of lease in this country. They came about because institutions which invest in Property find it convenient to have clear rents and to be able to project their income with some degree of accuracy. This is the only country (I am told) in which they are common.

Personal Guarantees

Whenever possible, a landlord will require personal guarantees from the directors of any limited company taking a lease. This is to protect against the limited company building up arrears, failing to comply with lease covenants and then going into liquidation to avoid obligations[6].

Privity of contract

For leases granted before 1st January 1996, the original tenant is responsible throughout the term of the lease, for the defaults and breaches of covenant of his successors in title, even after he has assigned it to a third party. This is an extremely onerous obligation for a tenant and for the personal guarantors of a lease.

In my first job I recall managing a portfolio of mixed commercial properties, one of which was situated in a seedy suburb of Birmingham. There was one shop let to a firm known as K L Television Services Limited who were keen to assign their lease because the trading position had deteriorated.

K. L. Television Services Ltd. were a good and honorable tenant and came up with a number of potential assignees all of whom appeared to be weak and unacceptable judging by their references. This was not surprising because the trading position had deteriorated over the years and was likely to be attractive only to weak tenants.

Eventually they produced another potential tenant; a halal butcher; who also appeared weak but who had acceptable

---

[6] Or doing a hive down, which is much the same thing.

references. Reluctantly the landlord, Canas Properties Ltd. accepted the assignee. Time passed and the rent got into arrears. An inspection showed that the assignees had done a moonlight flit and disappeared leaving behind a tray filled with something described by the first person on the scene as a malodorous green furry camel hump.

A writ claiming possession was issued but the writ was not properly served upon the butcher. Then I remembered privity of contract and thought of the original tenant. Fortunately, since the writ claiming possession had not been properly served, the lease had not yet been determined and Canas were able to recover the rent arrears from K L Television Services Limited.

The Landlord and Tenant (Covenants) Act 1995

The Landlord and Tenant (Covenants) Act 1995 has changed the law for leases granted on or after 1st of January 1996 (unless pursuant to an agreement or order made before that date).

Assignments by Tenant

By section 5(2), where a tenant assigns the whole of his lease, he is released from the tenant covenants as from the assignment.

Assignments by Landlord

So far as the landlord is concerned, upon the assignment of the reversion, he is also released from his covenants by section 6, provided that he has served the appropriate notice on the tenant in accordance with section 8, before or within 4 weeks of the assignment *and* that the tenant does not object. Even if the tenant does object, the court can make a declaration that it is reasonable for the landlord to be released (section 8(2)(b)).

Schedules of Dilapidations are not a one way street

If you are a landlord who fails to carry out his repairing obligations under the terms of a lease, (the premises are not let on full repairing and insuring terms) your tenant can serve you with a repairs schedule, though it will not be under section 146 of the Law of Property Act, 1925. It will be for breach of the covenant to repair or breach of covenant for quiet enjoyment. Such covenants are often implied into the lease by statute, even where there is no express provision in the lease itself.

Just because the landlord is not liable for repairs, it does not follow automatically that the tenant is liable. Conversely, if the Tenant is not liable, the landlord may also be free from obligation to repair. Remember the homily. Check the lease.

CHAPTER 3

FOR THE TENANT

Lease terms

You need premises to carry on your business and naturally wish to obtain the best value you can get. You want the lowest rent, the lightest possible repairing and insuring obligations and if possible, an all inclusive rent. Whether you are able to achieve this will depend upon the market and whether tenants or letting space are in short supply.

Have the building surveyed before taking a lease

Having tested the market, you may have found premises which appear to be suitable. Do not rush. You could be taking on a repairing burden equivalent to several years rent. Have the building surveyed to establish the state of repair and the likely cost of putting and keeping it in repair. If it is really bad you can look elsewhere. You may be able to negotiate a rent free period or agree to a schedule of condition.

Schedule of Condition

If you are able to rent premises subject to a schedule of condition, as a tenant it is in your interests to refer to damage in general rather than specific terms. If, for example, the east elevation has a number of frost damaged bricks, it is better for you if the schedule says, "There are frost damaged bricks" rather than "There are 97 frost damaged bricks". If at the end of your lease there are now 343 frost damaged bricks, which ones do you repair and will it be cheaper for you to take down and rebuild?

Chapter 3 – For the Tenant

Neither landlord nor tenant liable to repair

If you take premises with a faulty rainwater disposal system which is noted on the schedule and water penetration starts to occur, and dry or wet rot becomes established, what are you to do? Let us assume that the landlord is not liable for repair. Your business will suffer if water gets in and damages your stock or equipment and there is no mention of dry rot on the schedule of condition, even if it does flow from the poor state in which you took the premises. You will have to repair, because there is an implied obligation on a tenant to use the premises in a tenant like manner. That means that regardless of whose obligation it is, if a slate slips from the roof, the tenant must replace it.

Landlord fails to repair

If the lack of repair is damaging your business or threatening your staff, you may be forced to do the repair. If it is the obligation of the landlord and he is refusing to honour his obligation, then you must seek recompense from him to recover the cost.

Rent to be paid "without deduction"

Before deducting the cost you have incurred carrying out the landlord's obligation to repair, from your rent, check the lease. Some leases have clauses requiring rent to be paid "without deduction" even if the tenant has a valid claim against the landlord. In such a case, the tenant must pursue his landlord for the cost as a separate issue

Statutory obligations

If you employ staff, you will be required under the Health and Safety at Work Act 1974 and other legislation, to maintain certain minimum working conditions. If your secretary injures herself by falling through the floor which is riddled with dry rot because you failed to repair a rainwater pipe, it will not assist you to argue in defence that neither you nor the landlord were responsible to repair.

Full Repairing and insuring leases

Full repairing and Insuring leases are the standard. Anything less is a bonus. Landlords like to have clear rents and to be able to avoid the uncertainty of the cost of maintaining and repairing their buildings, by passing the obligation to their tenants. There is some logic in the tenant being responsible for repairs. He is the one who has most to do with the building and the landlord may be several hundred miles away. Nevertheless, landlords are wise to periodically inspect their properties.

There is some pressure to move away from fully repairing and insuring leases but F.R. & I. leases are still the standard.

What is a schedule of dilapidations?

A schedule of dilapidations is a list of defects required to be remedied in order to bring the building into the state of repair required by the lease. It is not a specification. By reading the landlord's schedule, you must be able to understand what breaches of the repairing covenants are alleged.

Lack of clarity and particularity in a schedule

Lack of clarity and particularity in a schedule of dilapidations has resulted in the court deciding the schedule was bad. The inclusion of items which are not properly the tenant's liability (or the landlord's in appropriate cases) ought not in itself render the whole schedule bad. The landlord will not be able to enforce those parts for which the lease does not provide. If the good parts are clear and are the tenant's liability under the terms of the lease, they are enforceable.

Schedules used as levers

Some landlords use schedules of dilapidations as levers in rent review negotiations.

I once found myself in the High Court before a master with a lady who was representing herself in an application by the landlord. I was there because she had asked to attend in a telephone call the previous day and I thought I might get an instruction.

Counsel for the landlord addressed the Learned Master at length. Prefacing each sentence with "Master", he recounted a sorry tale of broken promises to do the repairs in the schedule. Finally, my client came to address the master and having spoken at length, said, "Master, I am going hell for leather to do the repairs." The master held up a hand to stop her. "Madam" he said. "At the rate you are going you will never get to hell." He then made an order against her.

Will she get to hell?

I mention this for two reasons. Firstly to opine that only time will tell if the Learned Master is right[7].

Establish a timetable for repairs

Secondly, to make the point that it is unwise to allow your premises to fall into disrepair, but if you do find they are in disrepair, you would be well advised to do something about

---

[7] She and her partner owned a great deal of very valuable property and I was informed by someone who knew them both well that each was waiting for the other to die so as to inherit. I cannot vouch for the truth of that.

it. If a schedule is served, agree a time scale for repairs with your landlord for the items for which you are liable, and stick to it. If the landlord will not agree a time scale, put forward what you think is reasonable. Provided the court thinks your proposals are reasonable it is unlikely to forfeit your lease.

Liability if Landlord in possession does repairs
Section 18 the Landlord and Tenant Act, 1927

If you are out of possession and the landlord enters and does repairs, the court is likely to find the cost of repairs to be equal to or less than the loss of reversionary value and you will have to pay:-

o   the cost of repairs incurred,

o   fees for administering of the works,

o   solicitors and surveyors fees for preparation and service of the schedule, if they are reserved in the lease,

o   rent during the time repairs are carried out.

Liability will not exceed the lesser of:-

o   the cost of the works; or

o   the loss of value to the landlord's reversion.

See section 18 the Landlord and Tenant Act, 1927.

If the tenant can prove that on the termination of the tenancy the landlord intends to demolish the building or so alter it that the benefit of any works done under the schedule will be lost, no liability will arise. Section 18 the Landlord and Tenant Act, 1927. The burden of proof is on the tenant.

Chapter 3 – For the Tenant

Privity of Contract

A landlord will wish to ensure that his tenant is likely to continue trading and be able to pay the rent and outgoings. If the tenant is a limited company, it is usual to require personal guarantees from the company's director(s). This is to safeguard the landlord if the company goes into liquidation. It is not in the tenant's directors' interest to give personal guarantees but it may be impossible to find premises on any other terms.

For leases granted before 1st January 1996 (or pursuant to an agreement or court order made before that date) the original lessee and guarantors of a lease are responsible for the liabilities of that lease throughout the term. Assignees are only liable for the period during which they are the tenant, unless they have agreed otherwise. Until 1996 it was therefore quite risky to be the first signatory to a lease.

The position for leases made after the 1st January 1996 (unless pursuant to an agreement or court order made before that date) is that the tenant (and hence the guarantor) is released from the tenant covenants upon assignment of the whole of the lease. Section 5 of the Landlord and Tenant (Covenants) Act 1995.

Effect of rent reviews

Bear in mind that most leases not only have repairing obligations but also obligations to pay rent which is regularly reviewed. You could have entered into a 21 year lease ten years ago. The financial climate may have changed and your assignee may have gone to the wall. The landlord comes looking for you and the rent is now ten times the rent you agreed when you signed the lease, because of upward only rent reviews. Arrears may have accrued. If you are the original tenant of a lease granted before 1st January 1996 (or pursuant to an agreement or court order made before that date), or the guarantor of such a tenant you will be likely to be liable for arrears.

Your only hope is to convince the landlord you are so impoverished that you are not worth powder and shot.

Schedules of Dilapidations are not a one way street

If you rent premises where your landlord is liable to carry out repairs and he fails to do so, you can serve him with a repairs schedule though it will not be under section 146 of the Law of Property Act 1925. It will be for breach of the covenant to repair or breach of the covenant for quiet enjoyment. It may be for a breach of statutory obligations in the case of statutory tenancies.

Because you are not liable for a particular repair under the terms of the lease, it does not necessarily follow that the landlord is liable. Check the lease or the appropriate statute.

Some years ago, I was instructed by two ladies who lived in a large detached house as statutory tenants. They were liable for internal repairs and the inside of the house was beautifully maintained. Not so the outside which was the landlord's responsibility.

Their landlord died and a niece inherited. Under the mistaken belief that she could winkle the tenants out, she kept sending potential purchasers to view. After she was served with a repairs notice she soon changed her tune and the two ladies managed to agree a very advantageous price for the freehold of the house they occupied.

CHAPTER 4

FOR THE SURVEYOR

Whether you are acting for landlord or for tenant, before embarking on any instruction you must do the following:-

Confirm your instructions in writing

Write to your client setting out the terms and the scope of what you intend to do and the basis of your remuneration. Particularly where the landlord clients expect the tenant to pay your fees, you must make it quite clear that regardless of the position between him and his tenant, you will look to him for your fees. If you are prepared to allow him time to pay, by all means say so. If you expect payment immediately, or upon certain occurrences you must also state what these are.

Obtain all the documents and read them

Make sure that you have all the documents in the case. If the client sends you the documents in response to request in your letter confirming instructions, this, in itself, is a tacit confirmation of instructions unless he raises some point concerning the terms you have quoted.

You will need a copy of:-

o   the actual lease which was signed:

o   any licences which have been granted:

o   copies of any relevant correspondence between the landlord and the tenant:

- o if you are acting for the tenant a copy of the schedule which has been served and the notice with which it was served.

It is very easy to make mistakes without the right documents, so be warned by me. I was instructed to prepare a Schedule of Dilapidations for a building in Kent. I was given a written instruction, advised of the location and the name of the occupying tenant, and told it was a fully repairing and insuring lease, a copy of which would follow later.

Street numbers were few and far between but I eventually located the property which was occupied by a multiple firm of estate agents. I scrutinized, measured and photographed it for the best part of a day and then prepared a detailed, priced Schedule of Dilapidations which I duly sent to my client. He had a good laugh and told me I had inspected the wrong building.

The correct building was a Grade I* listed building occupied by the same firm of estate agents. I reviewed the basement and the ground floor which were used by the estate agents[8]. They had sub-let the upper flat to a reporter on the local rag. He kindly allowed me access and followed me around, chatting all the while.

We came to a fine timbered living room with a fire place with Gothic lettering painted on the massive oak mantel beam, calling down a curse on the head of anyone who changed "this comfortable room". He then mentioned the ghost of a lady in red who occupied the attic. I continued my inspection with my "doggie". He was behind me on the stairs when I opened the attic door. "Oh, I do beg your pardon." I said, looking in; "Please excuse me." I turned round to my companion, expecting him to laugh, but he

---

[8] A national chain.

was aghast. He had gone rigid, turned the colour of paste and his hair virtually stood on end.

Statutory Consents

Ensure by inquiry with the local authority that if any alterations have been carried out which required statutory consent(s) that such consent(s) were obtained and a final inspection carried out and the works approved.

Means of Escape and other Fire Regulations

Check to see if any statutory notices are outstanding.

Bear in mind any special circumstances which may give rise for the need of:-

- o   a fire certificate;
- o   requirements for additional fire escape(s);
- o   Smoke and fire detectors;
- o   audible alarms; emergency lighting;
- o   call points;
- o   smoke lobbies;
- o   automatic smoke vents
- o   fire protection to doors, ceilings and or structural members;
- o   Vision panels in doors;
- o   Fire protection to escape routes;
- o   Fire protection to gas and electric meters and fuses;
- o   Fire protection to surface wiring;
- o   Automatic smoke vents;
- o   special requirements caused by the processes carried on or the materials stored at the premises;
- o   special requirements caused the numbers of staff and/or members of the public likely to be within the premises at any time;
- o   Special requirements because of the height of the premises;

o   Special requirements for old age homes, hostels hotels, rooming houses. etc.

o   Any special requirements peculiar to that particular property or use.

By all means pick the brains of local officials charged with enforcing fire regulations.

Bear in mind that if the premises are vacated, the position may be completely changed because if it is empty, compliance with fire safety and other public health provisions become much easier.   Unless a standard is specified in the lease you may have difficulty enforcing a standard on empty premises or explaining to a clever barrister why you wish to enforce high standards on an empty building.

Check the notice is valid

If you are acting for a tenant, check the notice against the lease, because if there is a significant discrepancy it may invalidate the schedule. It is more likely however, that only the bad part will be unenforceable.

Common errors are:-

o   requiring repairs under covenants not actually found in the lease. If the good parts can be identified, then those will most likely be enforceable if the tenant is liable under the lease and the defect actually exists.

or

o   the land is not an agricultural holding;

o   there are more than three years of the lease unexpired of an original term of seven years or more;

o   the notice does not contain a statement required by section 1(4) of the Leasehold Property (Repairs) Act, 1938;

o   The notice will be invalid but the landlord can serve another one.

If there is a glaring error, a consultation with the client's solicitors is worth while. It is sometimes wise to keep one's Powder dry.

CHAPTER 5

LANDLORDS AND TENANTS FIXTURES & FITTINGS

Fixtures and Fittings

Trade fixtures, ornamental and domestic fixtures, and agricultural fixtures are three categories of fixtures installed by the tenant which the tenant may usually remove at the expiration of the lease, provided that they have not become landlord's fixtures or an integral part of the demised land. He must make good any damage caused. Landlord's fixtures and fittings are such things as heating plant affixed to the premises, though not always so. In industrial units, such plant may belong to the tenant.

If a tenant put lighting in your factory at the start of a lease, unless the lease says otherwise he may remove it at the end of the term, making good any damage. The test of whether a fixture is the landlord's or the tenant's is, in essence, the degree of annexation to the property. How firmly is it fixed? Is it set in concrete? The answers are not always clear cut.

Compensation for Tenant's improvements on termination of the lease

The rules relating to compensation for tenants improvements are laid down in Part 1 of the Landlord and Tenant Act, 1927 as amended by the Landlord and Tenant Act, 1954.

Compensation limited to business premises

Section 17(1) of the Landlord and Tenant Act, 1927 provides that Part I of the Act only applies to premises used wholly or in part for trade or business purposes, including professional purposes. Agricultural holdings and most service tenancies are excluded.

Section 17(4) of the Landlord and Tenant Act, 1927 limits compensation to only those parts used for business purposes.

What are "improvements"?

"Improvements" are not defined in the Landlord and Tenant Act, 1927 but section 1(1) requires that the improvement must add to the letting value of the holding. Trade fixtures and items the tenant may remove at the end of his tenancy do not qualify for compensation under this Act.

However, regardless of the provisions for compensation for improvements, if the tenant's fixtures do make the premises more attractive for a future tenant, there is no reason why a landlord and tenant cannot reach agreement for one to purchase them from the other at the termination of the lease.

Often the fixtures are only valuable because they are where they are. If for example, a tenant has put a heating system into a warehouse, and the system is not so attached as to become a landlord's fixture. It may well be in both party's interest to reach an agreement. If the heating system is removed, its second hand value may not cover the cost of removal. Conversely, the cost to the landlord of installing heating may be large and the rental value with heating may be improved.

Safes are definitely not an advantage when left in premises. The cost of removing them can vastly exceed their value. It usually exceeds the value of their contents as well. I have only once found valuables in a safe left behind by a tenant. It was a vast quantity of blank airline tickets. The receiver of the erstwhile owner quickly claimed them. I have known cases where it was cheaper to excavate the basement and bury the safe, than to remove it[9].

Non qualifying improvements

Those made before 25th March, 1928.

Those made by a tenant or his predecessor in title under a contractual obligation for valuable consideration, which includes work done under a building lease. See section 2(1).

Improvements carried out before 1st October 1954 and within three years of the end of the lease.

Work done before 1st October 1954 in pursuance of a statutory obligation.

Qualifying improvements

Improvements carried out after 25th March 1928.

Where improvements are carried out on or after 1st October 1954 improvements carried out at any point before the end of the lease will qualify.

Work done on or after 1st October 1954 in pursuance of a statutory obligation.

Conditions for Qualification for compensation for tenant's improvements

---

[9] Nowadays, this could have party wall implications. One wonders what future archaeologists will make of it.

Tenant's Notice

Section 3(1) Landlord and Tenant Act, 1927

Before making improvements, the tenant must serve notice on the landlord of his intention to do so. Notice must be in writing and be accompanied by a plan and specification, but no form is laid down. If there are superior landlords above the immediate landlord, it or they are entitled to copies of the notice.

Objection
Section 3(1) Landlord and Tenant Act, 1927

The landlord has three months to respond in writing serving notice of objection.

No response within three months
Section 3(4) Landlord and Tenant Act, 1927

If no objection is received the tenant may proceed but he must proceed in accordance with his plan and specification.

Landlord's objection in writing within three months
Section 63 Landlord and Tenant Act 1954

Until the 1st of July, 1991 lessees of premises with a rateable value of less than £5,000 had to apply to the county court with those of £5,000 or more rateable value applying to the Chancery Division of the High Court. Now jurisdiction is unlimited.

Factors the court will take into account

- Whether the improvements will add to the letting value at the termination of the tenancy.

o   Whether the improvements are reasonable and suitable to the character of the holding. If the landlord can demonstrate that the proposed improvement will injure or damage the amenity or convenience of the neighbourhood it will not be suitable.

o   If the proposed improvement will injure the value of any other property belonging to the landlord or his superior(s) in title.

The court has the power to modify plans and to set time limits for completion under section 3(1).

The court finds for the tenant.
The landlord elects to do the works

The landlord may offer to execute the improvements himself for an enhanced rent which reasonably reflects the value of the improvements. Section 3(1). The court can then only give a certificate to the tenant if the landlord fails to do the works.

If the court finds for the tenant and the landlord does not elect to do the works

On completion of the improvements the tenant can require the landlord to give him a certificate. There is no set form for this request. If the landlord does not do so within a month the court is empowered to do so. Section 3(6)

Claims for Compensation for tenant's improvements

They must be made within three months of the notice to quit or to terminate.

They must be made no more than six months nor less than three months before the termination of a tenancy due to expire by effluxion of time.

They must be made within three months of the effective date of an order for possession in forfeiture proceedings or within three months of the date of peaceable re-entry.

These time limits cannot be extended or changed.

If the tenant continues to occupy the premises by obtaining a new tenancy under the 1954 Landlord and Tenant Act or for any other reason, no compensation is payable.

It does not become payable until he gives up possession of the premises and then only if he serves the correct notices within the strict time limits set out above.

Amount of compensation payable

Under section 1(1) of the Landlord and Tenant Act, 1927 compensation the must not exceed:-

(a) the net additional value of the holding as a whole, which may be determined to be the direct result of the improvements; or

(b) the reasonable cost of carrying out the improvement at the termination of the tenancy subject to a deduction of the cost of putting the works constituting the improvements into a reasonable state of repair, in so far as this is not covered by the tenant's repairing covenants.

If the landlord intends to alter or demolish the premises or to use them in a different way after the termination of the tenancy, this may reduce or eliminate the value of the improvements and the compensation payable. Section 1(2). If the court decided that no compensation or reduced compensation is payable to the tenant, it may at the same time fix a time within which the landlord must put his intentions into effect.

If he fails to do so within the time stipulated by the court, the court may permit a further application for compensation by the tenant. If the tenant has received valuable consideration from the landlord for the improvements, the court will take this into account in deciding whether compensation is payable and if so how much. Section 2(3)

CHAPTER 6

PREPARING A SCHEDULE OF DILAPIDATIONS

Practical knowledge of building construction assumed

It is assumed that you have a structural knowledge and are able to inspect a building and note defects. If this is not the case then you would benefit from our video and construction book "A Practical Guide to Residential Surveys" which is also useful for commercial buildings, though it does not cover some elements. Lifts and air conditioning, for example.

Plan and dimensions

It is extremely helpful to have a plan of the building with dimensions. This enables pricing to be done accurately in the event of any defect being found. If no plan is available it is useful to measure up and do a drawing. The drawing is also helpful for identifying areas so that the schedule can be clearly understood. When taking dimensions do not forget to take ceiling heights, and eaves and ridge heights in factories. Also take the dimensions of anything else where the price of repairs will have to be calculated by quantity. For example, if there are broken Georgian wired glass panes make sure you have their dimensions so that you can cost them accurately. Damaged floor or wall tiles should be measured or counted. And so on.

Rule for the number of measurements taken

There is a rule for the number of measurements taken, which is:-

     o   The number of measurements taken is equal to the taken number of measurements needed, less one or more.

or

     o   The number of measurements taken < the number of measurements needed.

Identification of parts

Many surveyors like to refer to "left" and "right" in their preamble and state that these terms are used facing the property; or some other variation on the theme.

Each must do as he thinks fit but I find this very confusing when I am checking a schedule prepared by another surveyor. I have to establish my orientation before I know where to look.

I prefer to refer to compass points which are likely to remain the same during my lifetime, though I am told that they reverse every few million years. A compass rose is usually included on the plan attached to my schedules.

For clarity, name or number rooms on your plan. If there are a number of roofs, do a plan so that they can be clearly identified. The same will apply for drain inspection chambers, where appropriate or any other feature which may not otherwise be pinpointed with certainty.

Whatever system you adopt, make sure that it is clear.

Have clear calculations for pricing

When preparing your schedule it is useful to do it in tabular form. The defect should be on the left and the pricing quantities and calculation as to value developed to the right

It is helpful to number each item for quick reference.

Column heading could read:-

- o Line Number – for quick reference.

- o Item number.

- o Description – recording and reciting the details of the part inspected.

- o Breach of clause number – some surveyors do not credit the recipient and the court with the ability to decide which clause applies to each defect and to avoid doubt, they list the clauses breached.

- o Breach complained of.

- o Remedy required. This is not essential for the schedule but you have to take a view as to the remedy required if you are going to value the cost of remedial measures.

Then come the calculations of cost. Continuing across the sheet, headings will read:-

- o Quantity

- o Unit

- o Price per unit

- o Total cost

I use a spreadsheet so that the calculations can be performed automatically and totalled automatically with any changes immediately reflecting in the bottom line. The layout is professional and clear and makes argument by an opposing surveyor more difficult. Judges like this form of presentation because they can understand the build up of a price.

Use of published pricing schedules

It is useful to refer to pricing books. Spons, Laxtons, Griffiths, and Wessex are some of the better known pricing books available and each person has their own preferences. Depending upon the building, some will be better than others for the purpose.

When using a pricing book I often add another column giving a reference as to where my price came from. Prices do not have to come from a pricing book and your own experience of cost is of value when giving evidence. If you are being cross examined on a schedule of costs, the counsel facing you will wish to destroy your credibility by making you appear inept. If you have to hand chapter and verse and can extract a photocopy of the page with the item highlighted, you will improve your credibility as a witness.

Just because there is a price in a book does not mean that it must be adopted if in your experience it is out of step with the real World. However, do not succumb to the temptation to over egg the pudding. Be honest but conservative in your pricing.

Leasehold Property(Repairs) Act, 1938

After you have prepared and priced the schedule, you may wish to pass it to your client's solicitors for service on the tenant.

If the lease has:-

- o three years or more to run of an original term of seven years or more;   and

- o the demised premises are not part of an agricultural holding,

Do not forget to advise the solicitor to serve a notice with the schedule under the Leasehold Property (Repairs) Act, 1938. Surprisingly, not all solicitors will remember to serve such a notice without being reminded to do so and then the notice will be invalid.

To be valid under this Act, the notice must be in characters no less legible than those in the main notice, advising the tenants of his rights to claim protection under the Act and telling him how and where to serve the counter notice claiming the protection of the Act

Where a tenant claims protection of the Leasehold Property (Repairs) Act, 1938 by serving a counter notice on the landlord within 28 days of the date of service, the landlord needs leave of the court before he can apply for forfeiture and damages. The court will usually only give leave if the matter is one which affects the fabric of the property as opposed to being merely of a decorative or superficial nature.

The service by the tenant of a counter notice will also prevent the landlord claiming costs under section 146 of the Law of Property Act, 1925 without leave of the court. It will not, however, prevent the landlord from claiming the costs and expenses of serving a section 146 notice, where there is an express provision in the lease for recovery of such sums.

Such a notice will not protect a tenant where he has covenanted at the commencement of the tenancy to put the premises into a particular state of repair.

Priced or unpriced schedules

Some solicitors like to serve an schedule with the unpriced notice and others a priced one.

Section 146 Notice

A typical Section 146 notice served with the schedule will look like the specimen bellow:-

Notice to Lessee of Breach of Covenant to Repair
Under Section 146 of the Law Of Property Act, 1925
and the Leasehold Property (Repairs) Act, 1938

To: *insert the name and the correct address for serving the tenant which may not be the same as the address of the demised premises. Check what the lease has to say about service.*

lessee of the premises known as

insert the address of the demised premises

Pursuant to a lease dated

insert the date of the lease

Made between   *insert the name of the original landlord named in the lease, which may not be the same as the successor in title*

and   *insert the name of the original tenant named in the lease, which may not be the same as the successor in title*

(If there are successors in title it can add clarity to add the names of the current landlord and tenant)

We   *insert the name of the solicitor and agent for the landlord* solicitors and agents for your lessor, hereby give you notice as follows:-

1.   In the above lease, the lessee covenanted as follows:-

> *recite relevant covenants. These may include, the demised premises; the repairing covenants   which the lessor claims to have been breached and those allowing the lessor to recover his costs*

2.   The above covenants have been broken in that there exist defects, wants of repair and dilapidations as set out in the Schedule of Dilapidations served herewith, which you have failed to remedy.

3.   We hereby require you to remedy all the above breaches, in so far as they are capable of remedy, and to make compensation in money for those breaches to

> *insert the name and address of the lessor*

4.   If you fail to comply with this notice within a reasonable time, it is the intention of

> *insert the name of the lessor*

to forfeit the above lease and to claim damages for breach of covenant.

5.   [10]You are entitled under the provision of the Leasehold Property (Repairs) Act 1938 to serve on the lessor a counter-notice claiming the benefit of that Act. Such counter-notice must be served within 28 days from

---

[10] Omit this if the holding is an agricultural holding or the lease was for an original term of less than 7 years and has 3 years or less unexpired.

the date of service of this notice upon you, and may be served in any of the following ways:

(i)   by handing it to the lessor personally;

(ii)   by leaving it at the last known place of abode or business in the United kingdom of the lessor;

(iii)   by sending it by post in a registered letter or by recorded delivery addressed to the lessor by name at such last known place of abode or business in the United Kingdom, if the letter is not returned through the post office undelivered; and service in this manner shall be deemed to be made at the time at which the letter would in the ordinary course of post be delivered.

6.   The name and address for service of the lessor is:

insert the appropriate details

Signed:

Dated:

Check the lease document and schedule and   inspect subject property

If you are instructed by a tenant and receive a copy of the schedule; after checking the lease and other documents and you will wish to inspect the property. Check the dimensions if any are given. If there are none, and if there is no plan, it is quite useful for you to do your own plan and schedules of areas so that you can argue on a quantitative basis. If you have to appear in court, you will give a good account of yourself because you have done your homework.

Advantageous for tenant to do the work himself

If the tenant still has possession it will almost certainly be in his interest to proceed with any work required with his own builders while he still able to do so. He will be in a position to determine the standard and scope of the work and the cost. He may well save money. Once he has lost possession he is entirely in the landlord's hands as to the quotations the landlord obtains and the time it takes for the works to be carried out. The landlord can quite reasonably look to his erstwhile tenant for:-

o payment of rent during the period the works are being carried out

o for fees for supervision and other professional services required, such as planning supervisor and engineer for example.

He may well adopt a higher standard of repair than your client thinks necessary for that sort of property and take longer than the tenant thinks reasonable to obtain tenders and carry out the works. The tenant will have an uphill task to prove that the landlord has not acted reasonably if it can be shown that he took advice and obtained a number of arms length tenders.

If the landlord is after a cash settlement, the threat that the tenant might comply with the schedule whilst still in possession and thus draw the landlord's teeth, can be a powerful negotiating instrument.

I once defeated a fraudulent claim by a landlord who was seeking damages from my client. The landlord claimed to have done the work with his own direct labour. I was able to show that the dates on the time sheets did not correspond with the dates on the materials invoices he produced. The action was dropped.

Standard of Repair

The standard of repair required will vary from property to property. It is self evident that a much higher standard will be required from a luxury office or residence in Mayfair than would be required from a residence or office situated in the Old Kent Road or Hackney.

Landlord's Claim for Damages and Forfeiture

The courts are loath to grant forfeiture against a tenant where the lease is valuable and the unexpired term is lengthy.

I was involved in a case where a tenant did lose his valuable lease because it emerged during the course of the trial that he had failed to insure the premises and there had been a number of fires. Although he had done nearly all the work required under the Schedule of Dilapidations, the court felt he was an unsuitable person to be a tenant. This is an unusual result and courts tend to lean in the tenants' favour.

Statutory obligations

Whilst in occupation tenants have to comply with statutory requirements. If they are employing staff they must, for example, ensure that the toilet accommodation is sufficient; that the temperatures are maintained at the appropriate temperature range, and that they comply with the Offices, Shops and Railway Premises Act, 1963; The Fire Precautions Act, 1971; the Health and Safety at Work Act, 1974 and any other statutory requirements that may pertain to their particular calling.

These statutory requirements are quite separate from the requirements under the lease which are contractual require ments. Once the premises are vacant they no longer have to be met because they concern working conditions of staff employed. The next tenant may have only his family working for him and be exempt from compliance with these statutes[11]. The lease itself may have something to say on the matter of statutes so check it carefully.

Check the lease against the notice

Each lease will set out the repairing obligations. Check the lease carefully against the notice which is served and bear in mind the lessees obligations when checking the schedule itself.

Improvement

Some landlords will ask for improvements. For example, if there is no damp proof course they may ask for one to be installed. A tenant does not have to improve the landlord's premises unless he has covenanted to do so. However, if an original part of the property has come to the end of its life, a modern equivalent is usually the appropriate replacement. For example, if the wiring is at the end of its life, you will not replace it as it was but at the current[12] standard.

Investigation

Some schedules may ask the tenant to investigate something. He does not have to do that either. The landlord must make clear what breaches he requires his tenant to remedy. It is up to the landlord, not the tenant, to investigate potential defects. The investigations may be carried out at the tenant's expense if the lease so provides.

---

[11] For some reason, tenant's families are not thought to be in need of protection required for ordinary employees.
[12] No pun intended.

Waiver of Breaches

A landlord will waive his right to forfeit the lease for breach if he accepts rent. If the breach is a continuing one (provided the property remains in disrepair of course), the landlord's right to forfeit accrues from day to day. Although on the present state of the law, acceptance of rent after service of a section 146 notice appears not to 'waive' the notice, a landlord would be well advised not to accept rent after service of the notice, if he wishes to forfeit the lease, and certainly not where rent is payable in respect of any period after the notice.

The sort of breach he might waive is an unauthorised assignment of the lease. If he, or one of his servants or agents, has notice of the unauthorised assignment and continues to accept rent, he will have waived the breach. His servants and agents should have told the landlord and if they have not, he will nevertheless be credited with having notice.

Section 148(1) of the Law and Property Act 1925 provides:-

148(1) Where any actual waiver by a lessor or the persons deriving title under him of the benefit of any covenant or condition in any lease is proved to have taken place in any particular instance, such waiver shall not be deemed to extend to any instance, or to any breach of the covenant or condition save that to which such waiver specially relates, nor operate as a general waiver of the benefit of any such covenant or condition.

The effect of this is that if a landlord accepts rent in the knowledge that the premises are out of repair, this does not prevent him in the future from taking action against his tenant for failure to repair the premises, assuming that the tenant has an obligation under the lease to do so.

Meaning of Covenants

Covenants tend to be given their natural meaning by the courts. "To put and keep in repair", is no different in effect than "to keep in repair". You cannot keep something in repair until you have put it into repair. If a tenant takes a building in a poor state of repair and has an obligation to keep the premises in repair, then he must first put them into repair. However, it should be noted that breach of an obligation to "put into repair" is a once-and-for-all breach, for which the right to forfeit can be waived once-and-for-all.

It is a breach of an obligation to 'keep in repair' which is a continuing breach.

If he is required to "leave them in repair" this does not become enforceable until the end of the lease.

Costs and Settling Disputes

It is in the interests of both the landlord and the tenant to reach a settlement without going to court. Many leases will make the tenant responsible for the costs of preparing, serving and enforcing a schedule of dilapidations. If the landlord is not justified in bringing his action he may, nevertheless, find that he has an obligation to pay the tenants' costs. The scenario is unlikely to be clear cut. It may happen that the tenant believes he has a certain obligation valued at £X and pays X plus a little bit extra into court. Should the court find that the tenant has an obligation smaller than the sum he has paid into court, costs following the date of payment in, are likely to be awarded against the landlord.

Calderbank Letter

Alternatively, without paying in he may write a Calderbank letter making an offer. A Calderbank letter is a letter written "without prejudice" save as to costs.

The advantage is that the tenant may negotiate without prejudice but no money has to be paid into court. Should the court's award be less than the offer in the Calderbank letter, costs may be awarded against the landlord. The disadvantage is that, where the claim is for money so that payment-in could have been made, the use of a mere offer letter will not necessarily provide the 'costs protection'. Whether it does or not will be at the judge's discretion.

Going to court is extremely expensive. Landlord and tenant cases are complex and it is not unusual for a case concerning dilapidations to last three days, five days or even more. Assuming one barrister, one solicitor and one expert on each side, the costs can easily be in the region of £3,000 per day at the time of writing and that is for each side. If counsel of long call or QC's are instructed, the sky is the limit. The loser could therefore end up with a substantial bill at the end of the hearing. He may also be responsible for pre hearing costs of his opponent as well as his own.

Detailed Assessment of Costs

After the hearing and following the award of costs, these are either summarily assessed by the judge at the hearing itself or referred to 'detailed assessment'. If referred to 'detailed assessment', this process itself incurs costs and if you are represented at the detailed assessment, you will incur further professional fees. If you are not represented, the bill of costs may well go through unopposed.

On detailed assessment, the court will examine the bill of costs which has been presented to the court by the winning side and decide what costs can be allowed under each head. Usually the court reduce costs and an average would be by about a third. If the case lasted five days the bill to the unsuccessful litigant could easily be £15,000 plus pre court costs say £5,000, plus his own costs. Two thirds of £20,000, is not far off £13,000 and by the time his own costs are included, the unsuccessful litigant could be facing a bill of well over £30,000.

A litigant aggrieved at his own solicitor's costs may also elect to have his solicitor's bill assessed but must pay the costs of the detailed assessment.

Legal Aid[13]

Costs are not often awarded against legally aided litigants but if they are they are awarded it is usually with the proviso "but not to be enforced without leave of the court". It is therefore often cheaper to settle a dispute with a legally aided opponent because someone with a legal aid certificate is indeed rich. However, legal aid is becoming increasingly difficult to obtain.

Wearing my Aesop's hat, the moral is;

You must be rich
Or very poor
If you wish
To go to law

Alternative Dispute Resolution - Conciliation

Anyone can be named as a conciliator provided he is acceptable to both parties in the dispute.

The Centre for Dispute Resolution will be able to assist anyone interested in resolving their disputes in this way.

---

[13] Now referred to as being supported by the Legal Services Commission

They are to be found at 100 Fetter Lane, London EC4A 1DD. Telephone 020 7430 1852. Unlike arbitration, the parties to the dispute are free to walk away from the proceedings at any time.

Arbitration

The Chartered Institute of Arbitrators are situated at 24 Angel Gate, City Road, London EC1 2RS. Telephone 020 7837 4483

In the case of arbitration, each party to the dispute is bound by an arbitration agreement and is not free to stop the arbitration process if they suddenly decide they do not like it. Costs of the arbitration are at the award of the arbitrator regardless of any agreements made by the disputing parties to the contrary

Both the conciliator and the arbitrator, unlike a High Court judge have to be paid by the disputing parties. If you intend to go into this form of dispute resolution with a battery of lawyers and experts, you may find yourself better off to use the courts because you will have the arbitrator or conciliator to pay, as well as your team of advisors. The advantage of arbitration or conciliation is that you will probably be able to arrange an earlier hearing at a time and place to suit the parties.

Other means of resolving disputes

Better still; instruct me to resolve the dispute. I will toss my coin and you can spend the money you have saved in Las Vegas.

CHAPTER 7

PREPARING FOR A COURT HEARING

Should the dispute be beyond resolution and headed for Court, it is advantageous to have your case in good order.

The schedule of dilapidations will be a very important part of your report. It should be developed and extended with quantities and prices because the action will be one for damages. Each item of claim should be numbered. If costs are developed across the schedule in a logical way, the judge can see how prices are arrived at. Photographs are also useful and desirable. If a photograph relates to a particular defect then a column in the Scott Schedule, giving a photograph number, will also assist the court. It is helpful and convenient to bind photographs separately and if there are captions each caption should be visible with its photograph.

A plan identifying the areas will help the court to understand what the dispute is about, particularly when linked to photographs. This should also be accessible so that the elements of your report can be viewed simultaneously whilst the hearing develops.

A photographic identification plan, clearly showing which photographs relate to which area, will further clarify your evidence. A number with a circle round it and an arrow pointing in the direction the photograph was taken assists identification. Try to make your photographs clear and crisp.

New Requirements for Experts Reports

Under the Woolf reforms there are new rules for experts reports. These rules reproduced below are published by the

Lord Chancellor's department. The report must contain the following:

- o   it must be addressed to the court;

- o   details of the expert's qualifications and details of any materials upon which the expert has relied when making the report;

- o   where tests or experiments have been carried out state who performed them, giving the qualifications of that person and state whether or not they were carried out under the expert's supervision;

- o   where there is a range of opinion on matters dealt with in the report summarise the range of opinion and give reasons for the expert's own opinion;

- o   a summary of the conclusions reached;

- o   a statement setting out the substance of all material instructions (whether written or oral) on the basis of which the report was written; (CPR 35.10(3)

- o   summarise the facts and instructions given to the expert which are material to the opinions expressed in his report or upon which his opinions are based; (CPR 35.10(3)   in the Commercial Court where any of the facts stated are within the expert's direct knowledge this should be made clear and where any stated assumptions are also in the opinion of the expert unreasonable or unlikely, this should also be stated; (Commercial Court Guide, Section H2.12)

○ be verified by a statement of truth signed by the expert in which he confirms that he understands his duty to the court and that he has complied with that duty.' (CPR 35.10(2) and Pt 35, practice direction, para 1.4)

○ If the report is prepared by a member of the Royal Institution of Chartered Surveyors it must contain the following statement: -

> "This report complies with the requirements of the Royal Institution of Chartered Surveyors, as set down in *Surveyors Acting as Expert Witness: Practise Statement.*"

Scott Schedule

Before the full hearing it is likely that in preliminary hearings the parties will be directed either to appoint a joint expert(s) or to exchange reports and to be given a chance to comment on each other's reports. They may be instructed to agree what can be agreed so as to limit the areas of dispute, but this may emerge in the form of a Scott Schedule. Any expert appointed without leave of the court will not be allowed to give evidence[14].

A Scott. Schedule is a schedule with comments by the claimants expert in one set of columns; the defendant's expert's response in adjacent columns; and space left to the right hand side for comments by the judge.

There is no particular format for a Scott Schedule save that it is in three sections and developed across the sheets in order to give a clear picture of the position of each side in the dispute and for the judge to comment with his own

---

[14] I have known this happen where instructing solicitors have been incompetent.

views. Such schedules are often long and unwieldy and stuck with tape.

If you are going into court it is as well to have your papers in good order and to be familiar with all aspects of your client's case and the opposing case. During the trial you will have to advise your client's solicitor and counsel on points which arise as evidence is given, and to give evidence yourself.

Taking Instructions

Try to ensure that the client and instructing solicitor have given you all the facts. When clients do not reveal important facts until they are in court, cases can start to unravel.

Conference in chambers

Before you even get as far as the court it is important that you confer with the client, the instructing solicitor and counsel. Such meetings are usually held in chambers and can be extremely useful. Litigation is one of those expensive team sports and therefore to be avoided if possible. If there is a possibility of a settlement it should not be lost without careful thought. As a result of conferences with counsel and clients it may be necessary to revise the report. However, an expert who gives evidence which he does not believe to be true is betraying himself and his client and may be committing perjury. The current requirement that the expert must address his evidence to the court underlines this duty.

Do not swear black is white

If there are unpalatable facts in your client's case, the fact that you admit them only adds to your status and credibility as an expert and makes the rest of your evidence more plausible. Clear reports will also add to your stature. In the final analysis, expert witnesses are judged on their performance in presenting and giving their evidence. The weight attached to the evidence given will depend upon the clarity of thought of the expert and his ability to answer questions concisely and honestly.

Number of copies

Try to make your reports and photographs look presentable and appear to be in a logical order. I normally prepare eight copies for a High Court case:

o One for myself.

o one for my client;

o one each for my instructing solicitor and counsel;

o one for the judge;

o one for opposing counsel;

o one for the witness;

o have an additional copy against contingencies. Sometimes it comes in useful.

When giving evidence, just answer the question that you are asked. Counsel for your client will treat you gently. I was going to say lead you gently but leading a witness (indicating the answer required in the question) is a breach of the rules of evidence. Evidence given when being examined by your client's counsel is called "evidence in chief".

The opposing counsel will "cross examine" you and will no doubt have a plan of campaign.

It is no good trying to anticipate what counsel is thinking when cross examining you. You probably will not see it coming until it hits you. Just answer truthfully. Take time to think before answering. This adds gravity to your evidence as long as you do not appear indecisive.

- Do not try to be funny or flippant.

- Do not be aggressive.

- Do not be put off what you believe to be true by aggressive cross examination by counsel.

Your client's counsel is there to protect you in the event of the opposing counsel taking undue liberties. It is part of the process of the law that counsel can chew up experts and spit them on the carpet if they are not up to muster.

I once found myself acting for a tenant against two experts one of whom argued that the value of the reversion was reduced by more than the cost of the works. This was a stupid argument because the ceiling for damages was the cost of the works provided they did not exceed the loss of reversionary value[15]. Nevertheless, his counsel made great play of this evidence and the pseudo scientific graph he produced. It was easy to demolish. The opposing surveyor had not established a standard method of measurement or a group of control properties against which to measure his evidence. It was just so much nonsense and even if he had proved his theory, his client stood to gain nothing. His credibility was damaged by his ridiculous assertions[16].

Settling on the steps of the court.

---

[15] S 18(1) of the Landlord and Tenant Act 1927
[16] Strangely enough, this argument was upheld by a trial judge in the subsequent case Culworth Estates Ltd v Society Of Licensed Victuallers Court of Appeal [1991] 39 EG 132

You will probably find that the vast majority of cases are settled on the steps of the court. By the time the experts have exchanged their evidence, each side has a very good idea of the strengths and weaknesses of the opposing case. This means that counsel can guess the likely outcome of any hearing and it is better to settle these disputes earlier rather than later because the costs gallop on at a frightening pace.

Fees

Concerning fees it is always an advantage for experts to take interim payments of fees in litigious matters. The outcome of litigation is always in doubt even with the best prepared case

CHAPTER 8

Scott Schedule

This is named after a Surveyor who invented the format. A Scott Schedule is in three parts. It has:-

o   columns for the Landlord's Surveyor;

o   columns for the Tenant's Surveyor; and

o   columns for the Judge.

There is no particular format. Whenever I draft a schedule of dilapidations I always set it out in a tabular form using a spreadsheet. An example of a schedule served on the tenant of a small floor of offices on an internal repairing lease is set out later in this chapter. It has not been annotated with the tenant's surveyor's comments for reasons of space. However, in the next chapter, I set out some of the counter arguments to this schedule. With the tenant's surveyor's comments, it could form the basis of a Scott Schedule, needing only a column for the judge.

It is courteous to offer one's opposite number the information on disk so that he can easily add his comments. In days gone by a pot of paste used to come in handy.

When pricing a schedule, keep a note of the source of your prices and the reference. If you have used a pricing book, copy the page, highlight the line and place a reference in a column, which you do not need to print except on your own copy. It can save you a lot of embarrassment during cross examination if the matter comes to court.

Chapter 8 – Scott Schedule

In preparing a schedule of dilapidations the following are customary :-

1. The Title Sheet

- detailing the address of the premises;

- the parties to the lease;

- the date of the lease;

- if the Landlord or tenant have changed, the current Landlord and tenant;

- the date inspected; and

- who the premises were inspected by.

2. Extracts of relevant lease covenants

- the demised premises;

- repairing covenants;

- charging covenants which, for example allow for recovery of fees and costs

3. The Schedule of Dilapidations

If the schedule is an interim schedule of dilapidations and the landlord wants the tenant to actually do some repairs, then it is not always priced. This will save costs.

Terminal schedules of dilapidations may be priced, or the landlord can go to tender for the repairs and the priced specification based upon the schedule of dilapidations will usually be acceptable, provided more than one arms length estimate has been obtained from reputable builders.

Valuation of work

Where instructed to value the work you may wish to split the schedule up into a number of columns.

Column 1

- Consecutive line numbers, inserted after the schedule is complete. In a Excel spread sheets - put *1* on the first line and on the line below

= (the address of the first line) + 1.

This can be dragged down and will automatically add 1 to the previous number. This will help to find a particular item or part of an item easily, particularly in court.

Column 2

- The item number.

Column 3

- A description of the premises.

Column 4

- The number of the clause of the lease alleged to have been breached.

Column 5

- The breach complained of.

Column 6

- The remedy required.

Columns 7 – 10

Pricing information:-

- Quantity (a number)

- Unit (for example, square feet or cubic metres)

- Price per unit

- Total cost. This will be the number of units multiplied by the price per unit

- VAT can be added at the end if the landlord is not registered for VAT and is therefore not in a position to recover it.

Wherever possible, I like to base my values on published pricing tables. This may be slightly less than the current market cost, but it can be supported in Court. Sometimes these schedules are so out of line that one has to use one's common sense. There is nothing wrong with basing pricing on experience, but the Courts do like a structured approach and they like to see that you have applied some sort of science before arriving at the price and have not just pulled it out of the air.

Schedule of Areas

A schedule of areas of each part of the property is useful to the court and in pricing repairs.

Identification Plan

Courts like an identification plan. It helps to identify which part of the property is referred to in the schedule. If the schedule cannot be understood then it will not be enforceable so it is worth while taking the time and trouble to prepare such a plan.

If it is done using a computer aided design package, this will greatly assist in calculating quantities, particularly for strangely shaped areas.

Photographs

Photographs taken on site illustrating the defects and showing general views are useful, both when pricing the schedule and in the event that the dispute arrives in court.

Should it come to court then the photographs should be bound in a separate book with an identification plan showing which photograph relates to what part with arrows pointing in the right direction. The plan should be accessible whilst the book of photographs is open so that it can be referred to.

Further Columns

The opposing surveyor will normally add his comments in adjacent columns and it is courteous to offer the Schedule on disk. The judge will then write his notes against the two surveyor's columns.

Terminal
Schedule of Dilapidations

and wants of repair

found to have accrued and required to be remedied

at the premises known as

First Floor
121 Brent Cross Road
London, NW99

Contrary to the terms of a lease

Dated: 17th August 1984

Between

Lessor: Pedicular Properties Limited

And

Lessee: Hebetudinous Limited

Premises Inspected 2nd April 2001

By Landlord's Surveyor

Vegoda and Co. Ltd.
5 Beech Avenue
London, N20 9JT

Tel: 020 8446 2653
Fax: 020 8445 9594
email: expert@dilapidations.co.uk

Summary of Relevant Lease covenants

REPAIRS

(3)   At all times during the said term well and substantially to repair maintain cleanse and keep in good and substantial repair and condition the whole of the interior of the Demised Premises and every part thereof and all additions to the Demised Premises and the water and sanitary apparatus heating and hot water systems solely serving the same and the Landlords and other fixtures and fittings therein and all boundary walls and fences and other appurtenances thereto and all pipes drains wires cables meters channels and sewers therein and solely serving the Demised Premises including windows plate glass doors partitions locks fastenings (except in respect of damage by-fire and such other risks against which the Landlord shall have insured provided that the Policy of Insurance shall not have been vitiated or payment of any of the Policy moneys withheld or refused in whole. or in part by reason of any act omission neglect or default of the Tenant or any sub-tenant or their respective servants agents licensees or any invitees)

DECORATION

(4)   Without prejudice to the preceding sub-clause in a good and workmanlike manner and to the reasonable satisfaction of the Landlord or the Landlord's Surveyor to decorate with good quality materials the interior of the Demised Premises in the last year of the term (howsoever determined) and PROVIDED THAT the colours design and material of all work done in the last year of the term shall be such as the Landlord shall require

CONTRIBUTIONS/SERVICE CHARGE

(5)(a)   To pay a fair proportion of the costs incurred or to be incurred from time to time by the Landlord for or the cleansing and maintenance of all party walls fences gutters sewers drains passageways floors roads pavements forecourts gardens yards roofs and foundations of the Demised Premises and the building of which the Demised Premises forms part and other things the use of which is common to the Demised Premises and to any neighbouring property

(5)(b)   As soon as practicable after the end of the Landlord's financial year the Landlord shall furnish to the Tenant an account of sums expended by the Landlord pursuant to clause 5 (a) hereof for that year and within one month of the furnishing of such account there shall be paid by the Tenant to the Landlord his proportion of such expenditure

ALLOW ACCESS

(6)   To permit the Landlord and persons authorised by the Landlord with or without workmen and others at reasonable times upon appointment made to enter upon and examine the condition of the Demised Premises and thereupon the Landlord may serve upon the Tenant a notice in writing specifying any repairs or decorations necessary to be done and require the Tenant forthwith to execute the same and if the Tenant shall not within one month after service of such notice commence and thereafter proceed diligently with the execution of such repairs or decorations then to permit the Landlord to enter upon the Demised Premises and execute the same and the cost thereof shall be paid by the Tenant on demand and in default be forthwith recoverable as a debt due from the Tenant together with interest from the date of completion of the work to the date of payment by the Tenant

ALTERATIONS

(7)   Not at any time during the said term to make any alteration in or addition to the Demised Premises without the previous written consent of the Landlord

ACCESS

(9)   To permit the Landlord and persons authorised by the Landlord with or without workmen and others at reasonable times upon appointment made save in the case of emergency to enter upon the Demised Premises to view the state of repair and condition thereof and to execute repairs or alterations on any adjoining premises all damage to the Demised Premises thereby caused being made good at the Landlord's expense

USER

(10)   Not to carry on or permit or suffer to be carried on in or upon the Demised Premises or any part thereof any dangerous noxious noisy or offensive trade or business and not to permit any person to sleep or reside there but to use the Demised Premises only for the purpose described in the Third Schedule hereto

(11)   Not to do or permit or suffer to be done anything in or upon the Demised Premises or any part thereof which may be or become a nuisance or annoyance or cause damage to the Landlord or the owners or occupiers of the other property in the neighbourhood

(12)(a) Not to do or permit or suffer to be done on the Demised Premises anything which may render an increased or extra premium payable for the insurance of the Demised Premises or any other nearby premises of the Landlord or which may make void or voidable any policy of insurance effected in respect of the Demised Premises

(b) In the event of the Demised Premises or any part of the Demised Premises being destroyed or damaged by any of the insured risks to give immediate notice to the Landlord

(c) In the event of the Demised Premises or any part of the Demised Premises being destroyed or damaged by any of the insured risks and the insurance money under any policy of insurance effected by the Landlord being wholly or partly irrecoverable by reason of any act of default of the Tenant then and in every such case the Tenant will forthwith (in addition to the rent) pay the Landlord the whole or (as the case may require) the irrecoverable proportion of the cost of rebuilding and reinstating the Demised Premises

COMPLIANCE WITH STATUTORY MATTERS

(13) To comply forthwith at the Tenant's own expense with any nuisance sanitary or other statutory notice lawfully served by any local or public authority upon either the Landlord or the Tenant with respect to the Demised Premises and similarly to comply with all requirements of or made under or deriving validity from any local or national legislation or regulations which are now or may hereafter come into force whether as to the Demised Premises or any alteration addition or improvement thereto the use thereof the employment or residence therein of any person or in connection with any fixture machinery plant or chattel therein

(14) Not to do or omit to do or permit or suffer to be done or omitted to be done anything in or about the Demised Premises or any premises used for the

purpose of but not comprised in the Demised Premises whereby the Landlord may become exposed to the liability to pay any penalty damages compensation costs charges or expenses and to keep the Landlord indemnified against all such liabilities

ADVERTISEMENTS

(15)   Not without the Landlord's consent in writing first had and obtained to display any external sign or advertisement on the Premises or any part thereof save for visual trade signs or otherwise affect alter or modify the external appearance of the Demised Premises or any part thereof

COSTS AND EXPENSES

(16)   To pay all expenses together with any value added tax thereon (including solicitors' costs and disbursements and surveyors' fees) reasonably incurred by the Landlord:-

(a)   Incidental to the preparation and service of a notice under Section 146 of the Law of Property Act 1925 or incurred in or in contemplation of proceedings under Section 146 or 147 of that Act (notwithstanding in any such case that forfeiture is avoided otherwise than by relief granted by the Court) and in connection with every application for any consent made under this Lease whether such consent shall be granted or not

(b)   In or incidental to the services of all notices and schedules relating to wants of repair of the Demised Premises whether the same be served during or after the expiration or sooner determination of the term hereby granted (but relating in all cases to such wants of repair that accrued not later than the expiration or sooner determination of the said term aforesaid)

(c)   In or incidental to the collection and recovery of any rent payable hereunder which shall be in arrear (including the costs of any collection agency) or in any action reasonably taken by or on behalf of the Landlord in order to prevent or procure the remedying of any breach or non-performance by the Tenant of any of the covenants conditions or agreements herein contained and on the part of the Tenant to be observed and performed and the costs of the supervision of services and repairs to the property and common parts of which the demised premises forms part and generally for the, management thereof

YIELD UP

(21)   To yield up the Demised Premises with the fixtures and additions thereto at the determination of the term hereby granted with vacant possession and in substantial repair and condition in accordance with the covenants hereinbefore contained

(7)   Any notice under this Lease shall be in writing and shall be deemed to be sufficiently served if complying with the provisions of the Law of Property Act 1925 - Section 196 as amended by the Recorded Delivery Service Act 1962

THE FIRST SCHEDULE

The Demised Premises

ALL THOSE First Floor Offices being part of the building known as 311 New Cross Road, London SE14 for the purposes of identification edged red on the plan annexed hereto including:-

(a)   The paint paper and other decorative finishes applied to the interior of the exterior walls of the building but not to any other part of the exterior walls

(b)   The floor finishes so that the lower limit of the demised premises shall include such finishes but shall not extend to anything below them

(c)   The ceiling finishes so that the upper limits of the demised premises shall include such finishes but shall not extend to anything above them

(d)   The entirety of any non-load bearing internal walls within the demised premises

(e)   The inner half severed medially of the internal non-load bearing walls dividing the demised premises from other parts of the building

(f).   The windows and the window frames

(g)   All additions and improvements to the premises

(h)   All the Landlord's fixtures and fittings of every kind which shall from time to time be in or upon the demised premises whether originally affixed or fastened to or upon the same or otherwise except any such fixture installed by the Tenant and that can be removed from the. demised premises without defacing the same

(i)   Any pipes that exclusively serve the demised premises

Schedule of
Dilapidations

Chapter 8 – Scott Schedule

Remedy Required	Quantity	Unit	Price per Unit	Total Cost	
	Assume keys already exist				
Provide scaffolding front and rear as required	PC			£ 2,000.00	
	Allowed above				
	Allowed above				
Comply with CONDAM (Construction (Design and Management) Regulations 1994 requirements.	Say			£ 250.00	
				£ 9,774.00	
Builder's risk and profit				£ 1,954.80	
				£ 11,728.80	
Pay all costs in connection with the preparation, service and enforcement of this schedule.				£ 3,000.00	
				£ 14,728.80	
Add VAT @ 17½%				£ 2,577.54	
Total				£ 17,306.34	

	Description	Breach of Clause no.	Breach
	Keys		
58	Provide two clearly labelled keys to each lock.	2(21)	
	Access to the works		
59		2(3), (13) & (21)	
	Safety Certificates		
60	Provide a certificate of safe working for the burglar alarm system.	2(13) & (21)	
62	Provide a certificate of safe working for the fire alarm system.	2(13) & (21)	
	The Construction (Design and Management) Regulations 1994		
63		2(13)	
64			
	Costs		
65		2(16)	

Chapter 8 – Scott Schedule

Remedy Required	Quantity	Unit	Price per Unit	Total Cost	
Earth wiring	PC			£ 500.00	
Place electrical system in a safe working order.	No allowance made				
Produce an unqualified certificate from a member of the National Inspection Council for Electrical Installation Contracting and do such works as are necessary to enable the contractor to sign such a certificate.	PC			£ 200.00	
Provide a certificate of safe working for the entryphone system.	PC			£ 75.00	
Repair neutral fault in room 5					
Eliminate all sources of dampness and make good all damage caused thereby.	Repairs allowed above				
Ease and adjust all windows, replacing missing parts.		28 hours	£ 18.75	£ 525.00	7 no windows ½ day each
	PC			£ 100.00	Materials
Seal and paint windows externally and replace putties as necessary. Cut out soft spots and make good	see below				
Clean all glazing.	PC			£ 50.00	
Leave all doors in good working order.	small allowance above				
Bring forward and redecorate.	See composite price				
Bring forward and redecorate window joinery.	See below				
Repair cracked plaster. Hack off damaged plaster.		5 days	£ 120.00	£ 600.00	
Replaster damp walls with a waterproof render and where chimney breasts are involved, with a waterproof render with a sulphate resistant mix.	See above				
Bring forward and redecorate.		374 sq m	£ 6.00	£ 2,244.00	
		7 no	£ 120.00	£ 840.00	labour
	PC			£ 200.00	materoials

	Description	Breach of Clause no.	Breach
	Electrical Wiring		
43		2 (3) & (21)	The lighting and supply, where inspected, was not earthed. Earth all lighting wiring.
44			
45			
46			
47			
	Damp Proof Course		
48		2 (3) & (21)	Damp stains in rooms 2 and 4
	Windows		
49		2 (3) & (21)	Windows were difficult to operate and in some cases need balancing. There are missing parts to windows.
50		2 (3) & (21)	Externally putties are loose and joinery is unprotected with paint and sealant.
	Doors		
51		2 (3) & (21)	There are repairs needed to doors to rooms 4 and 5
	Internal Woodwork		
52		2 (3) & (21)	Decorations are worn
	External Timber		
53		2 (3) & (21)	External joinery is neglected
	Plaster		
54		2 (3) & (21)	There is cracked and damaged plaster
55			
	Decoration		
56		2(4) and (21)	Decorations are worn : -
57		2(4) and (21)	Internally and Externally

Chapter 8 – Scott Schedule

Remedy Required	Quantity	Unit	Price per Unit	Total Cost	
Repair and make good.	See composite item				
Remove carpeting and leave floors in good condition.	allowed bove				
Bring forward and redecorate.	See composite item				
Ease and balance sash window.	See composite item				
Reconnect with a bolt and nut.		1 hour		£ 15.00	
Ventilate chimneybreast.	PC			£ 30.00	
Hack off damp plaster. Re-render with a waterproof sulphate resistant mix to a smooth finish ready for redecoration.		6 sq m	£ 40.00	£ 240.00	
Cut out crack and repair.	See composite item				
Produce a certificate that the alarm is in good working order.	Prov sum			£ 75.00	
	allowed bove				
Bring forward and redecorate.	See composite item				
Ventilate chimneybreast.	PC			£ 30.00	

80

	Description	Breach of Clause no.	Breach
	Room 4		
27	Floor: carpeted		
	Walls: plaster		
	Ceiling: plaster		
	Radiator		
	There are 4 x 13 amp power points.		
	Ceiling light.		
	There is an entryphone handset.		
	There is an alarm key point.		
28		2(3) & (21)	There are cracks in the corners and at the junction with the ceiling.
29		2(21)	The room is carpeted
30		2(4) & (21)	Decorations are worn
31		2(3) & (21)	The sash window needs easing
32		2(3) & (21)	The door closer has been disconnected from the frame.
33		2(3) & (21)	There is an unventilated chimneybreast.
34		2(3) & (21)	There is a damp stain on the chimneybreast. This was very damp with a maximum reading on the Protimeter moisture meter.
35		2(3) & (21)	There is cracking underneath the window.
36		2(21)	There is an alarm
	Room 5		
37	Floor: carpeted, with a holed carpet.		
	Walls: plaster		
	Ceiling: plaster		
	Radiator		
	There is a sash window.		
38	The room was so over furnished that it was impossible to find any power points. There was a wander lead and this showed a neutral fault.		
39	There was an infrared alarm detector and a Control box.		
40	Remove carpeting and leave floors in good condition.		
41		2(4) & (21)	Decorations are worn
42		2 (3) & (21)	There is an unventilated chimneybreast.

Remedy Required	Quantity	Unit	Price per Unit	Total Cost	
Ventilate chimneybreast.	PC			£ 30.00	
Hack off water damaged plaster and renew with a render with a waterproof mix.		8 sq m	£ 40.00	£ 320.00	
Replace 3 no. cracked or missing caps to radiator valves.		3 no	£ 5.00	£ 15.00	
Repair and make good.	See composite item				
Repair and make good.	See composite item				
Replace missing brass furniture to allow lifting of right hand sash window.	PC			£ 20.00	
Remove carpeting and leave floors in good condition.	allowed bove				
Bring forward and redecorate.	See composite item				
Ventilate chimneybreast.	PC			£ 30.00	
Repair and make good.	See composite item				
Remove carpeting and leave floors in good condition.	allowed bove				
Bring forward and redecorate.	See composite item				

	Description	Breach of Clause no.	Breach
13		2(21)	There is an unventilated chimneybreast.
	Room 2		
14	Floor: carpeted Walls: plaster Ceiling: plaster 2 x radiators Timber sash windows with secondary double-glazing. 4 x 13 amp power points. Ceiling light. There is an entryphone handset.		
15		2(3) & (21)	There is a damp patch on the outside wall running into the chimney breast alcove at high level. This was dry when tested. However plaster has been damaged and blown and discoloured.
16		2(3) & (21)	1 cracked and two missing radiator valve caps
17		2(3) & (21)	There are cracks to plasterboard joints.
18		2(3) & (21)	There are cracks at joints to the walls and ceiling in the chimney breast alcove and in the alcove adjacent.
19		2(3) & (21)	Furniture is missing from the right hand sash window
20		2(21)	The room is carpeted
21		2(4) & (21)	Decorations are worn
22		2(3) & (21)	There is an unventilated chimneybreast.
	Room 3 – Rear		
23	Floor: carpeted Walls: plaster Ceiling: plaster Radiator Sash window 5 x 13 amp power points Ceiling light There is an entryphone handset.		
24		2(3) & (21)	There are cracks in the corners and at the junction with the ceiling.
25		2(21)	The room is carpeted
26		2(4) & (21)	Decorations are worn

Remedy Required	Quantity	Unit	Price per Unit	Total Cost	
Clear out all tenants' fixtures, fittings and all rubbish.		6 days	£ 120.00	£ 720.00	
Skips		2 no	£ 150.00	£ 300.00	
Make good all disturbance caused by the removal.	Prov sum			£ 240.00	
Reinstate premises to lease plan unless a licence for alterations has been granted.	No allowance made as yet				
Bring forward and redecorate.	See composite item				
Repair cracks in plasterwork.	See composite item				
Repair beading around glazed Georgian wired glass window to office 5.	PC	0.5 day	£ 150.00	£ 75.00	Labour
				£ 50.00	Materials
Remove carpeting and leave floors in good condition.	allowed in removals				
Repair window	See composite item				
Bring forward and redecorate.	See composite item				
Remove carpeting and leave floors in good condition.	allowed in removals				

84

The Dilapidations Handbook

	Description	Breach of Clause no.	Breach
	General		
1		2(21)	Premises contain the tenant's goods
2		2(21)	
3		2(7)	Premises have been altered changing acommodation shown on the lease plan
	Hall and Passage		
4	Floor: carpeted Walls: plaster Ceiling: plaster Windows: none Power: 2 x 13 amp power points 3 x ceiling lights Two small cupboards outside office 5: one large cupboard at the end of the passage. Audible alarm. Emergency light and fire extinguisher Infrared detector and alarm control box.		
5		2(4)	The premises are in poor decorative condition.
6		2(3) 2(21)	There are cracks at plasterboard joints.
7		2(3) 2(21)	The beads to the glazed window to room 5 office is damaged.
8		2(21)	The premises are carpeted throughout
	Room 1 – Front		
9	Floor: carpeted Walls: plaster Ceiling: plaster 2 x timber sash windows with secondary double-glazing. 4 x 13 amp power points Ceiling light.		
10		2(3) 2(21)	The secondary double glazing window to the left needs a new spiral balance.
11		2(4) & (21)	Decorations are worn
12		2(21)	There is carpeting

85

Chapter 8 – Scott Schedule

	All dimensions metric - because most areas are of an irregular shape, dimensions have been calculated by computer using a CAD Program

	Width	Depth	Height	Perim lin m	Wall Area	Floor/ceiling Area	Total Area
Hall and Passsage	7.10	2.65	3.09	19.93	11.06	61.58	72.64
Cupboard 1	0.91	0.31	3.09	2.60	0.35	8.03	8.38
Cupboard 2	0.91	0.31	3.09	2.60	0.35	8.03	8.38
Cupboard 3	1.06	0.78	3.09	3.65	0.81	11.28	12.09
Room 1	4.81	3.23	3.09	15.28	13.52	47.22	60.74
Room 2	4.84	3.19	3.03	15.34	13.61	46.48	60.09
Room 3	2.33	4.56	3.04	13.70	10.53	41.65	52.18
Room 4	2.55	4.52	3.05	14.97	11.02	45.66	56.68
Room 5	2.77	2.92	3.09	11.38	7.61	35.16	42.77
					68.86	305.10	373.96

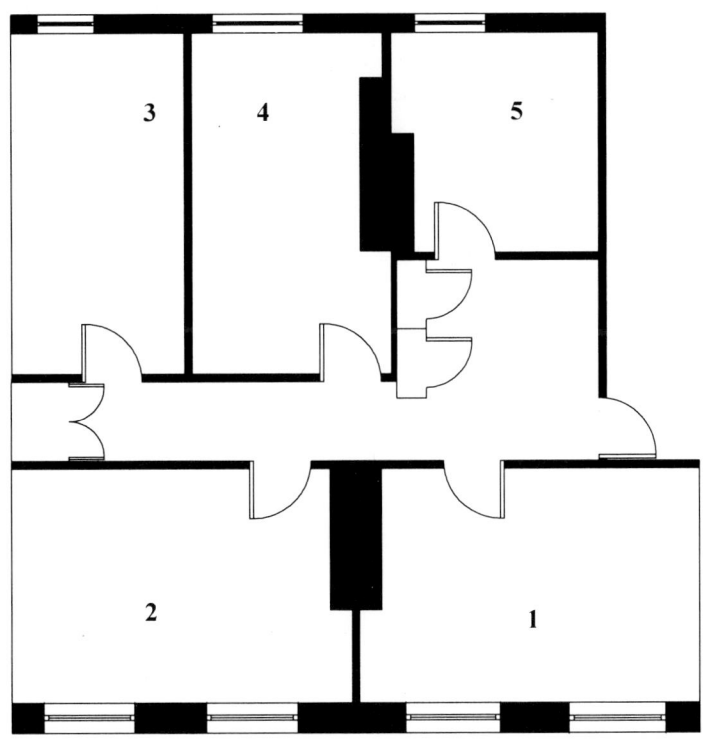

Identification Plan as at 2nd April, 2001

First Floor, 121 Brent Cross Road, London NW99

© Copyright Vegoda & Company Limited 2001

Do Not Scale

CHAPTER 9

Comments on Schedule of Dilapidations at the end of Chapter 8

Items 1 and 2, and others – cleaning/clearing out

The tenant's surveyor could argue that the tenant will have removed all his goods and rubbish prior to the determination of the lease.

Item 3 – reinstatement of floor plan according to the lease

In this particular case, the tenant had made unauthorised changes to the floor plan, but these improved the accommodation. It was therefore felt to be unnecessary to require reinstatement – though a hard landlord might.

Item 5 and other items of decoration

These have been consolidated and lumped together.

Item 6 – plaster cracks

There are a lot of plaster cracks and these items have also been consolidated. Unless cracks are very bad, their repair usually come into the category of "bringing forward" or preparation works.

Item 7 - joinery

This item of joinery repair was difficult to price using a published pricing book. It has therefore been broken down to labour and materials: a concept that a court can understand.

Chapter 9 – Comments on Schedule of Dilapidations
at the end of Chapter 8

Item 10 - Windows

Windows are fiddly to repair. Replacement windows can be priced using published information, with a fair degree of accuracy. Repairing sash windows can take a joiner half a day or a day each. If there are a lot of them it can amount to a pretty penny. It is a question of fact whether or not windows are in disrepair, but the degree of disrepair can be argued with the corresponding adjustments to the cost of repair.

Not so long ago I went to test a sash window in a building and when I unlocked one of the largest, the top frame fell like the blade of a guillotine. It had no sash cords. Dangerous being a surveyor.

Item 13 – ventilate chimney breast

The tenant's surveyor could argue that this would be an improvement. If the chimney breast was blocked when the premises were let and is not damp due to condensation, this might be arguable.

Item 15 – dampness

Plaster within the office was damp but the dampness was coming from outside. The tenant had an internal repairing lease with a liability to contribute to the cost of repairs of common parts. He could argue that the landlord should eliminate the damp penetration and make good the damage. If he gave notice of the defect to the Landlord, the Landlord would be in breach of the covenant for quiet enjoyment if he failed to remedy it.

Item 36 – plant and machinery

Provided the Tenant is liable for repair and maintenance, the Landlord can ask for an unqualified certificate for any plant. If the certificate is qualified, he can require the tenant to do the necessary repairs so that an unqualified certificate can be issued. Plant could include:-

- o air conditioning plant, particularly if there is a cooling tower and a risk of legionella disease. It is spread by dirty plant and aerosols or droplets;

- o alarms;

- o boilers;

- o cranes;

- o electrical systems;

- o hoists;

- o passenger lifts, car lifts and goods lifts;

- o plumbing and heating systems;

- o sewerage treatment equipment;

and any other plant and machinery.

Item 58 – Keys

Tenants should provide clearly labelled keys for the Landlord on giving up possession.

Item 59 – Scaffolding and access plant

Any costs for access or complying with Health and Safety requirements are legitimate costs.

Item 64 – Builder's risk and profit

This item can be added if the pricing book used is net of profit. Spons Architects and Builder's Price Book does not usually include builder's risk and profit whereas Griffith's Pricing Book usually does. Each pricing book differs and you should check how prices are computed in each case.

Item 65 – Costs

If the lease provides, you may seek to recover surveyors fees, solicitors costs and any other properly incurred professional fees and investigation costs connected with the preparation and enforcement of the schedule of dilapidations.

CHAPTER 10

Arguments between Landlord and Tenant

Carpets

The Landlord may require carpets to be cleaned. If the carpets have been left, then they become Landlord's fixtures and he can ask for them to be cleaned. If the tenant is still in occupation and he provided the carpets originally, he can take the up and cart them away, leaving the floor in repair.

Tanking of Basements

If a basement has not been tanked, then the Landlord cannot usually require an improvement, unless the lease says otherwise. Under common law, the Tenant is not obliged to improve the Landlord's property or to give something back which is different from that which he took.

Inherent Defects

If there is an inherent defect such as cladding, one can look at the cost in relation to the value of the property as a whole. If the cost is out of proportion to the value of the property as a whole then the tenant is not obliged to do the work, but if it is in proportion, then notwithstanding the fact that it is an inherent defect, the tenant can be required to do it, even if the cost is large. The test is, will the landlord be getting back something vastly different from that which he let.

Surveyors' Fees

Check the lease to see if these can be charged. If there is no charging clause in the lease, then refuse to pay. It is only if the matter goes to court that the Judge will then decide who pays for what. If there is a charging clause then you can argue that the hourly rate is out of proportion or the percentage rate, or whatever. No matter what level fees are pitched at, there is always an argument that they are too high.

Fees for Contract Administration

These are normally chargeable, but they must be sensible fees.

Fees for Condam

The Construction (Design and Management) Regulations 1994

If the works are such that the law requires the appointment of a Planning Supervisor, and the lease provides for recovery of fees, then they will be recoverable.

Loss of Rent

The Landlord is entitled to claim for loss of rent during the period in which the works are being carried out, but not while he is waiting to re-let.

Statutory Obligations

A Landlord can ask for a tenant to carry out works under statutory obligations. If the statutory obligations relate to the way in which the premises are occupied, then once the premises are empty there will be no breach of the statute. Unless a statutory notice has been served, nothing can be done.

A new tenant may occupy the premises in a different way.

Compensation for Tenants' Improvements

A tenant can apply for compensation provided that he has served the proper statutory notices and gone through the procedure under Section 3(1) of the Landlord and Tenant Act 1927.

If there have been improvements to the property, these may become the Landlord's depending upon the degree of annexation. If they are firmly fixed to the building, they may then be the Landlord's. For example, if the Tenant has installed a heating system which is bolted to the ground and plumbed in in such a way that it has become an inherent part of the building it might become the Landlord's. If it is an industrial premises where he has installed a free standing, oil fired heater which blows out hot air, this is not attached to the property and he can move it away.

Cost of Building

Where a Landlord has got possession of the building and has gone out to tender, it is difficult for a tenant to argue that the cost of repairs is not reasonable. In many cases the court will hold that the damage to the reversion is equal to the cost of the repairs.

Investigations

The Landlord cannot ask the tenant to investigate. If he finds dry rot in the property, he can say 'eliminate all dry rot' and then it is up to the tenant to follow the trail.

Drains reports and other specialist reports

The Landlord cannot tell the tenant to get a drains report, but if the lease provides, he can charge the tenant for a drains report which he has obtained: or an electrical report: or any other sort of report; whether or not it throws up work which needs to be done.

VAT

Where a Landlord carries out works and is registered for VAT, he cannot claim the VAT as part of his damages. The reason for this is that he can deduct the VAT as an input from the VAT he has to pay and therefore has not suffered that loss. If he is not registered for VAT then the VAT is part of his loss and he can add this to the sum sought from the tenant.

CASE SUMMARIES

Warning

Care has been taken in the preparation of these case summaries. However, they are intended to be no more than summaries of the main points of each case. Should anything of moment turn on interpretation of any of these cases, you are advised to read a reliable and full report. Neither the writer, the editor nor the publishers accept any responsibility for losses arising from their use.

Some of these summaries have been reproduced with the kind permission of :-

The Incorporated Council of Law Reporting for England and Wales;

and of

The Estates Gazette

All Rights Reserved

Grateful thanks are due to the very helpful librarians at the Royal Institution of Chartered Surveyors

Relief from forfeiture

Abbey National Building Society v Maybeech
Ltd. and Another

[1985] Ch 190

Landlord and Tenant - Forfeiture of lease - Relief from
forfeiture - Mortgagee's charge over lease - Lessee's failure
to pay maintenance contributions - Order for forfeiture of
lease - Lessor re-entering into possession - Whether
mortgagees application for statutory relief from forfeiture
too late - Whether equitable jurisdiction to grant relief -
Law of Property Act 1925 s. 146(4).

Held, that the forfeiture proceedings had been completed
on the lessor re-entering into possession of the premises
and, therefore, at the time the building society was
informed by the Land Registry of the lessor's application to
remove references to the title to the lease from the registers
there were no proceedings during the pendency[17] of which
the building society could apply for relief from forfeiture
under section 146(4) of the Law of Property Act 1925,
although the building society could not seek relief from
forfeiture under section 146, the section and its
predecessors were enabling provisions and did not
constitute exhaustive provisions which would have
precluded the court from exercising its equitable
jurisdiction to grant relief from forfeiture for a breach of a
covenant other than one to pay rent; and that, in the
circumstances, the court would exercise its equitable
jurisdiction to grant the building society relief from
forfeiture.

---

[17] Condition of being pending or undecided

98

Forfeiture - Repudiatory breach - Context had to be
taken into account - Section 145 of Law of Property Act
1925

Abidogun v Frolan Health
Care Ltd

Court of Appeal [2001] 45 EG 138 (CS)

Landlord seeking forfeiture on basis of non-payment of
rent and breaches of repairing covenants - Tenant disputing
landlord's title - Judge dismissing claim for forfeiture -
Whether tenant's denial of landlord's title amounting to
repudiatory breach - Section 145 of Law of Property Act
1925 - Appeal dismissed

The claimant was the owner Of 72 Marine Avenue,
Whitley Bay, which it let to the defendant under a three-
year lease. After the expiry of the lease, the tenancy
continued under the Landlord and Tenant Act 1954. In
1997 the claimant issued forfeiture proceedings against the
defendant, claiming breach of the tenancy for non-payment
of rent and breaches of repairing covenants. The defendant,
inter alia, denied the validity of any lease on the basis that
the claimant was not the legal owner. The judge found that
the claimant was the sole legal owner of the property, but
dismissed the claim for forfeiture on the ground that non-
payment of rent and breaches of repairing covenants had
not been proved.

The claimant appealed, contending that the defendant had
repudiated its lease by denying the claimant's title. The
claimant submitted that the repudiatory conduct had been
accepted, which had brought the lease to an end. It was
argued that, accordingly, there had been no need for the
service of a notice under section 146 of the Landlord and
Tenant Act 1925.

Held: The appeal was dismissed.

1. The defendant was claiming that the lease was not valid on the basis of a number of reasons that were rejected by the judge. Those reasons had to be seen in their context. There were no findings by the judge that the defendant no longer intended to be bound by the terms of the lease. A tenant could not be assumed to have repudiated a lease when it was simply seeking the determination of the court on issues that had arisen. It was not the law that a tenant could not submit issues to be determined by the court without the risk of a landlord trying to end the tenancy.

2. In any event, there had been no finding by the judge of any acceptance of a repudiation by the claimant. The claimant had not pleaded that he had a right to terminate the lease by reason of denial of title. The judge had clearly considered that the argument raised was one of forfeiture, rather than repudiation. Furthermore, section 146 of the 1925 Act had to apply in the case of a denial of title, since the right to forfeiture for denial of title was a right based upon an implied term "in the lease". Accordingly, the fact that no such notice had been served was another reason for the failure of the claimant's appeal: *Warner v Sampson [1995] 1 QB 297* and *WG Clark (Properties) Ltd v Dupre Properties Ltd [1991] 2 EGLR 59 considered.*

Forfeiture

Adagio Properties Ltd v Ansari

Court of Appeal: [1998] EGCS 9

Tenant dividing flat into two dwellings in breach of covenant - Landlord's section 146 notice complaining of such division but giving no particulars of relevant works - Whether notice defective Landlord's appeal allowed.

In 1985 the respondent tenant acquired, as an investment, a lease, then having 54 years unexpired, of a two bedroom ground-floor flat described as 17 Poynders Court, Clapham. By the terms of the lease, the tenant could not make alterations without the landlord's consent and was obliged to permit entry by the landlord from time to time to view the condition of the premises. In early October 1992 the landlord observed, from external inspection, various features, notably a rear entrance freshly numbered 17A, indicating that the flat had been converted into two separate dwellings. Following the tenant's refusal to permit an inspection of the interior, solicitors for the landlord served a notice under section 146 of the Law of Property Act 1925 stating, inter alia[18], that the tenant had breached his obligations by "making alterations so as to divide [the flat] into two separate studio flats without permission". At a subsequent county court hearing it was found as a fact that the tenant, having replaced the bathroom with two shower rooms with wc, had put a light partition wall across the flat so as to create two one-bedroom flats, each with its own kitchen. However, the judge, while accepting that the case lay on the borderline, found that the section 146 notice was defective in that it had failed to specify the particular breach complained of. The landlord appealed.

---

[18] among other things.

Held: The appeal was allowed.

It was plain on the highest authority that the statutory duty to specify the breach did not require the landlord to give particulars of each defect: see *Fox v Jolly [1916) 1 AC 1.* Given that it was addressed to someone who knew or ought reasonably to have known of the state of affairs complained of, the notice had fulfilled the statutory purpose of giving the tenant the opportunity of remedying the breach, the means to be adopted being a matter for the lessee, not the lessor. For that reason, and contrary to the view taken by the trial judge, it was immaterial that the landlord could have obtained a court order directing the tenant to permit a full inspection.

Fixtures and fittings

Aircool Installations v British Telecommunications

County Court (1995) CLY821

In this case, despite a Romalpa Clause stating that the property remained that of the installer until he had been paid; for air conditioning units which were installed over a period of two weeks. They were held to be fixtures. The units were bolted to the factory walls and external units rested on paving slabs. There was quite extensive cabling and pipework. This is, however, a County Court decision.

Fixtures and fittings

Alletson Limited v Morris

House of Lords (1997) 2All ER 513

Bungalows, which were not physically attached the land, but could not be relocated without demolition were held to be fixtures.

Privity of Contract

Amsprop Trading Ltd v Harris Distribution Ltd and Another

Chancery Division [1997] 47 EG 127

Landlord and tenant - Underlease - Privity of contract. Whether headlessor can enforce covenants in underlease a original subtenant and its assignee.

In October 1975 USF granted K a headlease of premises for a term of 99 years less three days from July 31 1973. In November 1987 USF transferred the reversion to the headlease to Amsprop Ltd. In December 1987 K granted an underlease to the first defendant for a term expiring in January 1994 pursuant to a licence granted by Amsprop Ltd. In February 1993 the first defendant assigned the underlease to the second defendant following a licence to consent to the assignment granted by Amsprop Ltd to K. The plaintiff, Amsprop Trading Ltd, acquired the reversion to the headlease from Amsprop in May 1993. In February 1996 the plaintiff gave notice to the second defendant, purportedly pursuant to a provision of the underlease, requiring the second defendant to carry out repairs. The covenants in the underlease permitted the landlord and superior landlord to enter to carry out repairs following notice and to recover the costs. In March 1996 the second defendant gave up possession and the plaintiff forfeited the headlease. The plaintiff claimed against the defendants damages for breach of the repairing covenants in the underlease and reimbursement of the costs of repair.

Held:

Amsprop Ltd could not have enforced the relevant covenants of the underlease under section 56 of the Law of Property Act 1925, notwithstanding the references therein to the superior landlord; the relevant covenants were made with K and no one else was mentioned who might benefit. It followed that the plaintiff could not enforce the covenants in the underlease against the defendants.

If Amsprop Ltd could have enforced the relevant covenants in the underlease:

(1) the plaintiff could have enforced the covenants by reason of section 78 of the 1925Act;

(2) the second defendant would not have been liable to the plaintiff;

and (3) because the underlease came to an end before the expiration of the three months' notice period under the covenant to repair on notice, the defendants would not have been liable to the plaintiff.

"Well and sufficiently repair" - To repair having regard to their age; and to their character and ordinary uses, or the requirements of tenants of the class likely to take them, at the time of the grant or at the end of the term.

Anstruther-Gough-Calthorpe v Mcoscar and Another

In The Court Of Appeal [1924] 1 KB 716

Landlord and Tenant - Lease - Covenant to repair – "Well and sufficiently repair" - Breach - Long Lease - Alteration in District - Change in Character of Tenants - Measure of Damages Requirements of Tenants at Commencement of Term.

A lease of three newly erected houses made in 1825 for a term of ninety-five years contained a covenant by the lessee in very wide terms, the effect of which was, put shortly, that he would during the term well and sufficiently repair the premises with all manner of necessary reparations and would yield up at the end of the term the said premises so being in all things well and sufficiently repaired.

At the end of the term the assignee of the reversion brought an action against the assignees of the lease for breach of the above covenant. By an order of the Court the assessment of the damages was referred to an arbitrator. At the beginning of the term the houses were country houses; at the end of the term the only tenants likely to occupy the houses or parts of them would be tenants on short terms. The arbitrator assessed the damages at two alternative sums. He computed the smaller sum on the basis that the defendants were liable to execute such repairs only as in view of the age, character, and locality of the premises would make them reasonably fit to satisfy the requirements of reasonably minded tenants of the class that would then be likely to occupy them. He found that tenants of this class would require only such repairs as would keep out wind and water:-

Held:

by Bankes, Scrutton and Atkin L.JJ. that this was not the proper measure of liability; but that the defendants were liable for the cost of doing all necessary acts well and sufficiently to repair the premises in the words of the covenant, that is to say, for the cost of putting them into that state of repair in which they would be found if they had been managed by a reasonably minded owner, having regard –

Per Bankes L.J., to their age;

Per Scrutton and Atkin L.JJ., to their character and ordinary uses, or the requirements of tenants of the class likely to take them, at the time of the demise or at the commencement of the term.

Correct date for assessment of damages

Associated Deliveries Ltd v Harrison and Another

Court of Appeal [1984] 272 EG 321

Landlord and tenant – Assessment of damages for breach of repairing covenant and failure to deliver up in repair – Appeal against official referee's decision - Question as to correct date at which damages should be assessed - Whether at date of service of writ or later date when plaintiff recovered possession of premises – Importance of date was due to extensive deterioration due in large part to vandalism which took place between the two dates – Official referee decided that damage must be assessed, according to established principles , at fate of service of writ – Appellants who were themselves underlessees, had been plaintiffs in action against subunderlesseees and assignees of the latter – Appellants had paid the superior lessees a sum in satisfaction of the latte's claim for breach of covenant - Appellants' main contention in present appeal was that, despite the principle illustrated in such cases as *Jones v Carter* and *Canas Property Co Ltd v KL Television Services Ltd,* that the service of a writ operated as a decisive election to forfeit, put an end to covenants and fixed the date for assessment of damages, the obligation to deliver the property up in repair survived during the "twilight period" between the service of the writ and the enforcement of an order for possession.

Held

That this contention was incorrect and various authorities cited failed to support it - *Wheeler v Keeble* was decisively against it - A claim by the appellants for recovery of sums which they had paid to the superior lessee, was rules out on various technical grounds - Appeal against official referee's decision dismissed.

"Good and substantial repair" - "observe" and "perform." contrasted and defined - "window" does not include a skylight

Ayling v Wade

Court Of Appeal [1961] 2 QB 228

Landlord and Tenant - Sublease - Repairs, covenant for - Covenant to observe covenants in head lease - Repairing covenant in head lease - Whether covenant merely of indemnity - Whether covenant imposes duty to repair – "Observe" - Meaning – "Window" - Meaning.

By a clause in an underlease the landlord covenanted with the tenant *"to pay the rent reserved by and to observe the covenants contained in the lease, under which the landlord holds the demised premises, and to keep the tenant indemnified against the same ..."* By the terms of the head lease, under which the landlord held the demised premises, he was required to keep the premises in good and substantial repair.

During the hearing the judge defined "observe" as *"to comply with an obligation and has a positive as well as a negative meaning"*.

The plaintiff was the tenant and the defendant the landlord under the underlease of a restaurant, which was part of the premises held by the landlord under the head lease. The tenant covenanted with the landlord to keep the interior of the premises, including all windows, in good and substantial repair. There was no express covenant with regard to exterior repairs.

The glass in the skylight in the flat roof on top of the restaurant had been broken and ineffectively repaired by the landlord. As a result rainwater poured into the restaurant and the tenant was compelled to close it temporarily, during which time the tenant suffered loss of profits amounting to £38 19s. On a claim by the tenant to recover this sum as damages for breach of covenant:-

The draftsman must have intended to distinguish between "observe" and "perform." Both these words appear in clause 3(2), the covenant on the landlord to give quiet enjoyment, and the absence of the word "perform" in clause 3(1) shows that no active obligation was to be imposed on the landlord by that covenant. Stroud's Judicial Dictionary, 3rd ed., vol. 3 (1953), p. 1948, supports the view that when "observe" is used in contrast to "perform," it does not cover positive obligations. "Observe" in clause 3(1) means that the landlord must see that he complies with the requirements of the superior lessor. If the superior lessor waives a breach by the landlord, the landlord cannot be under an obligation to the tenant in respect of the same breach. The tenant cannot impose a greater burden on the landlord than that imposed by the superior landlord. It would have been simple to have inserted an express repairing covenant on the landlord, if that was intended; its absence indicates the absence of any such intention.

DANCKWERTS L J   This appeal turns upon the proper construction to be given to the terms of an underlease dated December 31, 1957. In the underlease, the tenant's covenants included first, the usual covenant to pay the reserved rent, and, secondly, *"to keep the interior of the premises, including all doors, windows, and landlord's fixtures, in good and substantial repair and properly painted, limewashed, papered, and varnished as from time to time required."* Apparently, it is accepted that a window does not include the skylight in the present case, a matter on which 1 think 1 should have felt some doubt.

Held:

That the covenant by the landlord to observe the covenants contained in the head lease was not a covenant to indemnify the tenant in the event of the superior lessor's taking proceedings for forfeiture, but was a covenant requiring the landlord to perform the repairing obligations imposed on him by the head lease; therefore, the tenant's claim succeeded.

Leave of the court not required under section 146(3) of the Law of Property Act 1925 as modified by section 2 of the Leasehold Property (Repairs) Act 1938, where the basis of claim is the contract.

Waiver of Breach

Bader Properties Ltd. v Linley Property Investments Ltd.

[1968] 19 P&CR 620

The lease contained amongst others, the following covenants-

"Not to assign or underlet without consent, such consent not to be unreasonably withheld."

"Lessee to pay all expenses (including solicitors costs and surveyors fees) incurred by the lessor incidental to the preparation and service of a notice under Section 146 of The Law of Property Act 1925 notwithstanding forfeiture is avoided otherwise than by relief granted by the court."

"..... if any covenant on the part of the lessee herein contained shall not be performed or observed...it shall be lawful for the lessor at any time to re-enter upon the demised premises in the name of the whole and thereupon this demise shall absolutely determine without prejudice to the right of action of the lessor in respect of any breach of the lessee's covenant herein contained."

The tenant's solicitors wrote to the landlord's chasing up the license and the landlords' solicitors replied on October 8, 1965:-

We are pleased to inform you that we have now heard form our clients to the effect that they are willing to consent to your clients underletting the above property to Aircraft Furnishings Limited. We will prepare the necessary documents and will forward them to you in due course, but in the meantime we shall be most grateful if you would confirm that your client will be responsible for the costs of the licence.

The tenant's solicitor responded with an agreement to pay proper costs on November 2, 1965.

On November 3, 1965 an underlease for the residue of the term less a few days, was entered into at a profit rent. No formal licence had been granted at this time and the plaintiffs were not aware that the underletting had occurred until some time later.

The tenant argued that the letter dated October 8, 1965 was itself a licence and that even if it were not, the breach had been waived by the lessor accepting rent after he had knowledge of the breach, and subsequently attempting to purchase the head lessees interest with the benefit of the sub-lease. It was common ground that the lessor knew of the underletting at the time the rent was demanded and accepted but not of the precise terms of the underletting. On January 6, 1966 the head lessee applied to assign his lease and the reply required detailed information concerning the user of the property and '.... they require Aircraft Furnishings Ltd. (the sub tenant) to redecorate and reinstate the premises in accordance with the provisions of the lease.' They declined a licence until this work was done.

Aircraft Furnishings Ltd. vacated the premises on March 4, 1966. On March 18, 1966 a demand was received from the landlord for a quarter's rent and this was paid and a receipt was given. On April 1, 1966 the landlord made an offer for the lessee's interest. On April 15th the lessee sent a copy of the underlease for registration apologising for the technical breach and it was at this point the landlord realised it may be able to use the 'breach' to obtain possession.

The landlord's solicitors denied that their letter had been a licence but sent an engrossed licence for execution which tried to impose new onerous conditions on the tenant. The defendants and their undertenant proceeded with a sale of the underlease and subsequently the premises were sub-underlet.

Held. The letter dated October 8, 1965 constituted consent to an assignment. The attempted imposition of onerous conditions in the licence which was eventually engrossed were unreasonable. The lessor's acceptance of rent after knowledge of the underletting amounted to a waiver. The offer by the lessor to purchase their lessee's interest also amounted to a waiver of the breach.

Concerning the lessors solicitors and surveyor's costs of 105 guineas, in relation to Section 146(3) of the Law of Property Act 1925 as modified by section 2 of the Leasehold Property (Repairs) Act 1938. This states:-

"a lessor on whom a counter notice is served under the preceding section shall not be entitled to Section 146(3) of the Law of Property Act 1925 so far as regards any costs or expenses incurred in reference to the breach in question, unless he makes an application for leave for the purposes of the preceding section, and on such an application the court shall have power to direct whether and to what extent the lessor is to be entitled to the benefit thereof."

The plaintiffs however were seeking to recover these costs by virtue of the provisions of the lease itself, not by statute. The lessee was unable to show any statutory provision to the contrary. The plaintiffs claim for these costs succeeded but the claim for possession failed.

Defendant awarded costs in the action less £50.

Leasehold Property (Repairs) Act 1938 s 1 - Leave of court required only when more than 5 years unexpired[3].

Baker v Sims

Court Of Appeal [1959] 1 QB 114

Landlord and Tenant – Repairs - Act of 1938 - Effect of counter-notice claiming benefit - Subsequent proceedings by lessor for breach of repairing covenant - More than five years[19] of term not then unexpired - Whether Act applicable - Law of Property Act, 1925 s. 146 - Leasehold Property (Repairs) Act, 1938 s. 1.

The plaintiffs were the landlords of premises let for a term of 99 years less seven days expiring on December 18, 1959. In 1953 the landlords served on the defendant, in whom the lease was then vested, a notice under section 146 of the Law of Property Act, 1925,[20] alleging breaches of the

---

[19] Section 1 of the Leasehold Property (Repairs) Act 1938 was amended by section 51 of the Landlord and Tenant Act 1954 from the original 5 year time period (considered in Baker v Sims) to 3 years. The 1954 Act came into force on 1 October 1954 and section 51 reads as follows: "51. Extension of Leasehold Property (Repairs) Act 1938 (1) The Leasehold Property (Repairs) Act 1938 (which restricts the enforcement of repairing covenants in long leases of small houses) shall extend to every tenancy (whether of a house or of other property, and without regard to the rateable value) where the following conditions are fulfilled, that is to say,- ...(b) that three years or more of the term remain unexpired at the date of the service of the notice of dilapidations or, as the case may be, at the date of commencement of the action for damages;..."

[20] Law of Property Act, 1925, s. 146: "(1) A right of re-entry or forfeiture under any proviso or stipulations in a lease for a breach of any covenant or condition in the lease shall not be enforceable, by action or otherwise, unless and until the lessor serves on the lessee a notice - (a) specifying the particular breach complained of; and (b) if the breach is capable of remedy, requiring the lessee to remedy the breach; and (c) in any case, requiring the lessee to make compensation in money for the breach; and the lessee fails, within a reasonable time thereafter, to remedy the breach, if it is capable of remedy, and to make reasonable compensation in money, to the satisfaction of the lessor, for the breach."

repairing covenants in the lease. The defendant served a counter-notice pursuant to the Leasehold Property (Repairs) Act, 1938,[21] claiming the benefit of that Act.

In 1954 the defendant assigned the lease to a company and it was subsequently surrendered. These proceedings were started in 1957 by the landlords against the defendant for damages for breaches of the repairing covenants of the lease. The preliminary point was taken that the action was incompetent because the leave of the court under section 1 (3) of the Act of 1938 was a prerequisite to the jurisdiction of the court:-

Held:

That effect could not be given to the purpose of section 1 of the Leasehold Property (Repairs) Act, 1938, unless a limitation was read into subsection (3) to make it consistent with subsections (1) and (2), and that in subsection (3) the provision that "no proceedings shall be taken" by the lessor

---

[21] Leasehold Property (Repairs) Act, 1938, s. 1: "(1) Where a lessor serves on a lessee under subsection (1) of section 146 of the Law of Property Act, 1925, a notice that relates to a breach of a covenant ... to keep or put in repair ... and at the date of the service of the notice five years or more of the term of the lease remain unexpired, the lessee may within 28 days from that date serve on the lessor a counter-notice to the effect that he claims the benefit of this Act. (2) A right to damages for a breach of such a covenant as aforesaid shall not be enforceable by action commenced at any time at which five years or more of the term of the lease remain unexpired unless the lessor has served on the lessee not less than one month before the commencement of the action such a notice as is specified in subsection (1) of section 146 of the Law of Property Act, 1925, and where a notice is served under this subsection, the lessee may within 28 days from the date of the service thereof, serve on the lessor a counter-notice to the effect that he claims the benefit of this Act. (3) Where a counter-notice is served by a lessee under this section, then, notwithstanding anything in any enactment or rule of law, no proceedings, by action or otherwise, shall be taken by the lessor ... for damages for breach thereof, otherwise than with the leave of the court. ... (5) Leave for the purposes of this section shall not be given unless the lessor proves ... [etc.]. (6) The court may, in granting or in refusing leave for the purposes of this section, impose such terms and conditions on the lessor or on the lessee as it may think fit."

for breach of covenant or for damages for breach thereof must be read as "no proceedings contemplated in the preceding subsections shall be taken" and, accordingly, that the leave of the court was only required where more than five years of the term remained unexpired.

"....repair, uphold support amend and keep the premises when, where and as often as required".

Baylis v LeGros

[1858] 4 CB (NS) 537

Tenant covenanted to "....repair, uphold support amend and keep the premises when, where and as often as required". There was also a requirement to repair within three months following notice.

Held:

These are two separate covenants. One is a general covenant to repair and the other a covenant to repair within three months of notice. Notice had not been given therefore a right of re-entry would flow from the general repairing covenant.

Landlord and Tenant (Covenants) Act 1995 -
landlord's application for release from obligations -
"personal covenants" - "landlord covenants"

BHP Great Britain Petroleum Ltd v
Chesterfield Properties Ltd and another

Court of Appeal – 30th November, 2001
[2001] 50 EG 88 (CS)
[2001] EWCA Civ 1797

Appellant landlord entering into collateral agreement with
tenant - Landlord transferring interest in the property -
Landlord seeking release from obligations under the
tenancy and serving notice upon tenant - Whether landlord
released from obligations – Whether obligations amounting
to "landlord covenants" or "personal covenants" - Sections
3(1) and 28(1) of Landlord and Tenant (Covenants) Act
1995 – Appeal dismissed

The first defendant (Chesterfield) owned a commercial
building in London W1. By an agreement made with BHP
in April 1997, Chesterfield agreed to undertake
refurbishment works to the building and subsequently to
grant a 20-year lease of the property to BHP. Under the
agreement, Chesterfield was to be liable to BHP for any
defects in the works. Clause 1.18 defined "Building Works
Defect" as "any physical damage to the demised premises
manifesting itself during the defects period or any defect in
the demised premises which will result in physical damage
to the demised premises manifesting itself during the
defects period". The lease was granted in July 1997.
Chesterfield subsequently transferred its interest in the
property, subject to the lease, to Chesterfield (Neathouse)
Ltd. It then served a notice on BHP pursuant to section 8 of
the Landlord and Tenant (Covenants) Act 1995, in which it
applied to be released from the landlord's obligations under

the tenancy", with effect from the date of the transfer of its reversionary interest. BHP did not serve a counternotice on Chesterfield objecting to the release of obligations.

In September 1999 fractures appeared in two vertical units cladding the exterior of the property. BHP brought an action claiming that Chesterfield was liable under the terms of the agreement to replace all the non-vertical units in the property, on the ground that the use of toughened glass in a non-vertical unit constituted a defect in the property that Chesterfield was obliged to make good. Chesterfield contended that its liability was limited to replacing the two fractured units. In the alternative, Chesterfield argued that it had been released from its liability by operation of the notice. Both Chesterfield and BHP applied for summary judgment under CPR Part 24. The judge concluded that Chesterfield's liability under the agreement was limited to replacing the fractured units. The judge also found that Chesterfield's obligations under the agreement took the form of "personal covenants" and not "landlord covenants" for the purpose of the 1995 Act, so that Chesterfield was not released from its obligations by the operation of the section 8 notice.

Chesterfield appealed against the judge's conclusion as to the effect of the notice. It submitted that the 1997 agreement was a collateral agreement and that the obligations in question constituted "landlord covenants" within the terms of section 28(1) of the 1995 Act, so that, by virtue Of section 3 (1) of the Act, the burden of those obligations passed to Chesterfield (Neathouse) Ltd on the transfer of the reversion, notwithstanding that the obligations were expressed as personal obligations to Chesterfield.

BHP cross-appealed against the judge's conclusion as to the extent of Chesterfield's liability. It submitted that the second limb of the clause 1.1.8 definition had been fulfilled, and that Chesterfield was obliged to remedy the defect by replacing all the non-vertical units of toughened glass.

Held: The appeal was dismissed. The cross-appeal was allowed.

1. The crux of the matter was the definition of "landlord" in section 28(1) as meaning "the person for the time being entitled to the reversion expectant on the term of the tenancy". It was impossible to read that as meaning only the original landlord. It followed that if that definition was transposed into the definition of "landlord covenant", what one had was an obligation "failing to be complied with by [the person who may from time to time be entitled to the reversion on the tenancy". Therefore, an obligation that was personal to the original landlord was, by definition, not a "landlord covenant", since it did not fall to be performed by the person who might from time to time be entitled to the reversion on the tenancy. Chesterfield's obligations under the agreement, being expressed to be personal to Chesterfield, were not "landlord covenants" within the meaning of the 1995 Act, and the section 8 notice was accordingly ineffective to release it from its obligations. The judge had been correct to find as he did on that issue.

2. The first limb of the definition of "Building Works Defect" was directed at physical damage that had actually occurred, whereas the second limb was directed at the existence of an underlying defect that had either caused or would cause physical damage. Under that second limb, Chesterfield's liability extended to remedying the underlying defect not merely by repairing any damage that had already occurred, but also by ensuring that the defect was remedied so that it would not result in any physical damage in the future.

Relief from forfeiture - Courts can grant relief from peaceable re-entry

Billson and others v Residential Apartments Ltd

Chancery Division: [1993] EGCS 150

Property demised to original lessees - Assignees of lease breaching covenants - Landlords re-entering premises and claiming possession - Whether courts could grant relief - House of Lords remitting case to High Court to hear tenants' application for relief against forfeiture - Court hearing new evidence - Position materially different from that at first hearing - Application for relief refused

The plaintiffs were the trustees and reversioners of properties including 17 Gledhow Gardens, London SW5. In 1964 a lease of the property was demised to R. The lease, which was due to expire in 1997, contained a number of covenants and the property was to be used in letting furnished rooms during the lessees' personal occupation. In 1989 the lease was assigned to the defendants (RAL). Work was done on the premises without the trustees' permission and they re-entered the premises and sought possession. RAL sought relief from forfeiture.

At first instance it was held that the re-entry was lawful and that the court had no jurisdiction to grant relief under section 146 of the Law of Property Act 1925. However, the judge also stated that if he had jurisdiction he would have granted relief from forfeiture on stringent conditions. An appeal to the Court of Appeal was dismissed: [1991] 1 EGI.R 70.

The House of Lords allowed the appeal in 1991 and remitted the cast to the High Court stating that on the renewal of RAL's application for relief the parties would be at liberty to adduce further evidence for the judge to consider the issue on the basis of the facts at the date of the hearing: [1992] 1 EGLR 43.

Held

Relief was refused.

1. The application was heard nearly four years after the lawful re-entry: the approach was to assume that the decision at first instance should be followed; and RAL granted relief from forfeiture, if the court was satisfied that the position today was not materially different from what it has been In early 1990.

2. However, the court had been given the benefit of additional evidence which had not been available to that court. Further through the passage of time, there was a fuller picture as to what the premises had been used for and as to the position with regard to planning regulations.

3. In the court's judgment the position was materially different and there was no difficulty in concluding that it was not a case where it would be appropriate to grant relief.

4. In light of the evidence before it, the court took into account the fact that, inter alia[22], In June 1993, the council had served nine enforcement notices on RAL alleging breaches of planning permission and planning control.

5. It appeared that from the outset It was the intention of RAL's parent company to acquire and convert the premises for use as short-term lets and a responsible tenant seeking relief in the present circumstances would have made proper inquiries to ensure that the use to which they put the premises was feasible and lawful.

---

[22] among other things.

6. The present use of the premises was in breach of an express covenant; there was no reason why it was necessary for the court to imply a term that consent should not be unreasonably withheld in order to make business sense out of the bargain made by the parties at the time. It was not for the court to decide to allow a newcomer to carry on such a business In future other than in the landlords' absolute discretion. It was not appropriate for a court to grant relief on a basis which was in breach of the terms of the existing lease or which involved rewriting the bargain made by the parties. Otherwise a tenant who did not like parts of a lease could deliberately break Its provisions and then ask the court to write out the Parts that he did not like. That would not be a proper exercise of the court's discretion.

7. The lease had no value at the present time and the works done by RAL had substantially damaged the trustees' reversionary interest. Moreover, the breach of covenant entitling the trustees to forfeit had been deliberate.

8. The court had taken into account the trustees' behaviour which had been wholly inappropriate for any landlord, but now that the law was clarified one would hope that no other landlord would expect to gain anything from such conduct. However, there was no reliable evidence to suggest that RAL would comply with the lease whatever condition the court imposed so that it was inappropriate to give relief subject to conditions.

Damages awarded for cost of repairs and for loss of rent whilst the premises were not able to be let because they were undergoing repairs

Birch v Clifford

[1891] 8 TLR 103

The landlord was entitled to damages, not just for repairs required to premises yielded up in a state of disrepair, but also for loss of rent in respect of the loss suffered during the time the premises could not be rented while they were being repaired.

Statutory nuisance

Birmingham City Council v Oakley

House of Lords [2000] EGCS 144

House with separate lavatory and no washbasin – Only access to washing facilities in kitchen or via kitchen - Whether premises in such a state as to be prejudicial to health - Part Ill Section 79(1)(a) of Environmental Protection Act 1990 - Justices ordering that lavatory be moved - High Court dismissing council's appeal – House of Lords allowing appeal

The respondent tenant, his wife, three children and a grandson lived at 4c, Hunslett Road, Quinton, Birmingham. The ground floor of the house included a bathroom with a washbasin, next to a kitchen that had a sink. On the side of the kitchen, opposite the bathroom, was a door leading into a lavatory. There was no washbasin in the lavatory and no space to install one, so that anyone using the lavatory who wanted to wash his hands had to do so in the kitchen sink or the bathroom. In May 1996 the respondent preferred an information against the appellant council alleging that they had failed to abate a statutory nuisance. The magistrates found that it was unacceptable, in the interest of hygiene, to expect people using the lavatory to either wash their hands in the kitchen sink or to cross the kitchen to the bathroom to do so. They ordered that the lavatory be moved into the bathroom, with an extractor fan, and that the door to the bathroom be resited.

The High Court dismissed the council's appeal, holding that the premises were used as they were as a direct result of their layout, and that, since that use was, predictably so unhygienic as to create a health risk, the state of the premises was injurious to health and a statutory nuisance

within   Part III, section 79(i)(a) of the Environmental
Protection Act 1990. The council appealed.

Held

The appeal was allowed by a majority.

1   The matters listed In section 79 of the Act, such as
smoke, gases, or an accumulation or deposit of dust, were
capable being prejudicial to health in themselves.
Subsection (1)(a) was not limited to the specific items
listed in' other parts of the subsection, although those items
gave an Indication of the essential feature of the statutory
nuisance that was being dealt with. There had to be a factor
that was, in itself, prejudicial to health. The arrangement of
the rooms, which were not In themselves unsanitary, so as
to be prejudicial to health, did not fall within section
79(1)(a) of the Act.

2. In the instant case, there was nothing wrong With the
lavatory, nor was there any defect in the drain or the
handwash basin. There was, accordingly. nothing in the
premises themselves that was prejudicial to health. The fact
that the lavatory and the washbasin were In separate rooms,
or that, to get from one to the other, it was necessary to
pass through the kitchen, was not sufficient to render the
house itself "in such a state" as to be prejudicial to health.
The prejudice to health resulted from any failure to wash
hands, or from the use of the kitchen sink or the bathroom
basin after access through the kitchen. Undesirable though
that arrangement was, it was not permissible to give an
extended meaning to the words in section 79(1)(a) of the
Act, however socially or hygienically desirable it might be.

Relief from forfeiture - Equitable charge

Bland v Ingram's Estates Ltd and others

Court of Appeal

[2001] 24 EG 163

Landlord and tenant - Forfeiture - Relief – Registered equitable charge of lease - Whether equitable chargee entitled to relief from forfeiture

By an agreement dated 4 May 1994, the claimant surrendered a lease of restaurant premises to the first defendant landlord. The landlord granted a new lease to Mr and Mrs B, who agreed to pay the claimant £172,500 in instalments for the business. Following the failure to pay certain instalments, the claimant obtained summary judgment against Mr and Mrs B and, later, two charging orders, one against the assets of Mr and Mrs B and the other against the beneficial interests of Mrs B. Both orders included the lease. These orders were registered in January 1996, pursuant to the Land Charges Act 1972. In April 1996 the lease was forfeited by peaceable re-entry for arrears of rent and a new lease was granted to the second and third defendants. In proceedings by the claimant seeking relief from forfeiture on the basis that she was an unpaid vendor and equitable chargee with the benefit of registered charges over the forfeited lease, the claimant's application was dismissed. In a further action, Mr and Mrs B claimed ownership of chattels as against the second and third defendants; in that action an injunction was granted against the second defendant on cross-undertakings in damages by the claimant. The second defendant appealed against the dismissal of his claim that the injunction should not have been granted.

Held:

The appeal was allowed in the forfeiture action and dismissed in the chattels action. Although a claim by the claimant for direct relief from forfeiture, based upon the inherent jurisdiction of the court, was not advanced before the trial judge, such a claim failed. The cases in which the inherent jurisdiction to grant relief from forfeiture for non-payment of rent were restricted to those in which the person claiming relief was entitled to possession of land or had a legal estate or equitable interest in it. The court had no jurisdiction to grant relief to an equitable chargee who had no such interest. However, an equitable chargee of a lease that has been forfeited for non-payment of rent can seek relief from forfeiture indirectly. The basis of such a claim was an implied obligation upon the chargor, under an equitable charge, to take reasonable steps to preserve the chargee's security. The effect of the charging order was to impose upon Mr and Mrs B equitable obligations, enforceable by the claimant, that included an obligation to apply for relief from forfeiture. If relief were to be granted upon this indirect basis, Mr and Mrs B would have to be made parties for the purposes of the order for relief. The court was likely to exercise its discretion to grant relief on terms that the claimant made payment to the landlord, and the second and third defendants respectively, of all arrears of rent payable under the forfeited lease and costs. The second defendants appeal in relation to the action concerning chattels was dismissed.

Defective Notice should have been served on the Public Trustee

Blewett v Blewett

[1936] 2 All ER 188

Two cottages were leased to the defendant's father and the lease eventually passed to five children who were tenants in common. One of the children occupied a cottage rent free on condition he kept both cottages in repair.

The notice was not held to be bad simply because it contained work which was not the tenant's liability under the lease. It was defective because it was not served on all the lessees. The lease was vested in the Public Trustee by virtue of the Law of Property Act, 1925 and notice should have been served upon the Public Trustee.

A balustrade is not a wall - Repairs to a lead roof are structural repairs

Blundell v Obsdale Limited

[1958] EGD 144

A lease of a house contained the following covenant:-

"and also will at their or his expense during the said term well and substantially repair uphold support maintain and reinstate where necessary the foundations and party walls of the said messuage or tenement buildings and premises hereby demised. And also well and effectually repair lead paint paper cleanse amend and keep the demised premises with their appurtenances and all fixtures additions and improvements that shall during the said term be erected or made in or upon the same premises with all necessary reparations and amendments whatsoever when where and as often as occasion shall require"

In addition the tenant had covenanted to paint inside and out. There was a proviso permitting the landlord to re-enter in the event of breach of covenant.

The underlease contained the following covenant:-

"and also will at her expense during the said term well and substantially repair uphold support maintain and reinstate where necessary the foundations and party walls of the said messuage or tenement buildings and premises hereby demised (damage by fire excepted) but the lessee shall not be responsible for structural repairs to foundations roof main walls and drains. And also will well and effectually repair lead paint paper cleanse amend and keep the demised premises with their appurtenances and all fixtures, additions and improvements which shall during the said term be erected or made in or upon the said premises with

all necessary reparations and amendments whatsoever when where and as often as occasion shall require except structural repairs to the foundations roof main walls and drains".

The action claimed that the underlessee failed to repair a balustrade to a balcony on the first floor front room and also to repair a lead roof over the rear fourth floor level.

Held:

The balustrade was not a wall, merely a decorative feature and the defendant therefore had to repair it.

Repairs to a lead roof were structural repairs outside the repairing covenants of the lessee. However re-dressing and soldering cracks in the lead would not be structural repairs and would fall within the tenant's repairing covenant.

Each side bore their own costs.

Landlord's obligation to reinstate decorations following repairs - Housing Act 1961, sections 32 and 33

Bradley v Chorley Borough Council

Court of Appeal 275 EG 801-802

Landlord and tenant - Housing Act 1961, sections 32 and 33 - Obligation of local authority landlords under section 32 to carry out repairs - Whether obligation included liability to make good damage to decorations involved in work of repair - Repairs required to electric wiring - Landlords contended that they were under no obligation to make good damage to decorations and county court judge, on tenant's claim for cost of decorations, upheld this contention - Judge referred to fact that under the tenancy agreement it was the tenant's duty to maintain the dwelling-house in a clean condition and to be responsible for its interior decoration - Tenant appealed

Held, on appeal:

That whether or not the tenant's covenant imposed on him a positive duty to redecorate, which was by no means clear, this could not override the landlords' duty under section 32 - It was provided by section 33(7) that no contrary covenant could override the landlords' duty - *McGreal v Wake,* a decision of the Court of Appeal, was authority that the obligation to repair under section 32 included the reinstatement of decorations - *McGreal v Wake* was indistinguishable in this respect from the present case - The judge was wrong in attempting to distinguish it and in his view the tenant had forfeited his rights, if any, to require redecoration by failing to carry out his own covenant to redecorate - Landlords in present case were under an obligation to make good any consequential damage to the decorations - In some circumstances this may give a tenant the windfall of better decorations than he had before and there could be a claim for the inconvenience of having to live in an undecorated house pending the effecting of the decorations - Appeal allowed

"fixture" - windows

Boswell v Crucible Steel Company

In The Court Of Appeal [1925] 1 KB 119

Leave - Covenants - Landlord's Fixtures.

In a lease of a house the term means something which is affixed to the premises after the structure of the house is completed. It does not include things which form part of the original structure itself.

A tenant of business premises, the sides of which mainly consisted of plate-glass windows of the ordinary kind which do not open, covenanted to repair (inter alia[23]) the landlord's fixtures:-

Held:

That as the windows formed part of the structure of the house, the covenant did not extend to them.

---

[23] among other things.

Housing Act 1961 s 32(1)(a) - Steps form part of structure of house

Brown v Liverpool Corporation

[1969] 3ALL ER 1345 Court of Appeal

The tenant of a small house let by the Liverpool Corporation suffered injury falling down some steps which were in a state of neglect.

Held:

under Section 32(1)(a) of The Housing Act 1961 that the steps do form part of the structure and exterior of the house and The Corporation had to pay damages.

Breach of covenant

Botu v Brent London Borough Council

Court of Appeal [2000] EGCS 34

Landlords obtaining possession order and evicting claimant - Landlords letting out property to new tenant - Claimant obtaining order setting aside possession order - Claim for damages for breach of covenant for quiet enjoyment - Whether setting-aside order resuscitating secure tenancy apparently concluded by possession order and eviction - Judge awarding damages - Appeal allowed

The claimant was a secure tenant of premises at 93 Taylor's Lane, London NW10. In December 1996 he was arrested and remanded in custody. In April 1997 the council issued a notice seeking an order for possession on the ground of arrears of rent and, in July 1997, in the claimant's absence, they were granted an unsuspended possession order, to take effect in August 1997, together with a money order representing the arrears of rent.

On his release from prison, the claimant sought to persuade the council to take no further action on the possession order. By a letter of September 1997, the council informed the claimant's solicitors that they had applied for a warrant and were awaiting a date from the county court bailiff. The claimant's solicitors sought legal aid to apply for an order to suspend the warrant. In October 1997, before the application was decided, the eviction was carried out. Despite being informed by the claimant's solicitors that an application would be made to set aside the original order, the council proceeded to relet the premises to a new tenant, A, who moved in in November.

On 21 November the claimant obtained an order setting aside the possession order. He issued Proceedings for damages against the council claiming that as a result of the setting aside order, he had been entitled to exclusive possession of the premises and that the council had therefore been in breach of their covenants for quiet enjoyment. The judge held that the council was liable to compensate the claimant for breach of the covenant from 21 November 1997. The council appealed, and the claimant cross appealed against the conclusion that the breach of covenant had not been established prior to 21 November 1997.

Held

The appeal was allowed; the cross-appeal was dismissed.

1. The council had been acting under an order of the court when they evicted the claimant and relet the premises. The Interruption to the claimant's quiet enjoyment was therefore lawful at the time that it took place and could not retrospectively be made unlawful. A person should be entitled to act in pursuance of a court order without facing the risk of his action being rendered unlawful retrospectively. That was more pertinent where the interests of a third parties such as A, became Involved: see *Hillgate House Ltd v Expert Clothing Service & Sales Ltd [1987] 1 EGI.R 65* and *Isaacs v Robertson (1985] AC 97.*

2. There was nothing in the case of *Governors of the Peabody Donation Fund v Hay [1986] 19 HLR 145* to suggest that the possibility had been envisaged that liability could be established for actions carried out under the authority of the original judgment, or that the effect of an order to set aside could nullify a properly created secure tenancy or create two simultaneous secure tenancies. A's tenancy had clearly been lawful from its outset. A enjoyed the rights of a tenant at the premises, including the benefit of the covenant for quiet enjoyment, and the claimant could not enjoy them at the same time. Accordingly, the claimant was not entitled to damages for breach of quiet enjoyment.

Nuisance and negligence

Brew Brothers, Ltd. v Snax (Ross), Ltd. and another

High Court Of Justice
Queen's Bench Division
[1968] 207 EG 341

Nuisance and negligence - Flank wall in danger of collapse on to plaintiffs premises - Adjoining occupier and his landlord both liable to plaintiffs - Neither liable to the other - Reparations required not within occupier's repairing covenant - Matter of fact and degree - Doctrine in *Lister v Lane* applied - Further point of law on landlord's right to repair and consequent liability in nuisance to third party.

Service charge demanded in breach of landlord's
earlier undertaking - Estoppel - Equitable relief

Brikom Investments Ltd v Carr And Others

Court Of Appeal [1979] 251 EG 359

Landlord and tenant - Tenants of flats under long leases
liable to pay a maintenance charge and an excess
contribution, to be certified by the landlords' accountants in
respect of structural repairs to the block, including roof
repairs - Assurances by landlords that, despite tenants'
liability in the leases, the landlords would repair roofs at
their own cost - Subsequent demand for contributions from
tenants in accordance with leases towards cost of roof
repairs - In some cases tenants had assigned their leases
since the assurances – Tenants' refusal to pay upheld by
county court judge and Court of Appeal - some differences
of doctrine between members of Court of Appeal – Lord
Denning's view that tenants were protected by *"High
Trees"* principle of equitable estoppel - Roskill and
Cumming-Bruce LJJ preferred collateral warranty on
principle of *De Lassalle v Guildford*, or waiver in the case
of assignees or a principle of equitable relief, distinguished
from equitable estoppel, derived from *Hughes v
Metropolitan Railway Co*

Equitable Set-off

British Anzani (Felixstowe) Ltd v International Marine Management (UK) Ltd

Queen's Bench Division [1979] 250 EG 1183

Landlord and tenant - Preliminary issue on points of law - Discussion of principles governing equitable set-off to claim for non-payment of rent - Underlessees of warehouses sued for arrears of rent and for mesne profits - Cross-claim by underlessees under agreements preceding underleases for unliquidated damages in respect of defects in floors caused by inadequate design, faulty materials or workmanship - Whether sufficiently close connection existed between claims for rent and cross-claims for damages to satisfy conditions for equitable set-off - Review of authorities back to *Taylor v Beal* in 1591.

Held:

That underlessees were entitled to defend claim for rent and mesne profits by raising as set-off their claims for damages for breaches of agreements.

Service charges

Broomleigh Housing Association Limited v Hughes

Chancery Division The Times 26 November 1999

This concerned Section 148(1) of the Law of Property Act 1925. It was decided that notwithstanding that the tenant had carried out some of the works herself, in breach of covenant which was later waived by the Landlord, where works relating to the breach had been carried out by the Landlord, the full cost of service charge in respect of works on the exterior of the premises could be claimed by the landlord where works relating to the breach had been carried out by the landlord, the cost could be recovered in service charge.

Damages for breach of a landlords' repairing covenant

Calabar Properties Ltd v Stitcher

Court of Appeal [1983] 268 EG 697

Landlord and tenant - Damages for breach of a landlords' repairing covenant - Important decision but authority of somewhat weakened by procedural difficulties - Appeal by a defendant tenant claiming that the damages awarded to her on a counterclaim against her landlords should have been greater - Judge found the landlords liable for breach of covenant to repair, resulting in serious dampness and damage to tenant's flat, and there was no appeal by the landlords against the judge's decision on liability - Judge awarded tenant a sum in respect of the cost of making good and redecorating the flat, but reduced it by one third for the element of "betterment" - He also awarded a sum for the disappointment, discomfort, loss of enjoyment and bouts of ill-health suffered by the tenant's husband - These sums were not challenged on this appeal, but the landlords contested two further items which the judge had rejected but which were put forward again on appeal – The two items were (1) the rates, rent and running costs, including service charges, in respect of the flat, and (2) loss of use of the flat while uninhabitable, based on the capital or rental value of the flat - Landlords submitted that these items were irrecoverable and also objected that they were not pleaded in the tenant's defence and counterclaim - Court of Appeal dismissed tenant's appeal, but the judgments contain the following points of interest –

(1) Although the outgoings in respect of the flat were not as such recoverable, the tenant could have recovered, if pleaded and substantiated by evidence, the cost of alternative accommodation rented while the flat was

uninhabitable; *Green v Eales* was not an authority against the principle of such a claim –

(2) The claim for diminution in the value of the flat to the tenant, based on capital or rental value, was misconceived and had not in any case been pleaded as an item of special damage; it was inappropriate as the tenant did not wish to sell, but to continue to live in the flat -

(3) A tenant in these circumstances is entitled to claim the cost of redecoration and something for the unpleasantness of living in the flat until it becomes habitable –

(4) The judge should not have deducted a *"betterment element"* from the cost of repairs etc, as this was part of *"the unreal exercise of putting a price on the diminution in the value of the flat in circumstances when there was no need to do so"* -

(5) The object is to restore the tenant, so far as money can do it, to the position he would have been in had there been no breach; this object will not be achieved by applying rigid rules regardless of the circumstances but by looking to see how the tenant can be fairly compensated in the particular case.

"Wind and watertight" - repairs would not satisfy full repairing covenants despite deterioration of the neighbourhood during the period of the lease

Calthorp v McOscar

[1924] 1KB 716 Court of Appeal

In 1825 three new houses were let on full repairing terms. By the end of the lease the houses were in a state of neglect. The area in which the houses were situated had deteriorated. The Arbitrator valued the damages on two bases. One was the cost of repairs for tenants to whom the houses would now be lettable who would only want them on short lets and would be satisfied if they were wind and watertight. The second basis was to carry out proper repairs to a good standard.

Held:

That the higher standard of repair would be required. It was not sufficient to just make the houses wind and watertight to comply with the covenant.

Forfeiture - service of the writ - not mere issue - constitutes the notional re-entry in forfeiture proceedings

Canas Property Co. Ltd. v. K.L. Television Services Ltd.[24]

Court Of Appeal [1970] 2 QB 433

Landlord and Tenant - Forfeiture of lease - Date of forfeiture - Assignee of lease in breach of covenant to pay rent - Praecipe[25] for possession issued in count court against assignee - Service not effected - Claim against lessees for rent - Whether lease determined by issue of praecipe[26] or whether service of writ necessary - Mesne profits to be claimed from date of service of writ.

Landlord and Tenant - Forfeiture of lease - Mesne profits, claim for - Alteration of previous practice - Mesne profits to be claimed from date of service of writ for possession and not from date of issue of writ.

A lease dated July 15, 1964, for a term of 21 years at £800 a year payable quarterly in advance contained a proviso for re-entry in the usual form if rent was in arrear for 21 days. The lessees assigned the term to one M who failed to pay the rent due on December 25, 1967, and March 25, 1968, respectively. The lessors issued a praecipe[27] in the county court on April 25, claiming against M possession, the two quarters' rent, and liberty to apply for mesne profits from June 24 to the date of possession. As M had disappeared

---

[24] I had to include this case, because I instituted these proceedings. It is my claim to fame.
[25] Writ
[26] Writ
[27] Writ

the summons could not be served on him and was returned to the county court registrar by the post office.

The lessors discontinued the proceedings against M and on July 5 issued a writ against the original lessees claiming not only the two quarters' rent to March 25 but also the rent due on June 24 on the basis of a continuing lease. The lessees accepted liability for two quarters' rent but denied that they were liable for the June rent, contending that the lessors by issuing the praecipe[28] against M on April 25 had entered on the demised premises and determined the lease. The county court judge held in favour of the lessors that the mere issue of a writ or summons without serving it on the tenant or assignee did not suffice to forfeit the lease and that accordingly the lessees were liable for the June rent under the subsisting lease.

On appeal by the lessees:-

Held: dismissing the appeal

(1) that the lessees remained liable for the rent due and unpaid under the lease, for the lease had not been brought to an end by the mere issue of the summons for possession against M. To effect a forfeiture for breach of covenant in a lease, the lessor must not only issue but also serve the writ for possession on the lessee or assignee or, where personal service was impossible, affix a copy of the writ to some conspicuous part of the land.

Per curium. It is the service of the writ and not its mere issue which constitutes the notional re-entry in proceedings for forfeiture of a lease.

---

[28] Writ

Waiver of breach - Demand and acceptance of rent -
Use for immoral purposes

Central Estates (Belgravia) Ltd. v Woolgar (No. 2)

Court of Appeal [1972] 1 WLR 1048

Landlord and Tenant - Covenant - Waiver of breach -
Demand and acceptance of rent - Landlords' knowledge of
breach - Demand through clerical error - Tenant's
knowledge of landlords' intention to forfeit - Whether
waiver of breach

Landlord and Tenant - Forfeiture of lease - Relief from
forfeiture - Immoral user - Conviction for keeping brothel -
Many mitigating factors - Landlords' good name and value
of estate not damaged - Discretion to grant relief - Law of
Property Act 1925, s. 146 (2)

In 1957 the tenant, then aged about 60, took an assignment
of a long lease of a house in Pimlico. He supported himself
by letting furnished rooms in the house. The lease
contained a covenant against nuisance on the premises with
a proviso for re-entry in case of breach. On June 23, 1970,
the tenant was convicted of unlawfully keeping a brothel at
the house. He was discharged conditionally for 12 months.
On July 23, 1970, the landlords served notice under section
146 (1) of the Law of Property Act 1925 on the tenant
complaining that he had been unlawfully keeping a brothel
at the premises and had been convicted of that offence.

The landlords' agents, knowing of the tenant's conviction,
made internal office arrangements that no further rent
should be demanded or accepted. By a clerical error in

September 1970 a demand for £10, the quarter's rent due on September 29, was sent out. On September 22 the tenant paid the £10 and was given a receipt.

In December 1970 the plaintiffs claimed possession of the house. Judge Stockdale held that since the tenant, when he paid the September rent, knew that it was the landlords' intention to forfeit the lease there had been no waiver of the forfeiture. The judge allowed the tenant's counterclaim for relief under section 146 (2) of the Act of 1925 in view of circumstances which in combination he held to be wholly exceptional, including the tenant's age and health, the fact that there was no evidence that the landlords' good name or the value of their estate had suffered from the breach and that they stood to gain and the tenant to lose about £9,000 from a forfeiture.

On appeal by the landlords and cross-appeal by the tenant:-

Held:

(1), allowing the cross-appeal, that the landlords' demand for and acceptance of rent through their agents with knowledge of the breach of covenant effected a waiver of the forfeiture Per curiam[29]. The effect of an act relied upon as waiver of forfeiture must be considered objectively without regard to the state of mind of the landlord or the tenant.

(2) Dismissing the appeal (Buckley L.J. dubitante[30]), that in view of the many mitigating factors in favour of the tenant and the wholly exceptional circumstances, the judge's exercise of his discretion under section 146 (2) of the Act of 1925 would, if it were necessary, be affirmed.

---

[29] By the court – a precedent
[30] Doubting

Costs reserved on indemnity basis

Church Commissioners for England v Ibrahim and Another

Court of Appeal [1997] 03 EG 136

Costs were reserved in a lease on an indemnity basis. This was held to be binding by the Court of Appeal.

See also

Director General of Fair Trading v First National Bank Plc House of Lords
The Times 1st November 2001

A standard term that until payment of the borrowers debt *"after as well as before any judgment, such obligation to be independent of and to merge with the judgement"* was a default condition and not one which governed the adequacy of the interest earned by the bank for its loan. I therefore fell outside regulation 3(2)(b) of the Unfair Terms in consumer Contracts Regulations (SI 1994 No. 3159) and had to be fair in accordance with regulation 4. As the bank sent an explanatory letter to prevent the borrower being taken unawares and the bank's appeal was allowed.

Leasehold Property (Repairs) Act 1938 - Tenant not
protected by counter notice served by mortgagees,
though mortgagees "lessee" for the purpose of s 1(3)

Church Commissioners For England v Ve-Ri-Best Manufacturing Co. Ltd.

Queen's Bench Division [1957] 1 QB 238

Landlord and Tenant - Repairs - Act of 1938 - Mortgage -
Leasehold - Mortgage by way of legal charge - Proceedings
for forfeiture for breach of covenant - Notice of breach
served on tenant and mortgagee - Counter-notice by
mortgagee claiming benefit of Leasehold Property
(Repairs) Act, 1938 - No counter-notice by tenant -
Proceedings for forfeiture against tenant commenced
without leave of the court - Whether obligation to serve
mortgagee - Whether tenant entitled to invoke mortgagee's
counter-notice – "Lessee" - Law of Property Act, 1925 ss.
87, 146 - Leasehold Property (Repairs) Act, 1938 s. 1. –
Mortgage - Leasehold, of.

In November, 1946, the defendants, the tenants of premises
demised by a lease made in 1898 for a term of 78½ years
from March 25, 1898, mortgaged the premises by way of
legal charge to secure an advance. In June, 1955, the
landlords served on the tenants and on the mortgagees a
notice pursuant to section 146 of the Law of Property Act,
1925, alleging breach by the tenants of certain repairing
covenants in the lease and requiring the same to be
remedied within six months. In accordance with the
provisions of section 1(4) of the Leasehold Property
(Repairs) Act, 1938, the notice contained a statement to
the effect that a counter-notice claiming the benefit of that
Act might be served. On July 20, 1955, the mortgagees

served on the landlords a counter-notice claiming the benefit of the Act of 1938. No counter-notice was served by the tenants and on March 1, 1956, the landlords, without first obtaining the leave of the court, issued a writ against the tenants claiming damages for breach of covenant and possession. The tenants objected to the proceedings as being improperly constituted and invalid on the ground that the mortgagees were "a lessee" for the purposes of section 1 (3) of the Leasehold Property (Repairs) Act, 1938 and the counter-notice served by the mortgagees precluded the landlords from bringing the proceedings without the leave of the court:-

Held:

That a mortgagee by legal charge was to be regarded as included in the term "lessee" for the purposes of both section 146 of the Law of Property Act, 1925, and section 1 of the Leasehold Property (Repairs) Act, 1938, but that there was no obligation to serve a notice of breach of covenant on a mortgagee and that, therefore, since the landlords had served notice upon the tenants who were "the lessee" in possession, the tenants, who had chosen not to serve a counter-notice, could not, in an action against them by the landlords, take advantage of the fact that the mortgagees, who were not and had no right to be a party to the action, and who had no right to receive a notice, had also been served and had served a counter-notice; accordingly, there was no need for the landlords to obtain the leave of the court under section 1 (3) of the Act of 1938 before bringing the proceedings.

Water penetration from flat roof and gutters in possession of landlord - Landlord liable

Cockburn and Another v Smith And Others.

In The Court Of Appeal [1924] 2 KB 119

Landlord and Tenant - Flat - Roof - Possession of Landlord - Liability to Repair - Negligence - If Reasonable Care.

The owner of a block of flats let one of the top flats to a tenant, but kept the roof of the building and the guttering appurtenant thereto in his own possession and control. The guttering became defective, and rainwater which should have been carried away escaped and flowed upon the wall of the tenant's flat and made the flat so damp that the tenant suffered injury to her health and sustained damage. The landlord had notice of the defect, but was dilatory and negligent in remedying it. In an action by the tenant against the landlord:-

Held:

That the defendant was under an obligation to take reasonable care to remedy defects in the roof and guttering of which he had notice and which were a source of damage to the plaintiff., and that even if this duty was purely contractual it was not modified or excluded by the fact that the landlord had expressly agreed in the contract of tenancy to keep the staircases, passages, and landings in good repair.

Hart v Rogers [1916] 1 KB 646 is no longer an authority that a landlord who lets a flat and retains the roof is under an absolute obligation to repair the roof.

Improvement distinguished from Repair

Collins v Flynn [1963]

Court of Appeal 2 All ER 1068

The lessee covenanted to well and substantially repair, amend, renew, etc., the premises, and on determination of the term to yield them up so well and substantially repaired, amended and renewed. Due to inherently weak foundations, a pier supporting a girder upon which the large part of the rear wall and indirectly part of the side wall was bearing, subsided. As a result the foundations, walls and pier had to be reconstructed.

Held:

This was an important improvement and as the defect was an inherent one, the tenant was not liable. He would otherwise yield up in a better condition from that in which the premises were let.

Forfeiture
Crawford v Clarke

Court of Appeal [2000] EGCS 33

Tenant making unauthorised alterations - Tenant granted relief from forfeiture subject to performance of conditions - - Conditions not performed in due time - Whether right in all circumstances for tenant to be further relieved from forfeiture - County court ordering delivery up of property - Tenant's appeal dismissed

By a lease dated 25 December 1987, the claimant landlord demised part of a property known as 8 Eaton Garages, London NW1, to the defendant tenant for. a term of 99 years at a premium of £96,000. The lease contained standard covenants to keep the premises in repair and. not to make alterations without the consent of the landlord. In 1995 the landlord complained that the tenant had made unauthorised alterations and served a notice under section 146 of the Law of Property Act 1925. In 1996, under the Leasehold Repairs Act 1938, the, landlord obtained leave to bring proceedings complaining of disrepair, damage and alteration to the premises.

In March 1998, as a result of the proceedings, the parties entered into an order, by consent ordering forfeiture of the lease but granting relief from forfeiture on condition that the tenant complied with the terms set out in an agreed schedule. The schedule contained an agreed timetable for works and required them to be completed by October 1998.

The first stages were satisfactorily followed through but the works were later delayed due to the tenant's failure to make payments promptly. Ultimately the builder withdrew, and works ceased in October 1998 without being completed. The tenant duly made an application for an extension of time in order to comply with the requirements of the consent order. Such an extension was granted until January 1999 and a further extension was granted until September 1999, following which the tenant applied for a third. The county court held that although it was unusual to refuse such an application, it was no appropriate in the circumstances to grant further relief from forfeiture. Accordingly, it ordered delivery up of the property by the tenant within 28 days.

The tenant appealed, contending that the judge had failed to take into account sufficiently, or at all, the fact that the works were nearly completed and that a substantial windfall would accrue to the landlord if relief from forfeiture were not granted.

Held:

The appeal was dismissed.

The appeal amounted to an attack on the judge's exercise of discretion, and such an appeal would only be entertained on very limited grounds. In particular, the court would have to be satisfied that the judge had failed to take into account sufficiently, or at all, something that he should have taken into account or that he had taken something into account that he should not. The judge had taken account of the fact that the works had nearly been completed, and he had been entitled to balance that against all other circumstances, including the substantial, prolonged and lamentable failure by the tenant to fulfil the terms. Further, he had had valuation evidence of the freehold interest of the property before him and had been informed of how much the tenant had paid for the leasehold interest, which he had fully taken into account. Accordingly, although the judge's order was unusual, he was fully justified in the highly unfavourable view that he had taken of the tenant's conduct and had been entitled to exercise his discretion in the landlord's favour to order delivery-up of the premises: *Chandless-Chandless v Nicholson [1942] 2 KB 321* considered.

Landlord's covenant to repair - Water Penetration

Credit Suisse v Beegas Nominees Ltd

Chancery Division [1994] 11 EG 151

Landlord and tenant - Recently erected building - Covenant to repair - Cladding joints allowed ingress of water - Whether breach of covenant - Assessment of damages

By an agreement dated December 14 1977 D, a developer, contracted with a trustee for the defendant landlord that, in the events which happened, to erect a building to consist mainly of offices at 66 - 67 St James's Street, London SW1. The building was erected and clad by G, a subcontractor, in aluminium panels each of which interlocked both vertically and horizontally with its neighbours. The windows consisted of double-glazed units inserted into the panels. On January 28 1985 D, who had been granted a headlease of the building, and who had found R, who had taken possession under an agreement to take an underlease in July 1982, sold the headlease to the trustee; on the same date the underlease was granted to R for a term of 25 years from July 25 1983. On June 26 1985 the plaintiff tenant took an assignment of the underlease and at all material times held the term directly from the defendant landlord. Under the terms of the underlease the landlord covenanted by clause 5(c) (subject to payment of a service charge representing 75% of the costs) "to maintain repair amend renew ... and otherwise keep in good and tenantable condition ... the structure ... roof ... and walls . . .". From October 1982 water leaked through the panels into the building and both D and G were informed; by reason of the failure of D or G to cure the cause of those leaks no final certificate was issued in respect of the 1977 agreement. Water continued to penetrate the panels and in January 1988 the plaintiff resolved to move its West End office elsewhere. In January 1989 the rent was agreed at review at £365,000 (on the basis of £45 per sq ft). Thereafter the plaintiff sought to market the underlease but, because of the leaking panels, one prospective assignee withdrew and no further prospective assignee could be found. Meanwhile, in proceedings by the landlord against D and G, G consented to a Tomlin[31] order by which, in the events which happened, it agreed to pay the defendant £2.3m as compensation for the failed cladding. The tenant brought the present proceedings against the landlord, claiming damages for breach of clause 5(c). At the end of the trial, during closing speeches, the landlord applied to amend its pleading to enlarge its claim to seek recovery of the appropriate proportion of the costs of replacing the cladding under the service charge provisions of the underlease.

Held:

1. The landlord was in breach of clause 5(c). In order to put and keep premises in a specified condition of good and tenantable repair the work needed may not be a repair strictly so called. In such cases the required condition is not by reference to the state of the actual building at the date of the demise, but the requirements as to condition of reasonably minded tenants of the class likely to take the premises at that date. In the present case that meant a condition that the building would he substantially watertight. The cladding was not put into that condition. Having regard to "good and tenantable condition" the replacement of the cladding was within clause 5(c), it was not a substantial rebuilding and the cause of the water leaks was irrelevant. Further, having regard to the obligation "to repair, amend and renew" in the clause, the evidence showed that the water leaks had become worse owing to the movement of the panels and the failure of the seats at

---

[31] Records that an action is stayed by agreement of the parties on terms set out in a schedule.

their joints. Accordingly, there was a state of disrepair. Although the replacement of the cladding was too extensive to amount to a "repair" it fell within the obligation to "renew and amend".

2. The following damages were recoverable: (1) general damages for inconvenience suffered by staff and customers £40,000; loss of premium expected on sale of underlease and abortive costs in attempts to dispose of the same £260,173; rent, insurance and service charges payable after the date when the underlease would have been disposed to trial of £1.642m, and continuing liability to pay rent to the term date of 2008 in the sum of £2.298m after deducting the landlord's counterclaim for arrears of rent.

3. The landlord's application to amend the pleadings was disallowed on the ground, inter alia[32], that by reason of the recovery of £2.3m from G there was no injustice if the landlord could not recover the costs of replacing the cladding under the service charge provisions from the tenant.

---

[32] among other things.

Repairing covenants - Substitution of modern heating
for underfloor heating not permitted

Creska Ltd v Hammersmith and Fulham
London Borough Council

Court of Appeal: [1998] EGCS 96

Tenant's covenant to repair - Faulty under-floor heating
system - Whether tenants entitled to replace system with
storage heaters

The defendant council were the tenants of four floors of an
office building at 217-285 King Street, Hammersmith,
London W6, under a lease dated July 1993 for a period of
10 years from March 25 1993, with a rent review clause
operative at March 25 1998. Clause 3(6) of the lease
contained a covenant that the tenants would "repair and
maintain and in all respects keep in good and substantial
repair and condition the interior of the premises and every
part therefore including ... the pipes and all electrical
heating mechanical and ventilation installations therein
which exclusively serve the premises". The 10-year lease
took the place of five separate leases which were due to
expire in 1996. The building was constructed in the 1960s
and an under-floor heating system was installed. Electrical
power running through cables were embodied in the
concrete floors to produce heat during off-peak hours,
which was stored for later release. Some of the cables were
broken or their insulation was damaged. The tenants
occupied the premises for some years before 1993 and the
existence of defects in the under-floor heating installation
was already known to them when they took the 10-year
lease.

In 1996 Creska Ltd, the landlord, sought a declaration that the tenants were obliged by virtue of clause 3(6) to carry out repairs to the under-floor heating. The judge found that the tenants were obliged to repair the defects and that they were entitled to discharge that obligation by installing modem electric night storage wall heater units as and when requisite or by relaying the under-floor a cables in separate zones with flexible terminators. The landlord appealed contending that the clause meant what a it said, and that the under-floor heating system was capable of repair. The tenants submitted that a repairing covenant was capable of being performed by installing the modern equivalent of what was installed before, that repairing the existing installation was no longer a "sensible and practicable" way of maintaining the heating installation and that the party liable under the covenant to repair was entitled to perform the obligation under the covenant by substituting a different system, which performed the same function, in place of the old.

Held

The appeal was allowed.

The tenants had undertaken to maintain the existing under-floor installation in good repair. The system was defective and in need of repair and the repairs, although expensive, were capable of being carried out. The fact that repairs carried out now would incorporate some improvements in design did not mean that they would cease to be works of repair which the party liable under the repairing covenant was bound to perform. It was not a case where attempts to repair it would be futile or where the only "sensible and practicable" course was to substitute some other system.

The tenants, therefore, were not entitled to discharge their obligations under the repairing covenant by substituting individual storage heaters for the under-floor system, and the question whether they would be entitled or bound to do so, if repairs to the existing installation were no longer practicable, did not arise.

Landlord and Tenant Act 1927. section 18(1) --
Terminal damages for disrepair

Culworth Estates Ltd v Society Of Licensed Victuallers

Court of Appeal [1991] 39 EG 132

Landlord and tenant - Covenant to repair - Measure of damages for breach - Landlord and Tenant Act 1927. section 18(1) - Diminution in the value of the reversion - Cost of repair as a guide to diminution of value - Position where landlord has no intention of carrying out repairs - Landlords claimed damages based on cost of carrying out repairs but contended that the damage to the reversion was greater than such cost - Appeal from judge dismissed.

The lease in question in this case was for a term of 21 years from June 24 1965 - The premises were described as "factory premises office buildings and outbuildings" - The lease was a full repairing lease and it was common ground that at the expiration of the lease the premises were in disrepair - Despite this disrepair the landlords within a few months of the end of the term had sold the premises to a property company for £320,000 and this purchaser resold the property in March 1988 for £550,000, still in its dilapidated condition - It was agreed during the trial that the cost of carrying out the repairs required by the lease was £175,000 and judgment was given for this sum plus £21,875 for professional fees at 12½% and £31,000 for loss of rent, a total of £227,875 - An unusual feature of the case was that the landlords contended that the damage to their reversion was greater than the cost of carrying out the necessary repairs (plus fees and loss of rent) and the trial judge upheld that contention - It was entirely clear that the landlords never had any intention of themselves carrying out any repairs to the premises - The tenants appealed against the judge's decision, seeking either that the award should be set aside on the ground that the landlords had not suffered any actual damage or that the court should order a new trial.

The Court of Appeal considered authorities on the measure of damages for disrepair of property at the end of a lease and the impact of section 18(1) of the Landlord and Tenant Act 1927 - In principle the measure was the diminution in value of the landlord's reversion but it was accepted that the cost of repairs could be a guide to that diminution in value - It was recalled that Denning LJ had said in *Smiley v Townshend* that in cases where it is plain that the repairs are not going to be done by the landlord. the cost of them is little or no guide to the diminution in value of the reversion, which may be nominal" - Dillon LJ, however, observed in the present case that it did not follow that in such a case the diminution in value *must* be nominal and he referred to the judgment of Donaldson LJ in *Dodd Properties Ltd v Canterbury City Council.*

In the present case the judge found that the value of the reversion in its state of repair at the end of the lease was £320,000 (the amount paid by the first purchaser) and this was not challenged - There was, however, a substantial conflict of valuation evidence as to the value of the reversion in the state in which it would have been if the covenant to repair had been complied with. - Differences in the figure per sq ft in rental value and in the number of years' purchase produced substantial differences in capital value - Dillon LJ went into some detail in his consideration of the valuation submissions - The judge below had preferred the evidence of the landlords' valuer but had not found it necessary to be precise as the figures for the diminution of value exceeded by so very large a margin the agreed cost of repairs plus professional fees and loss of rent - Dillon LJ found the figures given by the landlords' valuer "startling" and he proceeded to take "a close look at the calculation" - In the end, however, he did feel able on the evidence to substitute any other figure of damages for that awarded by the judge below "even if (which was not the case) we had been invited by either party to make our own assessment of the damages" - He rejected the defendants' claim that the damages should be nil or nominal, since even on their valuer's figures the damages should be £134,083 - The court also refused to order a new trial - The appeal was accordingly dismissed, leaving the damages as awarded by the trial judge.

section 18(1) of the Landlord and Tenant Act 1927 -
Onus of tenant to prove landlord's definite intention on
termination

Cunliffe v Goodman

Court of Appeal [1950] 1 ALL ER 720

The tenant had a full repairing lease. On expiry of the lease,
the landlord was contemplating demolition and
redevelopment of the premises.

The landlord sought damages for breach of covenant to
repair. The tenant countered that there was no liability
because of section 18(1) of the Landlord and Tenant Act
1927 which says:-

*18(1) Damages for a breach of covenant or agreement to
keep or put premises in repair during the currency of a lease,
or to leave or put premises in repair at the termination of a
lease, ...*

*.... if it is shown that the premises, in whatever state of
repair they might be, would at or shortly after the
termination of the tenancy have been or be pulled down, or
such structural alterations made therein as would render
valueless the repairs covered by the covenant or agreement.*

The landlord had not fully decided on a course of action at
the date of determination because amongst other things she
needed building licences and conditions attached to the
licenses might render the whole scheme of development,
uneconomic.

Held:

The onus was on the tenant to prove the landlords definite intention at the date of termination. To show a conditional decision by the landlord was not sufficient.

Receiver appointed to manage block which was neglected by landlords

Daiches v Bluelake Investments Ltd and Another

Chancery Division [1985] 275 EG 462

Receiver appointed by court to carry out repairs urgently needed to block of flats allowed by lessors to fall into a serious condition of disrepair - Action by leaseholder on behalf of himself and 109 other long leaseholders – Lessors' covenant to maintain, repair, decorate and renew the structure not carried out - Substantial disrepair in respect of common parts, roof, external walls, guttering and so forth – Premises alleged to be deteriorating and becoming dangerous - Decision of Goulding J in *Hart v Emelkirk Ltd* cited as a precedent for appointment of a receiver - Leaseholders in present case paid fixed ground rents plus a service charge to meet the cost inter alia[33] of repairing the structure, including main walls, roofs, foundations, chimney stacks, gutters and rainwater pipes - Although there was a provision for a reserve or sinking fund to be built up in order to meet future liabilities for major works, no such fund had been created, at least in recent years - The enjoyment of the leaseholders had been affected and the value of their leasehold interests imperilled by the lessors' neglect - It was true that the case differed from *Hart v Emelkirk* in as much as the lessors here had not abandoned the property but had continued to perform some of their duties - Nevertheless, the properties here also demanded urgent action and the necessary works were unlikely to he done without the court's intervention.

---

[33] among other things.

Held:

Accordingly, that a receiver and manager would be appointed in the place of the lessors to receive the rents and exercise the powers, duties and authorities of the lessors, as he may be advised, in managing the block - Appointment made, with liberty to apply in Chambers.

Damages - Permissive Waste

Dayani v Bromley London Borough Council

[1999] PLSCS 260

The lease of three dwelling houses let to the Council contained the following covenant –

> *Keep... the interior of the Property in tenantable repair (reasonable wear and tear and damage by insured risk excepted) and [at the end of the agreement to give back the property in the same condition as that set out] in the Schedule of Condition (reasonable wear and tear and damage by insured risk...... excepted), up to a maximum value of eight weeks rent.*

The tenant claimed that the wording 'up to the maximum value of eight weeks rent' limited damages to that sum. The Landlord argued that this equally could be held to be the minimum amount of damage allowed before the tenant became liable. The Court ruled that the words had no meaning and should be disregarded. However, despite the tenants' contention to the contrary, the remainder of the covenant was good. The clause must be read as a tenants express covenant to keep the interior in tenantable repair and to return each house to the landlord in the condition recorded in the Schedule of Condition. Both of these obligations limited by the exceptions of reasonable wear and tear and insured risk.

The Judge went on to explore the position in relation to permissive waste. He examined case law going back to 1293 up to more modern, 19th Century authorities. He considered writings of Littleton, Coke and Blackstone. He accepted that a fixed term tenant was liable for permissive waste. He then considered Woodfall on the matter and considered the argument that the Statute of Marlborough might be thought inappropriate to impose liability for omissions. However he decided that to accept this argument would fly in the face of the overwhelming authority to the contrary.

Compensation for tenant's improvements - Landlord
and Tenant Act 1927, Part 1 s3(1) - Validity of notice
to landlord of tenant's improvements - Judge's
jurisdiction to certify execution of improvements

Deerfield Travel Services Ltd v Leathersellers' Company

Court of Appeal [1982] 2 EGLR 39, (1982) 263 EG 254

Landlord and Tenant Act 1927, Part 1 - Compensation for
Improvements - Appeal from decision of Peter Gibson J on
preliminary questions arising out of business tenants' claim
against livery company landlords - Conditions for
compensation claim under 1927 Act - Requirement of
section 3(1) that tenant must serve on landlord a notice of
his intention to make improvements, together with
specifications and plans - Question as to whether a letter by
tenants' solicitors constituted a proper notice under section
3(1) served within time laid down - Plans sent with letter
were outline plans, but these were followed by more
detailed plans - Various criticisms made of letter as a
notification of intention considered and rejected - Letter
held to be a valid notice of intention to make improvements
- Judge held to have had jurisdiction under the 1927 Act
Act to certify that improvement works had been duly
executed - Appeal dismissed

Unjust enrichment - Forfeiture

Dollar Land (Cumbernauld) Ltd v CIN Properties Ltd (Scotland)

House Of Lords [1998] 51 EG 83

Landlord and tenant - Conventional irritancy (forfeiture) Unjust enrichment - Irritancy clause invoked - Whether landlord unjustly enriched - Whether tenant entitled to recompense remedy against landlord.

In 1979 the respondents, CIN, and CDC made an agreement whereby CDC would develop a shopping centre and grant a headlease to CIN for a term of 125 years. CIN agreed, inter alia[34], to finance the development and, on completion, to grant a sublease to CDC for a term of 99 years. CIN were to obtain a return on their investment in the development from the rent paid under the sublease, and CDC would receive rents from the occupational subtenants of the shopping centre. The sublease contained a conventional irritancy clause (a forfeiture clause). CDC assigned the sublease to the appellants, DLC, who failed to pay the rent under the sublease. CIN, as landlords, invoked the irritancy clause, giving notice pursuant to section 4(2) of the Law Reform (Miscellaneous Provisions) (Scotland) Act 1985 and raised an action for declarator of irritancy of the sublease. The Lord Ordinary granted that decree and the Inner House adhered to his interlocutor. The effect of this on DLC was that they forfeited all rights under the sublease and sub-subleases granted by CDC. CIN became entitled to absolute possession. DLC appealed to the House of Lords, contending, inter alia[35]: that, in this complex commercial arrangement, there was no reason in principle why a claim by DLC against CIN for unjust enrichment was not

---

[34] among other things.
[35] among other things.

competent; that where the irritancy was reasonably invoked it did not prevent the court affording a remedy to the tenant where the adverse consequences to him and the enrichment to the landlord were wholly disproportionate to the breach; and that the court were entitled to consider the disequilibrium to the parties.

Held:

The appeal was dismissed. CIN were within their rights in enforcing the irritancy clause, having given notice of their intention to do so as required by section 4 of the 1985 Act. The events that had occurred were precisely those that flowed naturally from the operation of, and that are provided for in, the irritancy clause. It was inevitable that CIN would he enriched if the irritancy clause were enforced. The parties or their predecessors had specifically and willingly contracted for this result, which could not be said to be unjust. Where an irritancy clause is invoked, the result of its exercise will normally be to confer an advantage on the landlord to the disadvantage of the tenant whose rights are being brought to an end. The benefit obtained by the landlord will accrue to him without any corresponding right in the tenant to demand payment and will flow to him as a direct result of the remedy exercised under the contract to bring the lease to an end. The lease will normally have been preceded by a preliminary agreement in the implement of which it was granted. CIN was entitled under the contract to enjoy the entire fruits of the development; there were no words to the contrary used in the irritancy clause. The remedy sought by DLC was excluded by the irritancy clause.

Landlord's Failure to repair section 32 of Housing Act
1961 - "structure and exterior" not limited to demise

Douglas-Scott v Scorgie

Court of Appeal [1984] 269 EG 1164

Landlord and tenant - Application of section 32 of Housing
Act 1961 - Alleged failure of landlord to repair roof of
building over flat in breach of section 32 - Whether roof
was a part of "the structure and exterior of the flat" - It was
conceded that the roof was not part of the demised
premises - However, judge below accepted that it was
established by *Campden Hill Towers v Gardner*, by which
he was bound, that the phrase "structure and exterior" in
section 32 was not limited to the subject-matter of the
demise Nevertheless, he interpreted the enumeration of
items given in the judgment of Megaw L.J in the *Campden
Hill* case as indicating that the roof above a top-floor flat
could never form part of the structure and exterior unless it
was included in the demise –

Held:

That the judge was in error in coming to this conclusion, in
response to a preliminary point of law, without bearing
evidence - The mere fact that the roof was not part of the
demise did not conclude the matter - On the other hand, it
could not be said that the roof of every top, floor flat fell
within section 32(1)(a) of the 1961 Act; for example, there
might he a void space or an uninhabited loft between the
flat and the roof - Everything depended on the particular
facts of the case - Appeal from decision on preliminary
point allowed and case referred back to court for rehearing.

Damages for disrepair rent, mesne profits, VAT and costs of the action

Drummond v S & U Stores Ltd

Queen's Bench Division [1981] 258 EG 1293

Landlord and tenant - Main issue quantum of damages for which tenants of shop premises were liable to landlord for breach of the covenant to repair - Useful statement of the law as to the measure of damages and analysis of items in the schedule of works required to repair the premises - Proper measure the diminution in the value of the reversion - *Smiley v Townshend* - In the absence of direct evidence the cost of repairs may he a useful guide - Consideration of schedule in detail - Damages included value added tax, the landlord not being registered for such tax - Conflicting submissions as to the extent to which disrepair or lack of decoration would influence the bid of a new tenant - A landlord's arrangements with new tenant "res inter alios acta[36]" as regards old tenant - Judgment a practical lesson in how the-court deal's with a schedule of dilapidations.

---

[36] A transaction between others does not prejudice those who are not party to it.

Implied obligation of the Local Authority to paint the premises

Edmonton Borough Council v W.H. Knowles and Son Limited

[1962] 60 LGR 124

The tenants occupied the premises on an Industrial Estate. The lease contained the following Clause:

"to pay the council the cost (as certified by The Borough Architects for the time being) of painting in a workmanlike manner every third year of the term all outside wood and metalwork and other external parts of the demised premises and any addition thereto heretofore or usually painted."

There was no right of entry reserved to carry out the works.

Held:

There was an implied obligation of the Local Authority to paint the premises and therefore the licence to have access to do so must be implied.

Damages for breach of contract

Electricity Supply Nominees Ltd v National Magazine Co Ltd and others

Technology and Construction [1998] EGCS 162

Lessee of commercial premises alleging failure by landlord to use reasonable endeavours to maintain lifts and air-conditioning system - Extent to which diminution in rental value a proper measure of loss sustained.

By the terms of a 25-year lease, commencing September 18 1978, of a seven-floor office building in Soho, London W1, at a reviewable rent, the plaintiff landlord covenanted, inter alia[37], "to use its reasonable endeavours ... to provide and carry out or procure the provision or carrying out" of certain services specified in two schedules to the lease. There was a covenant by the defendant tenant to pay, by way of service charge, a percentage of the cost of those services. Sued by the landlord for non-payment of the service charge, the tenant counterclaimed for damages, alleging that the lifts and the air-conditioning system had, on an excessive number of occasions, broken down or failed to operate properly. As regards its alleged loss, the tenant pleaded that the premises had been rendered materially less valuable and that such loss of value should be measured by reference to the difference between: (i) the rent that it had agreed to pay, whether original or reviewed, (the top figure); and (ii) the rental value of the premises in their actual condition (the bottom figure). The correctness of that measure was disputed by the landlord and by three third parties, who bore contractual responsibilities for the installations in question.

---

[37] among other things.

The matter fell to be determined by way of preliminary issue, in the course of which counsel for the tenant suggested, as an alternative bottom figure, the rent that would have been agreed if the level of service contractually required had been no higher than the level in fact attained (the reformulation).

Held

The tenant's contentions were acceptable in part.

1. The correct measure was the diminution in value to the tenant of its occupation for the relevant period, evidence of rent payable being admissible (but not conclusive) as to such value had there been no breach: see *Hewitt v Rowlands (1924) 93 LJKB 1080,* which did not impose any single or universal method of quantifying the difference in value between the premises in their actual state during the relevant period and the condition in which they would have been if the landlord's covenant had been performed.

2. The rejection in *Calabar Properties Ltd v Stitcher [1983] 2 EGLR 46* of rental value as an appropriate measure did not assist the landlord as the facts of that case (which concerned a non-assignable residential tenancy) were materially different. Nor, in the case of a trading company that remained in occupation, was there anything in the authorities to limit damages to an unexplained global sum for inconvenience: *cf Wallace v Manchester City Council [1998] 41 EG 223; Credit Suisse v Beegas Nominees Ltd [1994] 1 EGLR 76.*

3. Since the relevant covenant was not a repairing covenant as such, it could not be objected that the tenant had alleged a general devaluation of his interest rather than attributing specific losses to specific instances of equipment malfunction. As evidence of failure to use reasonable endeavours, such instances were relevant as part of a statistical whole rather than for their own sake.

However, since there was no assumption as to the period or periods of breach, the court would reject the tenant's reformulation of the bottom figure as it seemed to require a single level of notional rent to be fixed for the whole of each review period.

4.There could be no objection to adducing expert valuation evidence. Judicial disparagement of such evidence had to be read in the light of the tenancies there under consideration: *cf Calabar and Wallace (supra).*

Repairs distinguished from improvement

Elite Investments Ltd. v T I Bainbridge Silencers Ltd.

Chancery Division [1986] EG 1001

Landlord and tenant – Dilapidations – Repairs – Liability for dilapidated industrial unit – Action by landlords against tenants – Whether works specified by landlords constituted works of repair within the scope of the repairing covenants or were works of renewal outside it – Action concerned two industrial units, but the main issue related to the larger, the lease of which had terminated – There was a general repairing covenant well and substantially to repair, replace etc. the demised premises including the roof – At the date of grant the roof was already deteriorating – Bitumastic coating had not been applied until galvanising had to a large extent worn off and by the date of the action the roof was beyond patching; it had come to the end of its useful life and needed to be replaced – Replacement of roof would cost £84, 364 – In its dilapidated condition the unit had virtually no value for tenants but its value as repaired would be about £140,000 or £150,000 – As the cost of repairs was less than the diminution in the value of the reversion, section 18 of the Landlord and Tenant Act 1927 did not apply – The only question in regard to this unit was whether the replacement of the roof constituted a repair –

Authorities referred to included *Lurcott v Wakely and Wheeler, Brew Brows Ltd v Snax (Ross) Ltd, Ravenseft Properties Ltd v Davstone Holdings Ltd, Halliard Property Co Ltd v Nicholas Clarke Investments Ltd and Post Office v Aquarius Properties Ltd*

Held

(rejecting arguments based on inherent defect, giving back to the landlords an entirely different thing, disproportionate cost of repair, and the test of what a reasonable landlord would do) that this was a repair of replacement of part within the meaning of the tenants' covenant – It was not a different thing, but merely an industrial building with a new roof – Consequently a claim for damages of £83, 364 in relation to the larger unit had been established by the landlords –

Held however,

that a claim by the landlords in relation to the smaller unit, based on a covenant by the tenants to allow the landlords to enter and carry out repairs on the tenants' default and recover the cost, failed on the facts – On the application of the Leasehold Property (Repairs) Act 1938, Judge Paul Baker, like Nourse J *Colchester Estates (Cardiff) v Carlton Industries Plc,* allowed the decision of Vinelott J in *Hamilton v Martell Securities Ltd* in preference to that of McNeill J in *Swallow Securities Lts v Brand*

Whether bungalow fixture or chattel

Elitestone Ltd. v Morris and another

House Of Lords [1997] 27 EG 116

Landlord and tenant – Rent Acts – Structure – whether tenancy of bungalow – whether bungalow fixture of chattel

The plaintiffs were the owners of a site, divided into 27 lots, which they acquired in 1989 for development. The first defendant, who had occupied a chalet or bungalow on one of the lots since 1971, when he paid £250 for it, was required to obtain an annual "licence" the fee for which rose steadily until the plaintiffs demanded £1,000 in 1990. In proceedings by the plaintiffs seeking possession of the lots, the defendants claimed yearly tenancies protected by the Rent Act 1977. At trial the assistant recorder held that the first defendant's claim to a protected tenancy depended upon whether the bungalow formed part of the realty; he decided that it did. The first defendant appealed the decision of the Court of Appeal which had held that the bungalow was not a fixture and part of the realty, and was owned by the first defendant.

Held:

The appeal was allowed. Recent photographs not before the Court of Appeal showed that the bungalow was not like a Portakabin or mobile home. The nature of the structure was that it could not be taken down and re-erected elsewhere. When the bungalow was being constructed the object of bringing the individual bits of wood on to the site seems clear, they all became part of the structure, which was itself part and parcel of the land and realty.

The absence of any attachment to the soil (save by gravity) becomes an irrelevance. The subjective intention of the parties cannot affect the question, whether a chattel has become part of the freehold.

Damp penetration of flats Counter claims for ground
rent and service charge

Elmcroft Developments Ltd v Tankersley-Sawyer;
Same v Iab Ltd And Another;
Same v Rogers

Court of Appeal [1984] 270 EG 140

Landlord and tenant - Dampness in flats - Tenants'
counterclaims for damages in landlords' actions claiming
arrears of ground rent and service charges - Three separate
actions - Landlords' appeal against county court judge's
decisions in favour of tenants on counterclaims - Judge
found evidence of penetrating damp in flats due to the
damp course having been positioned below ground level,
with consequent "bridging" causing rising damp in the
walls Remedial work required included insertion of damp-
course by silicone injection - Landlords' covenant was to
"maintain and keep the exterior of the building and the
roof, the main walls, timbers and drains thereof in good and
tenantable repair and condition" - Review of well-known
authorities from *Proudfoot v Hart* to *Ravenseft Properties
Ltd v Davstone (Holdings) Ltd - Court of Appeal* held that
judge (whose judgment was a "model of lucidity") had
correctly found that landlords were in breach of their
covenant to repair; that the remedial work required did not
go beyond repair as defined in the authorities; and that it
did not involve the provision of a wholly different thing
from that which was demised - Judge's findings on tenants'
subsidiary claims in respect of breaches of covenants to
clean and light premises also upheld. Criticism of judge's
calculation of damages rejected Landlords' appeals
dismissed

Damages for failure to repair - Section 18 of the Landlord and Tenant Act 1927

Espir v Basil Street Hotel Ltd.

[1936] 3 All ER 91

E was the tenant of part of a building for a term of 98 years. He sublet to B., less a reversion of 15 days. B then took a lease from the superior landlord of the whole building, subject to the lease to E, for a term of 999.

E brought an action against B for breach of the conditions of the sub lease because he had made some unauthorised structural alterations to the whole premises which were used as a hotel. The county court judge awarded E £60 damages assessed on the cost of reinstating that part of the hotel in which E had an interest before he could let it to some other person.

B Appealed. It was held that the proper damages due to E were the loss of value in the reversion. He only had a 15 day reversion and there was no evidence of loss of value on reversion. This is particularly interesting because B was not only E's tenant, but also his landlord. In view of this, the court rejected the argument that account must be taken of the possibility of the lease being determined by forfeiture or otherwise than by effluxion of time. It held that the holder of a nominal reversion was only entitled to claim damages limited to the value of such a reversion, which in this case was nominal.

Forfeiture - Section 146(1) of the Law of property Act 1925 - Waiver - Bad notice - Breaches incapable and capable of remedy discussed

Expert Clothing Service & Sales Ltd v Hillgate House Ltd and Another

Court of Appeal [1985] 275 EG 1011

Landlord and tenant - Appeal by tenants against judge's order granting landlords possession of premises and dismissing tenants' claim for relief against forfeiture Premises previously used for clothing manufacture on which appellants had originally wished to set up a gymnasium and health club - There had been litigation in the county court which had been compromised, resulting in a consent order in "Tomlin[38]" form staying the proceedings on the terms of a schedule which recorded agreed variations of the lease - A deed of variation had been engrossed but not executed - By these varied terms the tenants were placed under an obligation to reconstruct the demised premises either as offices or as a gymnasium or health club and to complete the reconstruction by a certain date - Tenants got into financial difficulties and failed even to begin the reconstruction by the due date Landlords served a notice under section 146(1) of the Law of property Act 1925 alleging failures to reconstruct the premises by the due date and to give notice of a bank charge, and asserting that the breaches were incapable of remedy - In the subsequent action before Judge Paul Baker QC, sitting as a deputy High Court judge,

---

[38] Records that an action is stayed by agreement of the parties on terms set out in a schedule.

the judge held

(1) that the main breach alleged (the failure to reconstruct) was incapable of remedy, although the lesser breach of failing to notify a bank charge was so capable;

(2) that the landlords had not waived their right to forfeit the lease by proffering documents which on their face treated the lease as subsisting; and

(3) that the tenants should not be given relief from forfeiture.

The tenants appealed

Held by the Court of Appeal:

allowing the appeal, that both the breaches were capable of remedy, the breach of obligation to reconstruct being capable of remedy within a reasonable time, and that the landlords' notice under section 146 (1) was wholly bad as not requiring the breaches to be remedied.

This was enough to dispose of the appeal but, having been invited to express an opinion on the issue of waiver, the court agreed with the judge below that in all the circumstances the proffering by the landlords of the unexecuted engrossment of the deed of variation was not an unequivocal recognition of the subsistence of the lease, so that there was no waiver - Questions of relief from forfeiture did not arise in view of the court's decision that the landlords' notice under section 146(1) was invalid - A number of authorities were analysed and some matters of importance in regard to the distinction between breaches capable and breaches not capable of remedy discussed - For example, it was not true without qualification that the breach of a negative covenant was never capable of remedy nor that a Once-and-for-all breach of a positive covenant was never so capable - There was, however, authority for the proposition that the breach of a negative covenant not to assign, underlet Or Part with possession was never capable of remedy - The breach of a positive covenant was ordinarily, but not Invariably, capable of remedy - Per O'Connor LJ, commenting on intricate reasoning in *Scala House & District Property Co Ltd v Forbes*, "It seems to me that it cannot be right to describe a breach which has been remedied as a breach which is incapable of remedy, and thereafter to say that it was Incapable of remedy before it was remedied".

Tenant yielded up in disrepair citing lack of "building licence" required shortly after World War II preventing repairs being carried out. - Found to be liable for damages

Eyre v Johnson.

King's Bench Division [1946] KB 481

Emergency legislation - Landlord and tenant - Lease - Covenants by tenant to keep and yield up premises in repair - Covenant to paint inside and outside in the last three months of the tenancy - Work unlawful, without licence - Licence refused - Claim for damages for breach of covenants - Defence (General) Regulations 1939, No. 56A.

In 1930, a landlord let a house for twenty-one years, the lease containing covenants by the tenant to keep and yield up the premises in repair. The tenant having given six months' notice, pursuant to the terms of the lease, to determine the tenancy in December, 1944, applied to the Minister of Health for licences to effect repairs, but these were refused[39] and the premises were yielded up to the landlord unrepaired. In an action for damages for breach of the covenants to repair, the tenant pleaded that performance of the covenants became illegal by reason of the Defence (General) Regulation, 1939, No. 56A, and that therefore he was not liable. The judge found that, since the outbreak of war in 1939 very little had been done to the premises by the tenant by way of repair. There was no regulation restricting the tenant from effecting repairs until 1941 and from 1941 to 1944 the limit of work which could be done without licence was at first £500 and then £100.

---

[39] Builders made fortunes during this period by doing wonders for £100 and some folding paper.

Held that:

(1.) the condition of non-repair of the house was due to a series of breaches of covenant to keep in repair; and

(2.) the landlord having performed his obligations under the lease, the fact that it had become difficult or even impossible for the tenant to perform certain of his obligations under the lease, did not amount in any sense of the word to frustration and did not relieve the tenant from the payment of damages for his breaches of covenant.

Landlord and Tenant Act, 1927 s. 18. - covenant not to alter - not to use otherwise than as a private dwelling-house

Eyre and Another v Rea.

King's Bench Division [1947] KB 567

Landlord and tenant - Lease - Covenant not to alter internal planning of premises or underlet any part thereof - Conversion of house into flats - Breach of covenant - Forfeiture - Measure of damages - Landlord and Tenant Act, 1927 s. 18.

The assignee of a lease which contained a covenant not to alter the internal planning of the premises, not to permit the premises to be used otherwise than as a private dwelling-house in one occupation, and not to underlet or part with the possession of any part of the premises, granted sub-leases of parts of the premises to sub-tenants who, by arrangement with him, converted the premises into five separate flats. In an action in which the landlord was granted a decree of forfeiture for breach of covenant, and an order for possession, it was contended for the defendant assignee that the measure of the damages to which the landlord was entitled was only that provided by s. 18 of the Landlord and Tenant Act, 1927, for breach of covenant to keep and put premises in repair.

Held:

That the measure of damages provided by s. 18 of the Act of 1927 could not be extended to cover a breach such as had been committed in the present case, and the landlord was entitled to the cost of restoring the premises to their original state, plus the loss of rent during the work of restoration, even though the premises, as flats, were from a financial point of view more valuable than they would be as a single dwelling-house.

S 18 of the Landlord and Tenant Act 1927 - Occupying lessees of FR & I leases renewed - Intermediate landlord argued no loss of reversionary value because no argument to diminish rent for want of repair

Family Management v Gray

Court of Appeal [1980] 253 EG 369
[1979] 253 EG 369

Two shops were let on building leases granted of full repairing terms in January 1887 and expiring in December 1974. The shops were sub-let on fully repairing terms to two tenants and they renewed their leases also on full repairing terms for a further 20 years, direct with the freeholder. The premises which were situated in an area which had deteriorated over the years, had been improved but were not in repair at the expiration of the term. Some £6,000 had to be spent to put them into repair.

Under section 18 of the Landlord and Tenant Act 1927 damages are limited to the loss of reversionary value. Asked the hypothetical question, 'what would be the diminution in rental value if the premises were let with vacant possession in the condition in which they were found at the end of the term?' the tenant's expert suggested a reduction of £100 per year but heavily qualified his answer saying it was hypothetical. The expert for the landlord put the loss considerably higher. The judge found the loss to be £100 per annum per shop and capitalised at 8 year purchase, this came to £1,600.

Mr. Gray, who had owned the intermediate interest prior to its termination by effluxion of time, appealed. For reasons of friendship, he did not join in the occupying tenants. The crux of his argument was that his tenants had previously had fully repairing leases and could not therefore argue the state of disrepair in negotiating a new lease.

Lord Denning's judgment in Smiley v Townsend [1950] 2 KB 311 was cited in which two illustrations were discussed. "....These illustrations show that although future events do not in themselves reduce or extinguish the damages, nevertheless they may properly be regarded in so far as they throw light on the value of the reversion at the end of the lease."

The appeal was allowed with costs in the court of appeal and a variation in the appellant's favour of the order for costs in the court below.

Unlawful re-entry and forfeiture - Failure to spend insurance monies not a breach of a repairing covenant and was a single breach of covenant, not a continuing one - Acceptance of rent waived breach

Farimani v Gates

[1984] 271 EG 887 Court of Appeal

A building, let on a long lease, was damaged by fire. The lease contained a covenant to insure and keep insured the demised premises and in the event of damage to lay out the insurance moneys for rebuilding or repairing the premises. The settlement of a claim took a long time. The Landlord served a Section 146 Notice and made a peaceful re-entry and forfeited the lease.

Held:

1. That the breach of the covenant to lay out insurance moneys was not a breach of a repairing covenant.

2. That the breach of the covenant to lay out insurance moneys was a single breach and not a continuing one.

3. That the covenant to lay out insurance moneys was subject to an implied obligation to do so within a reasonable time.

4. That the acceptance of rent by the Landlord following the breach acted as a waiver of the right to forfeit.

Peaceably entering into possession was therefore unlawful.

Damp basement - Whether tanking part of structure

Fincar SRL v Mount Street Management Co Ltd

Court of Appeal [1998] EGCS 173

Water penetration into basement partly caused by damaged rendering applied to inside of external wall - Whether tenant liable under covenant to keep exterior of building in structural repair.

By two leases made in 1932 (the 1932 leases) a six-floor building comprising nos 109 - 113 Mount Street, London W1, was demised for a term of 999 years. The ground floor and basement were occupied by shops. Included in the demise were a number of vaults designed for coal storage, which lay below ground at the front of the building. Each lease contained a covenant by the lessee to "keep the demised building (both inside and outside) in a proper state of structural and decorative repair". In 1971 B Ltd, a successor to the original lessees, carried out works designed to extend the existing basement area into the vaults and to create more space for commercial lettings. As a damp-proofing measure, referred to as "tanking", a waterproof rendering was applied to the inside surfaces of the exterior walls of the enlarged area. However, it was subsequently discovered that two sections (the non-rendered sections) were not so treated; in one place the contractors had used polythene secured by battens and, in another, erected a stud and plasterboard false wall. The resulting ground floor and basement units were then let to commercial tenants.

In 1986 B Ltd concluded a sale and lease-back transaction with a bank, as a result of which the bank became the landlord of the commercial tenants and B Ltd became a sublessee of the remainder of the building for a term of 34 years. By the terms of the sublease, B Ltd was obliged to "keep the exterior of the Building in a proper state of structural and decorative repair *in accordance with the terms of the Head Lease* ". (Emphasis added.) The plaintiff landlord and the defendant tenant were respectively successors to the bank and B Ltd. In December 1994 the landlord took High Court proceedings, alleging that penetration of water into the basement had put the tenant in breach of the 1986 covenant. On taking a number of preliminary issues, the judge, relying partly on *Granada Theatres Ltd v Freehold Investments (Leytonstone) Ltd [1959] Ch 592,* ruled that the tenant was liable in so far as the damage was caused by its failure to repair the exterior structure of the building, including the tanking of the basement. The tenant appealed, contending that the internal rendering did not form part of the structure of the building. Fresh evidence was admitted before the Court of Appeal as to the attempted protection of the non-rendered sections a matter not considered at first instance.

Held

The appeal succeeded only in relation to the non-rendered sections.

1. Because of the concluding words of the 1986 covenant, effect had to he given to the wording of the corresponding covenant in the 1932 leases, in particular the reference to both the inside and the outside of the structure.

Accordingly, the judge had been right to hold that the tanking fell within the repairing covenant. On the other hand, the temporary expedients adopted in dealing with the non-rendered sections did not become part of the wall or structure.

2. Since the provisions of more than one lease had to be construed, decisions on similar wording were of little assistance: cf *Pearlman v Keepers and Governors of Harrow School [197812 EGLR 61.*

3. Per Thorpe U (dissenting): The specialist tanking did nothing to contribute to the fundamental function of the "exterior" brickwork, which was to withstand the pressure of the surrounding subsoil. Its only function was to change the use to which the interior space was put. On a common-sense view of the sale and lease-back transaction, that matter was intended to be the concern of the occupying commercial tenants.

Notice of disrepair - Repair defects not clear

Fletcher v Nokes

[1897] 1 Ch 271

The lease of six houses contained covenants to keep and yield up at expiration of the term in tenantable repair. There was a proviso for re-entry for breach of covenant. A notice was served on lessee under section 14(1) of the Conveyancing Act, 1881 saying words to the effect ".... you have broken the covenants to repair the inside and outside ...... Repair the houses and pay me 20 pounds compensation and expenses for surveyors and solicitors fees. If you do not, I will re-enter and take possession...."

Held:

A notice must be one which would enable a tenant to understand with reasonable certainty what it is he is required to do. The action was dismissed with costs.

Service charges

Fluor Daniel Properties Ltd. and others v Shortlands Investments Ltd

Chancery Division [2001] EGCS 8

Modern commercial block equipped with extensive air-conditioning system - Leases requiring landlord to maintain equipment and to provide air-conditioning and other services - System well maintained and in good working order - Landlord making £2m demand under service charge provisions to recover intended expenditure on upgrading system - Landlord relying upon extended wording of repairing covenant and express power to make reasonable additions and variations to services - Tenants' objections largely upheld.

Held:

The amounts claimed by the landlord were largely irrecoverable.

1. While the words employed in clause 6(1) did extend to the doing of works going beyond repair strictly so-called (see the similarly-worded provision considered in Credit Suisse v Beegas Nominees Ltd [1994] EGLR 76), the lessees had correctly submitted that, in the case of plant, the obligations contained in the clause presupposed some malfunctioning such that repair, amendment or renewal was reasonably necessary, having regard to what was reasonably acceptable to an office tenant of the kind likely to take a lease of the building.

2. The intended works could not be carried out under the proviso to clause 6(2), as the relevant service was the treated air, electricity or hot water that the landlord had covenanted to provide. The landlord did not provide a

service by renewing or improving plant that was capable of delivering such a service.

3. Although widely drawn, clause 7(2)(e) did not entitle the landlord to incur expense on plant where it was in proper working order and capable of rendering the relevant service to the standard required by the landlord's obligations, and where the proposed works were not reasonably required to maintain the service and would not improve it. It was otherwise where a service, although supplied to the standard applicable at the date of the lease, had ceased to conform to the reasonable requirements of the tenants of the building.

4. The fact that the lessees were paying for works that the landlord was required to carry out did not displace the normal rule that it was for the landlord covenantor, provided that he acted reasonably, to choose the mode of performance. Plough Investments Ltd v Manchester City Council [1989] 1 EGLR 244 considered. However, on the issue of reasonableness, the standard had to be such as the tenants, given the lengths of their leases, could fairly be expected to pay for. The landlord could not reasonably overlook the relatively limited interest of the paying tenants: see Holding & Management Ltd v Property Holding & Investment Trust plc [1990] 1 EGLR 65.

5. The intended works could not be said to be reasonable merely because the plant had operated over the expected 'Industry-recognised lifespan" to be found in various professional tables. These could only serve as a starting point. Strong contrary indications were to be found in the relevant maintenance records, which did not show an increase in the frequency of breakdowns or a rise in the cost of maintenance.

6. Upon the evidence before the court, the lessees' objections succeeded in so far as they related to replacement work intended to be carried out to: the sumps, humidifiers and cooling blocks; the chillers and cooling towers; the motors driving the fans; the operation of the boilers; and the removal of two redundant oil tanks. The landlord was, however, entitled to claim for the replacement of the roofs of three external air-handling units and for an upgrading of the electricity supply to the air-conditioning system.

Notice of disrepair - words "examine and repair" - Notice good

Fox v Jolly

House of Lords [1916] 1 AC 1

A notice was served under section 14 of the Conveyancing and Law of Property Act 1881 by the lessor of six small houses stating the particular breaches complained of were allowing dilapidations listed in a schedule annexed to the notice, to accrue. In some instances the schedule required the lessee to "examine and repair".

It was held that the notice sufficiently particularised the breaches and had the words "examine and" been omitted the schedule still made sense. The lessor was not required to give a specification for repairs. Merely to specify the breaches sufficiently for the tenant to remedy them. The application for relief from forfeiture failed.

Specific performance - section 125 of the Housing Act
1974

Francis v Cowlcliff Ltd

Chancery Division [1976] 239 EG 972

Specific performance ordered of landlord's covenant to
provide and maintain lift in small block of flats - Landlord's
financial position no answer to tenant's claim - No case of
frustration made out, or of hardship which might justify
refusal of the remedy

This was a claim for specific performance of a covenant in
the lease obliging the lessor to provide and maintain a lift
for tenants' use, alternatively for damages.

On October 16 1969 City & West End Properties Ltd, the
then landlords, granted the tenant a new lease of her flat for
a term of five years calculated from September 29 1969. By
clause 3 (2) of that lease the lessor covenanted to keep the
exterior of the premises and all parts of the building,
including the hall, staircase and passages not the subject of
that or any other letting, in good repair. Further, by clause 3
(4) the lessor covenanted to provide the services set out in
the schedule to the lease. Paragraph 2 of that schedule
provided: "Where facilities exist to provide and maintain a
lift or lifts for the use of tenants in the building." Such
facilities did exist, as the building was provided with a lift
operated by hydraulic power. This continued to operate
until February 1972. At that time a company which had
formerly provided a supply of water under pressure to
operate the lift ceased its supply. Also, it was common
ground between the parties that by February 1972 the lift
was in a very bad state of repair.

On August 13 1972 the reversion in the block was assigned
to the defendant company.

The company took proceedings against three other tenants, including Mrs Francis. Their action against Mrs Francis was heard in the West London County Court on July 13 1973. An order for possession was made but suspended on terms which Mrs Francis had performed. It was not disputed that she remained in possession as a protected tenant.

By its original defence to the present action the defendant company did not dispute that there had been a breach of covenant, but disputed the plaintiff's right to have the covenant specifically performed, on the basis that it was unpractical for the company to provide a lift. At the trial the company sought leave to amend its defence by raising for the first time the contention that it was impossible to provide a lift and accordingly that its obligations under the covenants had been frustrated. His Lordship had granted leave so to amend on terms that the company paid the whole of the costs of the action up to the amendment in any event.

There were therefore three issues in the action:

(1) whether the defendant company was excused from performing its obligations under the covenants because performance had been frustrated;

(2) if not, whether the plaintiff was entitled to specific performance of those covenants; and

(3) if not, what measure of damages was appropriate in lieu of specific performance.

Mrs Francis was a widow of over 70 years of age. His Lordship accepted that it was not impossible for her to continue to live in her flat without the help of a working lift, but in his judgment that lack of a lift caused her grave inconvenience. Her access to her third-floor flat had been made less convenient and must be a burden on a person of her age. Mrs Francis also said, and he accepted, that since the lift ceased to operate her friends, and particularly those who used to visit her for bridge afternoons, had been reluctant to come to her flat. In his judgment the lack of a working lift had been a serious inconvenience to Mrs Francis, as indeed to all tenants on the upper floors of this mansion, and amounted over a period of time to a hardship which now continued.

The reason, and the only reason, advanced by the defendant company for not proceeding with the installation of the lift was that it did not have adequate finance.

It was now said on behalf of the defendant company that the refusal of the mortgagee to make further advances had released the company from further performance of the covenants because it had not and could not raise the money required for the completion of the lift scheme. His Lordship accepted that the doctrine of frustration could apply to a covenant in a lease so long as it created a continuing or future obligation. In the course of argument counsel for the defendant company had referred him to the decision of the House of Lords in *Davis Contractors Ltd v Farehant Urban District Council [1956] AC 696*, and in particular to the speeches of Lord Reid and Lord Radcliffe.

In his (Judge Rubin's) judgment, the defence of frustration failed.

In support of her claim for specific performance the plaintiff, in respect of the repairing covenant in clause 3 (2), relied on section 125 of the Housing Act 1974. The defendants said only that their default was not a breach of clause (2) as the lift was not a part of the building not subject to any lease. (The lift had been removed and a new lift delivered and stored in the basement, but not installed.) The argument was that not being fixed it could not be part of the building. It seemed to His Lordship that in fact it was as much part of a building as a door which swung on its hinges. As far as the other covenant was concerned, clause 3 (4) and paragraph 2 of the schedule, the plaintiff relied upon the general principle that in an appropriate case the court would decree specific performance of an agreement to build if certain conditions were satisfied. *Jeune v Queens Cross Properties [1974] Ch 97*

The rule has now become settled that the court will order specific performance of an agreement to build if

(i) the building work is sufficiently defined by the contract, e.g. by reference to detailed plans;

(ii) the plaintiff has a substantial interest in the performance of the contract of such a nature that damages would not compensate him for the defendant's failure to build;

and

(iii) the defendant is in possession of the land so that the plaintiff cannot employ another person to build without committing a trespass.

The defendant company did not dispute that the first and third conditions were satisfied. In his (Judge Rubin's) judgment, on his finding of fact, the second condition was also satisfied. Prima facie[40], therefore, the plaintiff was entitled to specific performance, but as the remedy was equitable and discretionary the court would not grant it where it would inflict great hardship on a defendant.

Snell at p 598 put the matter in this way: To constitute a defence, however, the hardship must have existed at the date of the contract; specific performance will not be refused merely because, owing to events which have happened since the contract was made, the completion of the contract will cause hardship. Financial inability to

---

[40] On the face of it – as things seem.

complete is not hardship. This last proposition received support from *Nicholas v Ingram, a decision of the Supreme Court in New Zealand reported in [1958] NZI-R 972.* In Fry on Specific Performance 6th ed para 426 the proposition was stated as follows: The cases which have been already quoted as showing that the hardship must be judged of at the time of the contract also illustrate another obvious principle, namely that where the hardship has been brought upon the defendant by himself, it shall not be allowed to furnish any defence against the specific performance of the contract.

In this case there was no hardship at all at the time of the contract. If ever there was a case in which the defendants had brought the hardship on themselves, this must be it. They chose to purchase and embark upon an expensive scheme for development of the property without any or any adequate finance and without making any but the most speculative arrangements for such finance. Accordingly he (his Lordship) proposed to make the order for specific performance which the plaintiff sought. It was said that this would inevitably result in the company being wound up. Even if that were so, it did not seem to him to be any reason why the plaintiff should not have her order.

Mrs Francis did not seek an award of damages in addition to the order for specific performance.

An order was made accordingly. A stay of execution pending a possible appeal was granted on condition that notice of appeal was served, and the appeal pursued, with due diligence.

[An appeal was not entered.- Ed.]

Set Off - Distraint - Human Rights Act

Fuller v Happy Shopper Markets Ltd and another

Chancery Division

[2001] 25 EG 159

Landlord and tenant - Distress - Legal and equitable set-off - Overpayment of rent - Damages - Whether tenant entitled to legal and/or equitable set-off against rent Whether landlord must have regard to tenant's rights of set-off on levying distress - Whether distress interference with human rights

The claimant tenant held a lease of premises owned by the first defendant landlord. The lease was granted pursuant to the terms of a settlement of a dispute that had arisen between the parties. By clause 4(2) of the lease, the rent would be suspended if the premises were unfit for occupation due to an insured risk. The tenant alleged that, in January 1994, a storm damaged the roof of part of the demised property. Following the storm damage, the tenant paid two quarters' rent, and thereafter made no further payments. In February 1997 the landlord instructed bailiffs to levy a distress on the basis of rent arrears Of £22,737.67. In proceedings by the tenant alleging that the distress was unlawful, the master dismissed the defendants' applications for summary judgment against the tenant.

Following the defendants' appeal against those decisions, the parties agreed that the court should decide four preliminary issues of law, namely whether:

(1) the tenant can set off against rent due at the date of distress sums claimed against the second defendant (of which the first defendant was a subsidiary) for breach of the settlement agreement;

(2) part of the rent paid after the storm damage was, because of clause 4(2) of the lease, an overpayment, to which the tenant had an immediate entitlement without any prior demand;

(3) in exercising the right of distress and in determining the amount of rent due, the tenant's right of legal set-off must be taken into account; and

(4) the tenant had an equitable right of set-off in respect of the rent overpayments.

Held:

(1) On the proper construction of the settlement agreement, and in the taking of accounts to ascertain what, if any, rent was due from the tenant at the date of levying the distress, the sums claimed in damages were to be ignored.

(2) Where there is an overpayment under a mistake of fact and/or law, the payer (here, the claimant) has an immediate entitlement to repayment without any prior demand for such payment: *Freeman v Jefferies (1868-69) LR 4 Ex 189* distinguished.

(3) Where a landlord is exercising his remedy of distress, the legal right of set-off (unlike an equitable set-off) does not operate to reduce the indebtedness of the tenant to the landlord, and therefore cannot be offset against arrears of rent accrued due at the date when the distress was levied.

(4) However, the claimant was entitled to invoke the doctrine of equitable set-off. Equitable set-off arises where the relationship between the claims is such that equity insists that the one should operate in defeasance of the other. The self-help remedy of distress involves a serious interference with the right of the tenant, under Article 8 of the European Convention on Human Rights, to respect for his privacy and home, and, under Article 1 of the First Protocol, to the peaceful enjoyment of his possessions.

Set Off

Garrow v The Society of Lloyd's

Court of Appeal, October 13 1999

The contract of names with Lloyd's required them to pay sums demanded without "any set off, counter claim or other deduction".

A name, against whom Lloyd's had obtained a judgement applied to set aside a statutory demand on the grounds that he had a counter claim alleging fraudulent misrepresentation and that his claim was at least equal to his liability to Lloyds.

The demand was for just over £196,000 and Mr. Garrow claimed that his counter claim exceeded this amount. The judge who had described it as a test case, set aside the statutory demand pursuant to rule 6.5(4) of the Insolvency Rules (Section 1 1986, number 1925). Under this rule the court might grant application to set aside a statutory demand "if (4)(a) the debtor appears to have a counter claim, set off or cross demand which equals or exceeds the amount of the debt..... or (b) the debt is disputed on the grounds which appear to the court to be substantial".

Lloyd's claimed that Mr. Garrow could not rely on the counter claim because of clause 5.5 of the contract which was described as a 'pay now sue later' clause. Mr. Garrow did not challenge his liability for the insurance premium.

He said that he had a genuine and serious counter claim and asked the court to exercise its discretion.

In Arbuthnott −v− Fagan [1995] CLC 1396, an action brought by Lloyd's names against members agents and managing agents, foundered on a similar clause. The court held that its purpose was to ensure that agents calls on names were met promptly so that claims could be met promptly.

The Society of Lloyds –v- Leighs (The Times August 11 1997; [1997] CLC 1398) was directly concerned with clause 5.5.

The argument by the names that their claims for damage for fraud were a 'pure' defence transcending the words in clause 5.5, was not accepted. However the court did say that 'whilst it is agreed that the clause cannot oust the court's jurisdiction, it has potent effect. The insulation of the set off and counter claim was intended to achieve the speedy discharge of the indebtedness, which intention would be avoided and the whole function of the clause subverted by a stay of execution.'

Lloyds claimed that Mr. Garrow was making the same argument. Mr. Garrow did not dispute his liability for the re-insurance premium. However he claimed a genuine and serious counter claim sufficient to ask the bankruptcy court to exercise its discretion and set aside the statutory demand served by Lloyds. The issue was whether the 'procedural insulation' achieved by clause 5.5 was fairly construed in accordance with the Arbuthnott and Leighs principles and prevented Garrow from claiming an offset.

His Lordship did not believe that Clause 5.5 had that effect for the reasons stated in Arbuthnott. The court in Arbuthnott emphasised the need for a purposive construction of a vague phrase 'in connection with'. It follows that Lloyds was unable to rely on Clause 5.5 in the matter of construction. There were no grounds for interfering with the Judge's exercise of discretion under Rule 6.5 of the 1986 rules for Justice Brook and Lord Justice Morritt agreed.

In the absence of context to the contrary, the demise of a room includes the external walls

Goldfoot v Welch.

Chancery Division [1914] 1 Ch. 213

Landlord and Tenant - Demise of Room - Right to Outside Wall - Evidence.

A demise in writing of the "rooms situate on the first and second floors" of business premises.

Held:

In the absence of context to the contrary, to include the external walls of the two floors.

Carlisle Café Co. v. Muse Brothers & Co. (1897) 67 L. J. (Ch.) 53; 77 L. T. 515, and dictum of Joyce J. in Hope Brothers, Ld. v. Cowan [1913] 2 Ch. 312, followed.

Held, also, that parol evidence that the external walls were to be excluded from the demise was not admissible.

Semble, in Carlisle Café Co. v. Muse Brothers & Co. Byrne J. determined that, in the absence of context to the contrary, the demise of a room includes the external walls of the room.

**"Whole of the demised premises modern and up-to-date
and in good repair and operating condition"**

Gooderham and Worts, Limited   Appellants;

and

Canadian Broadcasting   Respondents
Corporation

[And Connected Appeal.]

On Appeal From The Court Of Appeal For Ontario.

Privy Council [1947] AC 66

Viscount Simon,
Lord Macmillan,
Lord Porter,
Lord Goddard and
Lord Uthwatt.

Canada (Ontario) - Lease - Radio broadcasting station -
Validity - Interpretation - Effect - Covenant to keep
*"Whole of the demised premises modern and up-to-date
and in good repair and operating condition"* -
Construction.

By an indenture of lease *"as of May 15, 1933"* the
appellants, the owners of a private radio station, leased to
the Canadian Radio Broadcasting Commission their land
and premises and all plant and equipment *"2. for and
during the term of three years .... to be complete and ended
on May 15, 1936,"* at a rent of $12,000 yearly, payable in
advance in equal quarterly instalments. It was provided by
cl. 4 of the lease that *"the lessee covenants with the lessor*

to keep the whole of the demised premises modem and up-to-date and in good repair and operating condition," and by cl. 12 that *"at the expiration of die term hereby granted and of every succeeding term of three years to be granted by the lessor to the lessee as hereinafter provided the lessor will .... grant a new lease for a further term of three years from the determination of the present or then existing lease .... and if no such new lease be entered into as aforesaid the present or then existing lease, as the case may be, and all the terms and conditions thereof shall continue until terminated by the lessor upon one month's notice in writing to the lessee ...."* The necessary statutory approval of the lease by the Governor in Council under s.9 of the Canadian Broadcasting Act, 1932, as amended by s. 2 of c. 35 of the Statutes of 1932-33, was explicitly stated to be of a lease *"for a period of three years at a price of $12,000 per annum,"* and no reference was made to any conditions. On the expiry of the term of three years on May 15, 1936, no new lease was entered into, but the Commission remained in occupation and continued to pay the rent quarterly. On January 26, 1938, the Canadian Broadcasting Corporation, the respondents, which were constituted under the Canadian Broadcasting Act, 1936, and took over thereunder all the obligations and liabilities of the Commission, gave notice to terminate the lease at May 15, 1938. Thereupon, the appellants, in April, 1938, instituted the present proceedings claiming, inter alia[41], a declaration that the lease was valid and subsisting and for specific performance; alternatively, they claimed a declaration that the respondents were tenants under a yearly tenancy expiring on May 15 in each year on the terms of the lease so far as applicable; they also claimed damages in respect of the respondents' alleged failure to keep the demised premises modern and up-to-date and in good repair and operating condition

---

[41] among other things.

Held first:

that cl. 12 of the lease, which modified cl. 2 by providing
that in the absence of a month's notice the parties were to
remain indefinitely in the relation of landlord and tenant,
was unauthorized by the Order in Council, which had
approved a lease for a period of three years only, and was
invalid ab initio[42], and ineffectual to extend the relation of
tenancy beyond May 15, 1936. Clause 12 was, however,
severable, and its elimination left an effective three years'
lease. The payment and acceptance of rent and the
continuance of the respondents' possession after May 15,
1936, had in law the result that from and after that date the
relation of the parties was by presumption of law that of
landlord and tenant under a year to year tenancy terminable
by six months' notice on either side before May 15 in any
year, and all the terms of the original lease, so far as
consistent with a yearly tenancy, were thenceforth by law
binding on the respondents, including the obligations of cl.
4. The notice to the appellants to terminate the lease as
from May 15, 1938, being dated less than six months
before that date, was accordingly bad, and was ineffective
to all intents and purposes.

Held secondly:

that the respondents were at the time the action was
brought in breach of the covenant contained in cl. 4, and
the matter must be referred to the Master of the Supreme
Court at Toronto to determine the amount of the damages
in accordance with the law and practice of the court. The
terms of the covenant were unusual and of very wide scope,
but having regard to the nature of the premises and the
purpose for which they were designed and used it was
enforceable as a condition of the respondents' yearly
tenancy and must receive a fair and reasonable

---

[42] from the beginning

interpretation. While it was not possible to devise a precise formula for the instruction of the referee, the covenant must be construed in a business sense. The obligations of the lessee were to be construed as being obligations to keep the whole of the demised premises modem and up-to-date in so far as the thing demised was capable of being kept modem and up-to-date, so that if the existing site of the station was inadequate for the accommodation of the plant necessary for a modem station the respondents were under no obligation to acquire additional land, and the duty imposed on them by the covenant did not extend to the substitution of an installation involving the use of higher power than that of the station demised. The damages for breach must depend on the loss suffered by the appellants from the respondents' failure to fulfil the covenant.

Section 125 of the Housing Act 1974 - Specific performance - Liability for deceit – damages - Enforcement of trusts of various lease clauses

Gordon and Another v Selico Co Ltd and Another

Court of Appeal [1986] 278 EG 53

Landlord and tenant- Appeal from decision of Goulding J in favour of long leaseholders of flat in action by them against lessors (Selico Co Ltd) and management agents (Select Managements Ltd) on grounds of fraudulent misrepresentation by lessors and breaches of obligations and trusts under the lease - Goulding J had awarded the plaintiff leaseholders (the present respondents) damages for deceit and he had made an order under section 125 of the Housing Act 1974 by way of specific performance, requiring the lessors to put so much of the block of flats as was in their possession or control into such reasonable condition as not to cause damage to the lessees or their flat by the incursion of water, propagation of dry rot or otherwise - One of the lessees' main complaints had been of an extensive outbreak of dry rot in the flat, indications of which, it was alleged, had been deliberately covered up before the purchase - The lessors and the agents appealed - There was no challenge on the appeal against Goulding J's finding of a deliberate and fraudulent cover-up by a building contractor instructed by the management agents, but it was claimed by the lessors and the agents that neither were answerable for the tort of the contractor on the basis of actual or ostensible authority - Goulding J had held that the lessors were liable for the deceit on the ground that the dishonest act was done by the contractor in the course of work ordered by the management agents within the scope of their authority as the lessors' agents.

The Court of Appeal, while upholding the judge's finding of deceit against the lessors, arrived at the same conclusion by a different route - In their view the management company was, through its main shareholder, a party to the deceit and, as the lessors had entrusted the company with sufficiently wide authority, they were vicariously liable for the fraudulent misrepresentation.

The Court of Appeal also agreed with the judge that both the lessors and the agents had been guilty of breaches of covenant and breaches of trust under the lease. As regards relief, damages were not by themselves a sufficient remedy and an order for the enforcement of the trusts of the lease was required - In view of the complexity, the Chief Chancery Master would be charged with the working out of the order Accordingly, the court ordered the lessors to pay the lessees damages for the tort of deceit and for breaches of contractual obligations under the lease and made orders for the execution of the trusts of various clauses in the lease and for specific performance of the lessors' covenants to keep certain parts of the block in good repair in pursuance of section 125 of the Housing Act 1974 -

The Chief Chancery Master was entrusted with the authority to give all necessary directions for the working out of these orders

Appeal dismissed with variations of Goulding J's order as indicated in the judgment Of the court.

Landlord's failure to repair - Meaning of "structural repairs" - Meaning of "substantial" - Render is part of wall - Assignee of lease not liable for previous tenant's breaches of repairing covenants, though he is liable for the disrepair of the premises as they stand when he takes over so far as their then state of disrepair falls within the scope of the tenant's repairing covenants

Granada Theatres Ltd. v Freehold Investment (Leytonstone) Ltd

Court of Appeal [1959] 1 WLR 570

Landlord and Tenant - Repairs - Covenant – "Structural repairs of a substantial nature" Meaning of "structural repairs" - Meaning of "substantial" - Notice to landlords of disrepair - Disrepair due to failure of tenants' predecessors to repair - Liability of landlords - Long delay by landlords in complying with notice - Refusal of landlords to give specification of proposed repairs Landlords' workmen prevented from doing repairs - Repairs done by tenants - Whether tenants entitled to damages.

By clause 2 (3) of a lease made in 1941 of a cinema the tenant covenanted to keep the demised premises

"in good and substantial repair and condition and properly decorated ... but nothing in this clause contained shall render the [tenants] liable for structural repairs of a substantial nature to the main walls roofs foundations or main drains of the demised building."

By clause 3 (2) the landlords covenanted, except so far as the tenants were liable under their covenants, to

"repair maintain and keep the main structure walls roofs and drains of the demised premises in good structural repair and condition."

On December 13, 1954, the lease was assigned to the plaintiffs (the tenants).

The roof being in disrepair and the cement rendering and brickwork of the front main elevation being defective, the tenants, on January 31, 1955, served a schedule of dilapidations on the landlords in respect of these. Long negotiations followed. The tenants contended that the roofs required re-roofing at a cost of £961, the landlords, on the other hand, alleged that they had obtained a tender of £130 10s for the work, and that £961 was excessive. The landlords further contended that the repairs were the liability of the tenants, being due to the failure of the tenants' predecessors in title to keep the premises in good repair in accordance with their repairing covenants. The tenants required the landlords to furnish their surveyor with a written specification of the repairs the landlords proposed to do. The landlords failed to do so but, after a long correspondence, on September 19, 1955, on their instructions, a builder with his men entered on the premises and started to repair the roof. They were ordered off the premises by the tenants, who subsequently did the repairs themselves at a cost of £961 and in this action claimed damages for breach of the landlords' covenant to repair the roof, and a declaration that the landlords were liable to repair the front elevation:-

Held:

(1) that making good the rendering and brickwork of the front elevation were structural repairs of a substantial nature and fell within the landlords' covenant to repair.

(2) That the repairs to the roof also fell within the landlords' covenant.

(3) That an assignee of a term is not liable for particular breaches of a tenant's repairing covenants committed by his predecessor, though he is liable for the disrepair of the premises as they stand when he takes over so far as their then state of disrepair falls within the scope of the tenant's repairing covenants; but that particular breaches committed before the assignment to him, as distinct from the state of the premises when he takes over, are matters, generally speaking, with which he is not concerned; and that, in the short time which elapsed between the assignment of the premises to the plaintiffs and the service of the notice of dilapidations, no appreciable part of the disrepair could be attributed to breach of the lessees' covenant by the plaintiffs as tenants; accordingly, the accumulated breaches of the lessees' repairing covenants could not be set off against the claim against the landlords for breach of covenant.

(4) (Jenkins L.J. dissenting), that, assuming that the repairs which the landlords proposed to do to the roof would have constituted a sufficient performance of their covenant under clause 3(2) of the lease, the landlords had, on the facts, given to the tenants a sufficient warning of their intention to do the repairs, and of the nature of the work they proposed to do, and that the tenants having prevented the landlords from doing the work, the landlords were not in breach of their repairing covenants in regard to the roof and the tenants had no cause of action in respect of the landlords' failure to repair the roof.

(5) That the case must be remitted back to the trial judge to determine whether the landlords' proposed repairs would have, if completed, have complied with the landlords' repairing covenant.

JENKINS L J

"It appears, rather surprisingly, that the expression 'structural repairs' has never been judicially defined, a fact to which attention is drawn in Woodfall on Landlord and Tenant, 25th ed., p. 770, para. 1732, and counsel in the present case have accepted that statement as correct. The writer of the textbook submits on the same page that 'structural repairs' are those which involve interference with, or alteration to, the framework of the building, and I would myself say that 'structural repairs' means repairs of, or to, a structure. It is sometimes said that repairs must always be either structural or decorative, and if that is the simple criterion we are, in this case, certainly not dealing with decorative repairs.

"Next, what is meant by the words 'of a substantial nature'? In a South Australian case, *Terry's Motors v. Rinder, [1948] SASR (Aus) 167* the word 'substantial' is pilloried as a word devoid of any fixed meaning, and as being an unsatisfactory medium for conveying the idea of some ascertainable proportion of a whole. In *Palser v. Grinling [1948] AC 291* a question arose as to what was a 'substantial portion' of a rent, and the decision is summarised (not perhaps very helpfully) in the headnote, saying that 'substantial' does not mean 'unsubstantial' but is equivalent to 'considerable,' and that the judge of fact must decide the matter according to circumstances in each case. See also *Thorneloe and Clarkson Ltd. v. Board of Trade. [1950] 66 TLR (Pt 1) 1117* Again, what is a 'structure'? And what ought to be regarded as part of a structure? We are dealing here with (1) the roof, and (2) one of the main walls of a cinema, and surely those are parts of the structure of the building."

As to the specific items of disrepair upon which the dispute turns, I may deal first with the front elevation of the premises. The competing views are, on the one hand, that you have here a wall, which no doubt is part of the structure, coated with a cement rendering, which can be regarded for this purpose as equivalent to paint. The cement rendering is merely, one might say, decorative, perhaps to some extent protective, but is no more part of the structure than a coat of paint would be. On the other hand, it is said that the front elevation of the cinema consists not of a wall with the incidental application of cement rendering, but it consists of a 9-inch wall rendered in cement. The bricks and the cement should be taken together, and they together constitute the front elevation. In my view, the latter way of regarding this cement rendering and the wall behind it is correct. On the evidence as a whole, the proper conclusion appears to me to be that the cement rendering (which appears to have been from $^3/_8$ to $^7/_8$ inches in thickness) set up a chemical reaction in the bricks of the 9-inch wall, and that this chemical reaction, coupled with the effect of water seeping down between the rendering and the wall and the effects of frost, caused the bricks to deteriorate and the rendering to come away from the wall, taking with it a considerable proportion of the outer ends and sides of the bricks. Moreover, the rendering, where it had come loose from the wall, was liable to fall, and was thus a potential source of danger. The operations necessary to make good the frontage to the premises would, therefore, consist of removing the rendering, making good the defective brickwork, and replacing the rendering. These operations appear to me, as they did to the judge, to amount to structural repairs, and, moreover, in view of their extent, to amount to structural repairs of a substantial nature, and, therefore, these were repairs which fell to be included in the landlords' repairing covenant.

Who own space in false ceiling of a flat?

Graystone Property Investments Limited v Margulies

[1984] 269 EG 538 Court of Appeal

A Victorian house was split into a number of flats. During the course of the works for conversion a number of false ceilings were inserted to give the rooms better proportions. These were at various heights and, in some cases, did not exist at all. It was therefore obvious that the premises had false ceilings. The tenant wanted to use the space above the ceiling to form a mezzanine floor and improve his flat.

Held:

1. The demise includes all the space between the floor of the flat and the underside of the flat above it unless there are good reasons to assume otherwise.

2. It is entirely unlikely that the Landlords would want to keep various irregularly shaped spaces between flats which were of no use to them.

3. The space in the false ceiling therefore passed to the tenant of the flat.

Alternative accommodation during repairs

Green v Eales

[1841] 3 QB 235

A Landlord who has to repair a house does not have to provide alternative accommodation for the tenant during the course of the repairs.

Cleaning flue is "executing repairs" - "making good all damage thereby occasioned" includes damage to stock-in-trade - Damages to take into account whether appellant had taken precautions to minimise damage

Greg v Planque.

Court Of Appeal [1936] 1 KB 669

Landlord and Tenant - Demise of ground floor of larger building - Flue serving other parts of building running through demised premises - Right reserved to lessor to enter demised premises to execute repairs upon other parts of the building – "Making good all damage thereby occasioned" - Cleaning of flue - Whether "repair" - Damage by soot to lessee's stock-in-trade - Liability of lessor.

The ground floor of a larger building was demised to the appellant, who carried on business therein as a court dressmaker. Through the part so demised, but not forming part of the demise, there ran a flue which served the other parts of the building. The lease provided that the appellant would *"permit the lessor or his .... agents and workmen .... to enter the said premises .... for executing repairs and alterations of or upon the other parts of the said messuage .... making good all damage thereby occasioned."* During the currency of the lease the lessor by his agents entered the demised premises for the purpose of cleaning the flue, and as a consequence of the work that was done a quantity of soot was scattered over the appellant's stock of dresses, thereby damaging them. On a claim in respect of this damage:-

Held:

(1.) that the cleaning of the flue was *"executing repairs"* within the meaning of the lease;

(2) that the words *"making good all damage thereby occasioned"* were not to be restricted to structural damage to the premises but were wide enough to cover damage to the appellant's stock-in-trade; and

(3) that in assessing the quantum of damage regard must be had to the question whether the appellant had taken reasonable precautions for minimizing the amount of damage.

Notice of disrepair

Griffin v Pillett

[1921] KB 17

The Landlord of a house covenanted to keep the exterior of the premises in good and substantial repair.

The lessee wrote to the Landlord on 2nd April 1924 saying *"the steps to the front door want attention"*.

On 8th April, following the letter from the Landlord, the builders inspected the steps and advised him that *"the front steps are in a dangerous condition and being so defective we have to put the matter in hand"*.

The builders carried out repairs on 16th April, but on 14th April, the tenant, who was not aware of the danger, fell into the cellar below when the steps collapsed. As a result he was seriously injured. The tenant sued the Landlord for damages for breach of the Landlord's covenant to repair.

Held:

1. The 2nd April letter was sufficient notice to the Landlord of disrepair.

2. It gave the Landlord the right of entry.

3. The letter from the builders on 8th April prevented him from pleading that he did not have express notice.

4. That having notice on 8th April of the dangerous condition, the Landlord should have taken immediate action to make the steps safe.

5. The Landlord had committed a breach of covenant.

The tenant was entitled to damages.

Bad Notice - Good parts inseparable from bad parts

Guillemard v Silverthorn

[1908] 99 LT 584

A notice under section 14 of the Conveyancing and Law of Property Act 1881 set out general covenants to repair contained in a lease and then set out two further special painting covenants which the lease did not contain. It comprised a schedule of work to be done generally, some of which was not properly referable to the general covenant.

The notice was held to be invalid because the good parts could not be severed from the bad parts, it not being clear to the tenant which bits of the notice were good and which were not.

Acceptance of rent on three quarter days following the service of the notice waived the forfeiture.

No obligation upon a tenant to improve the property

Gutteridge v Munyard

[1834] 7 C & P 129

A lease contained a covenant *"well and sufficiently repair, uphold, support, maintain, glaze.... and keep the said messuage or tenement .... in, by, and with all and all manner of needful and necessary reparations..."* The Landlord claimed that the tenant allowed the premises to be in a state of disrepair and dilapidated.

Held:

Where a very old building is let with the usual covenants to repair and yield up in repair, there is no obligation on the tenant to yield up the property in an improved state. The tenant has an obligation to keep the house in the state of repair in which it was found at the time of the demise by carrying out repairs as and when necessary.

Inherent   defect   -   Repair   distinguished   from
improvement

Halliard Property Co Ltd v Nicholas Clarke Investments Ltd

Queen's Bench Division [1984] 269 EG 1257

Landlord and tenant - Alleged breach of repairing covenant - Landlords' claim for forfeiture and damages - Lease included a covenant by tenants to repair the demised premises both internally and externally, including all fences, walls, roofs, gates etc appertaining to the premises - There was a jerry-built structure at the rear of the premises which included a wall 4½ inches thick which was virtually unsupported apart from two brick piers on either side of a door leading into a lane The judge found that at the time of the demise there was nothing to indicate to the tenants that the wall was in danger of imminent collapse - The wall did collapse and the landlords claimed that the tenants were liable under their covenant to rebuild the jerry-built structure and in so doing to reinstate it in accordance with applicable building byelaws The tenants invoked, among other submissions, the doctrine of "inherent defect" - Authorities, from *Lister v Lane* to *Ravenseft Properties Ltd v Davstone (Holdings) Ltd,* considered - Correct principle stated by Forbes J in latter case that "it is always a question of degree whether that which the tenant is being asked to do can properly be described as repair, or whether on the contrary it would involve giving back to the landlord a wholly different thing from that which he demised,"

Held:

That in the present case the reinstatement claimed would involve handing back an edifice entirely different from the unstable and jerry-built structure of which the tenants took possession at the start of the lease - Judgment on this issue in favour of tenants

Repair of roof terrace the responsibility of the landlord

Hallisey v Petmoor Developments Ltd

Chancery Division   The Times 7 November 2000

Under the terms of the lease, the landlord was responsible for repairing the structure main parts of the building. On the top floor, the roof terrace doubled as the roof of the building, protecting tenants below it from the elements.

On a proper construction of the lease, the court decided that the surface of the roof belonged to the tenant but the waterproof membrane was the responsibility of the landlord to repair because otherwise, the landlord would have ceded control and responsibility for the repair and maintenance of part of the fabric of the building to a tenant rather than retain the right to maintain the fabric of the building and the value of the reversion.

Where a tenant fails to comply with a repairing covenant in a lease which expressly confers on the landlord the right to enter on the demised premises and carry out the repairs and recover the cost from the tenant, an action by the landlord to recover the cost from the tenant is a claim for debt due under the lease, rather than a claim for damages within s1(1) and (2) of the Leasehold Property (Repairs) Act 1938 and does not require leave under s1(3) to bring an action against the tenant.

Hamilton v Martell

[1984] Ch 266 [1984] 665 1 All ER

By landlord's licences, a school was assigned and by further licence turned into a hotel. A condition of one of the licences was that the lessees paid the entire cost of repairing the green road (rather than one-third of the cost as originally covenanted), so far as it was not maintainable at public expense, in consideration for the right to use it. It also provided for the use of the brown road and the bridge by the lessor free from cost of repairing them.

Notice of disrepair of the brown road was served on the lessee in writing in January 1981 but despite reminders in writing the lessee did nothing. In January 1982 a further letter was written stating the 1981 letter was being treated as notice under the lease. Delaying tactics by the tenant followed and he asked for time to consider. In September 1982 the lessor wrote saying that if no works were done the road would become impassable and works would be put in hand forthwith unless they heard by return of post that the lessees were themselves doing the work. On 12th October 1982 the lessors wrote to their tenants saying that the condition of the roads (green and brown) was such that urgent and substantial works were necessary and that instructions had been given for the work to be put in hand at a cost of £14,680 exclusive of VAT of which £5,718 was attributable to the brown road.

The lessors concern was real. They were liable for injury under the s4(1) of the Defective Premises Act, 1972 and there was a real risk that injury would occur if nothing was done.

By an originating summons dated 8th September 1983, the lessor applied for an order:-

1: giving him leave under s1(3) of the Leasehold Property (Repairs) Act 1938 to take action for damages for breach of repairing covenants;

2: a direction under s2 of the Leasehold Property (Repairs) Act 1938 that the lessor should have the benefit of s146(3) of the Law of Property Act 1925 in respect of the costs and expenses incurred in relation to the breaches of covenant;

3: an order that the costs of the action be taxed by the taxing master and paid by the lessee to the lessor; and

4: alternatively, a declaration that the lessor was entitled to claim from the lessee the cost of the works, without leave of the court.

The summons was dismissed and the lessor appealed.

Held on appeal:

Where a tenant fails to comply with a repairing covenant in a lease which expressly confers on the landlord the right to enter on the demised premises and carry out the repairs and recover the cost from the tenant, an action by the landlord to recover the cost from the tenant is a claim for debt due under the lease, rather than a claim for damages within s1(1) and (20 of the Leasehold Property (Repairs) Act 1938 and does not require leave under s1(3) to bring an action against the tenant.

See Jervis v Harris Court of Appeal [1996]. 10 EG 159 and SEDAC Investments Ltd v Tanner (1982) 2 CH 44, [1982] 44 P & CR 319

Section 18 of the Landlord and Tenant Act 1927 - The tenant who is in breach of covenant cannot set off the value of early possession by the landlord.

Hanson v Newman

[1934] Ch 298

A lessee in breach of repairing covenants was sued for possession by his landlord. The tenant did not defend the action and possession and damages were awarded by the Master. Damages were assessed by the Master at the amount by which the reversion in possession was diminished by non repair at the date of the writ.

The tenant requested the judge to find that he was entitled to set off the difference between the value of the reversion expectant at the expiration of the lease and the value in possession at the date of forfeiture. The judge rejected the claim and upheld the approach of the Master.

The tenant, relying on section 18 of the Landlord and Tenant Act, 1927 appealed. It was held that there could be no set off. The court had to decide, at the date of re-entry, the difference between the actual value of the property in its unrepaired state and the value as it would have been if the property had there been no breach of covenant. This was the maximum damages which could be awarded.

Nuisance

Haringey London Borough Council v Jowett

Queen's Bench Division: Divisional Court
[1999] EGCS 64

Tenant complaining of traffic noise - Whether traffic noise constituted a nuisance injurious to health – Whether nuisance attributable to council as landlords - Environmental Protection Act 1990, sections 79(1)(a), 79(1)(ga), 79(6A), 82(4)(a) - Magistrates' court finding council liable - Appeal allowed.

The appellant council owned a property at 8 Coulding Court, Turnpike Lane, London Ns, which was occupied by the respondent tenant. The respondent issued a summons against the council, under the provisions of section 79(1) (a) of the Environmental Protection Act 1990, which stated that, on 7 July 1997 and on sundry dates thereto, a statutory nuisance existed and continued to exist at the property. The respondent alleged that the property lacked sufficient sound insulation and acoustic ventilation to prevent the transmission of external noise and that, accordingly, the premises were prejudicial to health. The magistrates' court found that the traffic noise constituted a nuisance that was potentially injurious to health, and that the council were responsible for the statutory nuisance by virtue of section 82(4) (a) of the Act. The council were ordered to abate the nuisance within six months and execute any works required.

The council appealed by way of case stated, contending that the complaint should have been brought under section 79 (1) (ga) of the Act, which dealt specifically with noise that was prejudicial to health or a nuisance and emitted from or caused by a vehicle, machinery or equipment in the street. It was submitted that section 79(1) (ga) of the Act did not apply to traffic noise by virtue of section 79(6A) (a), which could not be avoided by proceeding under section 79(1) (a). It was further submitted that in any event, it could not be concluded that the council were responsible for any nuisance caused by the noise of the traffic under section 82(4) of the Act.

Held:

The appeal was allowed.

1. Section 79(1)(a) of the 1990 Act re-enacted the words used in section 92(1)(a) of the Public Health Act 1936, and those words were wide enough to embrace traffic noise: see Southwark London Borough Council v Ince (1989) 21 HLR 504. However, parliament had subsequently enacted the Noise and Statutory Nuisance Act 1993, which by section 2 introduced into section 79 of the 1990 Act sections 79(1)(ga) and 79(6A). Since then, section 79(1)(a) was to be read together with, and in the light of, the additional provisions that formed part of section 79.

2. In the light of the additional provisions, it was clear that section 79(1)(a) did not embrace external traffic noise because if it was intended that such noise was to be capable of constituting a statutory nuisance, section 79(1)(ga), which dealt directly with vehicle noise, would not have been limited by section 79(6A).

3. Although it might have been possible for a claimant in similar circumstances to prove that the nuisance was attributable to the landlord by virtue of section 82(4)(a) of the 1990 Act, the magistrates' court should hesitate before coming to that conclusion in relation to a local authority with wide housing responsibilities and limited resources.

Landlord's failure to repair insure and to collect rent and service charge - Appointment a receiver in accordance with section 37 of the Supreme Court Act 1981

Hart and others v Emelkirk Ltd
Howroyd and others v Emelkirk Ltd

Chancery Division [1982] 267 EG 946

Landlord and tenant - Novel relief sought - Landlord's covenants to keep if repair, and even to insure, not performed during the past two or three years and rents and service charges not collected - Properties, consisting of two blocks of flats, seriously deteriorating - Plaintiffs in present action tenants of flats. Defendants a company which sold the reversionary interest in 1979 to a purchaser who had neither registered his title nor exercised any rights attached to his reversion - Plaintiffs brought the action against defendants seeking a mandatory injunction to compel compliance with covenants and also damages. Present motion was for the appointment, pending the trial, of an independent surveyor to receive the rents of the flats and other moneys payable and to manage the blocks in accordance with the landlord's obligations - Although knowing of no precedent for this form of relief in these circumstances, Goulding J appointed a receiver in accordance with section 37 of the Supreme Court Act 1981

These were separate motions in two actions relating to two blocks of flats in Battersea in which the same situation had arisen requiring some immediate action.

Giving judgment, GOULDING J said: These are motions in two actions relating to blocks of flats in Battersea. A situation has arisen, which I believe is not, by any means, unprecedented in the suburbs of London but which does not seem before to have been, so far as reported cases go, the subject-matter of a similar application to that I have today.

The several flats in each block are let under separate long leases - not expiring until far into the next century - made by a freeholder who was the predecessor in title of the defendant company. For two or three years past, the reversioner has neither attempted to collect the rent and the contributions to maintenance and services provided for by the leases nor performed the covenants by the landlord contained in the leases to keep the property in repair, or even to effect insurance. The evidence adduced by the plaintiffs shows that the properties are now in a condition where serious deterioration is taking place and where, in more than one of the flats, reasonably comfortable occupation is threatened by the incursion of damp and the propagation of moulds and rots.

The defendant company says by counsel, as it has already alleged in correspondence, that in 1979 it sold the freehold reversion and completed the sale by transfer, but the purchaser has neither registered his title nor sought, as I have said, to exercise any of the rights attached to the reversion. It is, indeed, suggested on the defendant's behalf that the purchaser may have sold on to yet a further party.

The action is brought to obtain a mandatory injunction against the defendant company to comply with the landlord's covenants and also for damages, and counsel for the defendant company tells me that third party proceedings are likely. But what I am asked to do today by the plaintiffs in each of the two actions dealing with adjoining blocks of flats is to appoint a named surveyor to receive the rents and profits of each property and all other moneys payable under the lease or any part thereof and to manage the property in accordance with the rights and obligations of the reversioner until trial or further order. I am asked to say that the person so appointed may give a good receipt for certain sums of money which one of the plaintiffs in each case has received as representing (or apparently representing) what remains of a reserve fund, intended under the leases to be built up by tenants' contributions, and that he (the receiver) may have to resort to those funds in course of management.

Now, I know of no precedent for such relief, but I also know of no authority that forbids it under the provisions of the Judicature Acts now represented by the Supreme Court Act 1981, section 37:

The High Court may by order (whether interlocutory or final) ... appoint a receiver in all cases in which it appears to the court to be just and convenient to do so ...

It clearly appears to me to be just to appoint a receiver in this case because it is done to support the enforcement by the court of covenants affecting property: compare *Riches v Owen (1868) 3 Ch App 820.* It is also convenient because, as I said, the properties are in a condition that demands urgent action.

I propose, therefore, in each action to appoint the nominated surveyor, in respect of whom an affidavit of fitness has been provided. I am assuming, of course, that his formal consent to act will be forthcoming. I will appoint him to receive the rents and profits and other moneys payable under the leases in the form of the notice of motion and to manage, in accordance with the rights and obligations of the reversioner, again as stated in the notice of motion, until trial or further order. I think the court has a wide jurisdiction to invest a receiver with such powers as the court, in its discretion, thinks necessary for the preservation of the property, the income of which he is to receive. I see no reason to dispense with security. I think the order should be that he be appointed upon giving security, and subject to such security I will include a direction that he may give a good receipt to one of the plaintiffs, Mr Murr, for the two sums that are in his hands.

As regards the position of the defendant, whose legal advisers appear not yet to be fully instructed in the matter, I think I can safeguard that and also assist generally if I direct that the parties be at liberty to apply as they may be advised in the most general terms.

The costs of the motion are reserved to trial.

"Good repair and condition (reasonable wear and tear excepted)"

Haskell and Another v Marlow and Others

Divisional Court [1928] 2 K.B. 45

Will - Devise of Dwelling-house to Tenant for Life - Direction to keep "in good repair and condition (reasonable wear and tear excepted)" - Failure by Tenant for Life to repair - Damage arising from natural Decay - Liability.

A testator devised a dwelling-house to his wife for her life, she insuring the same against loss by fire, "and also keeping the same in good repair and condition (reasonable wear and tear excepted)," and after her death he directed that the same should fall into his residuary estate, which was to be divided among his children in equal shares. The testator's widow occupied the devised premises until her death, a period of forty-two years. She did nothing actively to injure the premises, but did nothing substantially to counteract the natural process of decay. The plaintiffs, the trustees of the will, alleged that she had neglected to keep the premises in good repair and condition in conformity with the terms of the will, and claimed from the defendants, her executors, the cost of the necessary repairs-

Held:

That the testator's widow, having accepted and occupied the premises, was bound by the terms of the devise, that the words of the exception were not to be treated as mere surplusage, and that a reasonable meaning must be given to them, but that having regard to the length of time during which no substantial repairs had been done to the premises, and to the extent of the damage thereby caused, the widow, as tenant for life, was not protected by the words of the exception, and that her executors were liable for the damage arising from the natural process of decay.

Section 18 (1) of the Landlord and Tenant Act, 1927 - Previous tenant liable for damages even though subsequent tenant had agreed with landlord to do repairs

Haviland and Others v Long and Another (Dunn Trust Ltd., Third Parties)

Court Of Appeal [1952] 2 QB 80

Landlord and Tenant - Breach of covenant to repair - Landlord's claim for dilapidations - Repairs paid for by succeeding tenant - Diminution in value of reversion - Tenant's liability - Sufficient that work had to be executed - Landlord and Tenant Act, 1927 s. 18.

By section 18 (1) of the Landlord and Tenant Act, 1927: *"Damages for a breach of a covenant or agreement to keep or put premises in repair during the currency of a lease, or to leave or put premises in repair at the termination of a lease ... shall in no case exceed the amount (if any) by which the value of the reversion (whether immediate or not) in the premises is diminished owing to the breach of such covenant or agreement as aforesaid. ..."*

The defendant tenants being in breach of their covenant to keep and leave the premises in repair, the plaintiff landlords, shortly before the lease terminated, entered into a fresh lease with other tenants, who, while paying what was a full economic rent for premises in repair, agreed to carry out the repairs, the landlords undertaking to reimburse them out of any sum recovered from the old tenants by way of dilapidations. It was contended for the defendants that having regard to the terms of the new lease the value of the reversion had not been diminished, that the landlords had therefore suffered no loss, and had lost their right to recover damages.

Held:

That at the time when the new lease was entered into the landlords had a contingent right to recover damages should the original tenants eventually be in breach of their covenants, and did not lose that right by reason of the bargain made with the new tenants. It was the fact that the repairs required to be done and not the circumstances in which the landlords and their new tenants agreed upon the manner of meeting the charge which was the governing consideration.

Per DENNING L.J.: The fact that the landlord has an undertaking from a new tenant to do the repairs does not go in diminution of damages. It is res inter alios acta[43].

---

[43] A transaction between others does not prejudice those who are not party to it.

Value of dilapidations where damages previously paid

Henderson v Thorn

[1893] 2 QB 164

During a lease the lessor brought an action for damages against a lessee for breaches of covenant to keep the premises in repair. The lessee paid a sum of money into court and the landlords accepted it and discontinued the action. No repairs were actually done. On the expiry of the lease a further schedule of dilapidations was served including items for which damages had been paid under the original action.

The official referee awarded the cost of putting the premises into repair at the end of the lease less the damages accepted in the previous action. The landlords applied for this decision to be set aside but it was upheld.

The Rent and Mortgage Interest (Restrictions) Act 1920
- Notice of defect - Damages for landlord's failure to
repair

Hewitt v Rowlands

[1924] All ER 344 Court of Appeal

On 8th March 1875 an agreement was entered into for a
term of five years at a rent of £50 p.a. The Landlord
covenanted to:-

"keep the cottage dry and the outside in repair".

After the lease expired the tenant held over as the tenant
from year to year. During this time his original Landlord
sold to the present Landlord. The purchase occurred in
1920 and on 1st October 1921 the landlord served a Notice
to Quit.

The house fell within the scope of The Rent and Mortgage
Interest (Restrictions) Act 1920 so the tenant remained in
possession as a statutory tenant. In 1921 the tenant
complained of dampness to the Landlord and on 25th
November 1921 gave written Notice to the Landlord's
solicitors stating that the premises were *"very damp"* and
requesting the Landlord to *"take immediate steps to make
the premises damp proof".* The Landlord did nothing.

Held:

1. The tenant could not claim damages for any period
    before Notice was served.

2. Damages were calculated on the difference between the value to the tenant of the premises from the date of the Notice to Repair to the date of the assessment of damages in their present condition. The damages could only be calculated on the defects which the Landlord was liable and were calculated on the difference of the value in repaired state and in the actual state.

3. The fact that the tenant was a statutory tenant was of no consequence.

Housing Act 1957 s 42 (1) - compulsory purchase order
- Whether corporation liable for damage to reversion -
Acquiring authority cannot benefit by its own failure to
comply with the repairing covenants to plead Landlord
and Tenant Act 1927, s. 18 (1) defence

Hibernian Property Co. Ltd. v Liverpool Corporation

Queen's Bench Division [1973] 1 WLR 751

Compulsory purchase - Compensation - Damage to
reversion - Municipal corporation lessees in breach of
repairing covenants - House unfit for human habitation
included in clearance area and compulsory purchase order -
Whether corporation liable for damage to reversion -
Landlord and Tenant Act 1927, s. 18 (1)

The plaintiffs were freehold reversioners of a house and
land held by a municipal corporation first under a lease and
then by holding over and paying rent. The corporation, who
covenanted to keep and leave the house in good and
tenantable repair and condition, were in breach of the
repairing covenants. The house was designated as unfit for
human habitation and was included in a clearance area
under section 42 (1) of the Housing Act 1957. Thereupon
the corporation made a compulsory purchase order in
respect of the house and served a notice to treat and a
notice of entry. If the corporation had complied with the
repairing covenants the house would either have been
excluded from the clearance area or would have had an
enhanced value because it would have been habitable and
in good repair. In an action against the corporation for

breach of covenant to repair the plaintiffs claimed damages as representing the difference between the compensation they would receive for the agreed market value of the house in covenanted repair and condition and the compensation payable to them as the agreed site value with the house designated as unfit for human habitation. The corporation relied on section 18 (1) of the Landlord and Tenant Act 1927', pleaded that only site value was payable to the plaintiffs, and called no evidence.

On the claim: -

Held: giving judgment for the plaintiffs,

(1) that the proper test was to define the extent to which the value of the reversion had been diminished.

(2) That section 18 (1) of the Act of 1927 was inapplicable on the facts, for it had not been shown that the house would at or shortly after the termination of the tenancy have been or be pulled down; and that, accordingly, there was damage to the reversion and the plaintiffs were entitled to recover the agreed amount of damages, assessed at the date of the notice of entry

Per curiam[44]. Section 18 (1) of the Act of 1927 contemplates the decision to pull down the house being that of the lessor only and the section cannot be construed as enabling a municipal corporation to contend that they are given relief on a claim against them for damages for their own failure to comply with covenants to repair so that the house has to be demolished.

---

[44] By a court decision which can be used as a precedent.

**Compensation for tenant's improvements - Part 1 of
Landlord and Tenant Act 1927 - Certification cannot
take place after completion of the improvement**

Hogarth Health Club Ltd and another v
Westbourne Investments Ltd and another

Court of Appeal [1990] 1 EGLR 89, [1990] 02 EG 69

Landlord and tenant - Improvements to business premises -
Part 1 of Landlord Landlord and Tenant Act 1927 -
Provisions for compensation at the end of the tenancy for
improvements carried out by the tenant - Machinery for
certification - certification by the county court that the
improvement is a proper one - Whether county court may
grant a certificate where the improvement has already been
carried out when the application comes before the court -
Appeal by landlords against decision of recorder reversing
order of deputy registrar who had struck out tenants'
originating application on the ground of delay

The events in this case followed a remarkably desultory
course - The tenants' notice of intention, the landlords`
notice of objection, the originating application for a
certificate all took place in 1979 - The works in question
were commenced at some point in 1979, probably after the
tenants' notice of intention but before the issue of the
originating application - The works were completed in
1981 - The next events of material interest, however, did
not take place until 1988, when the deputy registrar struck
out the originating application and the recorder reversed
that decision - Then followed the present appeal against
the recorders decision

The question for the Court of Appeal was whether an application for a certificate under section 3 of the 1927 Act could be heard and determined after the relevant improvements had been completed - The tenants conceded that the notice of intention had to be given before the works were carried out (as was in fact done in this case) but argued that the recorder was right in holding that the court still had discretion to grant a certificate even if the application was heard after the improvements had been completed - The court had no difficulty in rejecting this view - The whole tenor of section 3 of the 1927 Act was consistent only with a certificate being granted before the works were completed - This was implicit in subsections (1), (2), (3), (4) and particularly (5) - In the present case the improvements were completed as long ago as 1981

It was noted that Peter Gibson J in Deertield Travel Services Ltd v Society of Leathersellers had accepted a concession that the 1927 Act had the meaning at which the court had arrived in the present case - It was thus not a decision by Peter Gibson J, but the present court considered that the concession was rightly rightly made

The result was that the court concluded, disagreeing with the recorder and agreeing with the deputy registrar, that section 3 on its true construction did not allow for certification after completion of the improvement - The appeal was allowed and the tenants` originating application struck out

Whether wall includes window.

Holiday Fellowship Ltd. v Hereford

Court Of Appeal [1959] 1 WLR 211

Landlord and Tenant - Repairs - Covenant – "Wall" - Covenant to repair "main walls" - Whether windows part of "walls."
Fact or Law - Landlord and tenant - Construction of lease -

The lessee's covenants in a lease of a dwelling-house included a covenant to maintain the demised buildings and the fixtures and fittings therein *"(except the roofs and main walls of the said dwelling-house)"* in good repair and condition. By a complementary covenant of the lease the landlord covenanted *"to keep the main walls roofs ... in good repair and condition."* The tenants sought a declaration that under those covenants the landlord was liable to paint and repair the windows:-

Held:

That the question in each case was one of degree and, on the true construction of the lease, the windows of the demised premises were not part of the "main walls."

Lord Evershed M. R.

Mr. Stranders has, not unnaturally, relied somewhat strongly upon that case; (Boswell v Crucible Steel Co [1925] 1 KB 119) and, indeed, he is encouraged to do so by the use and citation of it in the last edition of Woodfall on Landlord and Tenant, 25th ed., p. 760, where there is the following sentence:

"It would appear that windows in the outer walls of a building are themselves to be regarded as part of the walls and therefore of the external parts."

That passage is based exclusively on *Boswell v. Crucible Steel Co.* With all respect to the editor, 1 think that is an over-statement or over-simplification of the matter. It would be correct to say:

"It would appear that windows in the outer walls of a building may, in certain contexts and for certain purposes, be regarded as part of the walls".

but 1 do not think that Boswell's case justifies any more extensive proposition. Nor can 1 agree with Mr. Stranders that because, in Boswell's case, the conclusion is regarded as a matter of law, therefore it is impossible to say, as a matter of fact or degree in another case and in another context, that windows are not to be regarded as part of the main walls: the one thing by no means follows from the other.

So far, therefore, I am unable to hold (and I agree entirely with Harman J. that Boswell's case does not bind us to hold) that these windows are part of the main walls of this edifice for the purposes of this lease.

A further case was cited of *Taylor v. Webb, [1937] 2 KB 283* in which a somewhat similar problem arose. There was an obligation to keep *"outside walls and roofs in good and tenantable repair";* and the question was: What of skylights: were they part of the roof? The building was a somewhat unusual one. It appears that there had been at some time an addition to the original structure: a passage had been built over the roof of the back ground floor premises leading to some upper storey behind. The passage and the upper storey behind were only lit from above; and the facts seem to show that the so-called "skylights" constituted a very substantial part of the roof - certainly of the passage. It was said by du Parcq J.

"I have no doubt that the skylights are part of the building, and 1 also think that they are part of the roofs, and that that was the intention of the parties."

But once again it is, to my mind, a fallacy to suggest that that case (and du Parcq J's view on this matter was affirmed) leads to the proposition that all skylights for all purposes are part of the roofs in which they appear.

I conclude, therefore (with Harman J.), that these cases do not have a binding and conclusive effect. In any case, I would add that there is in truth no evidence whether the windows, as I see them, were or were not part of the original structure of this house. But that is, perhaps, neither here nor there.

If I am right so far in thinking that the matter is not concluded by these authorities, then the question comes back to that

"structure and exterior" - Whether paving slabs in rear yard part of house

Hopwood v Cannock Chase District Council (Formerly Rugeley Urban District Council)

Court Of Appeal [1975] 1 WLR. 373

Housing - Repair - Implied covenant - Paving slabs in back yard constituting danger - Whether back yard means of access to house - Whether part of "structure and exterior" of dwelling house - Housing Act 1961 s. 32 (1) (a)

The plaintiff was the widow of the tenant of a dwelling house of which the defendants were the landlords, the tenancy being subject to the provisions of section 32 of the Housing Act 1961. Adjoining the back of the house was a concrete yard, crossed by a row of paving slabs, which gave access to an alley and to the next-door house. The ordinary means of access to the house was from the front. While crossing the back yard the plaintiff tripped on the edge of one of the paving slabs which was in a state of disrepair, fell and injured her knee. She brought an action for damages against the defendants, claiming that they were in breach of their implied covenant to repair in section 32 (1) of the Act of 1961. The county court judge held that the paving stones were not part of the structure or exterior of the dwelling house and that the defendants were under no obligation to repair them.

On appeal by the plaintiff.. -

Held: dismissing the appeal,

That the back yard, which was not a necessary means of access to the house, could not be described as part of the structure and exterior of the house within the meaning of section 32 (1), and that, accordingly, the implied covenant to repair did not apply.

Brown v. Liverpool Corporation [1969] 3 All E.R. 1345, C.A. distinguished.

Repair of drains are an external repair

Howe v Botwood

[1913] 2 KB 387

The lessor of a house covenanted *"to keep the exterior of the said dwelling house and building in repair"*. The lessee covenanted *"to pay and discharge all rates, taxes, assessments, charges and all outgoings whatsoever which now are or during the said term shall be imposed or*

charged on the premises or the Landlord or tenant in respect thereof (land tax and Landlord's property tax only excepted)".

A Notice was served on the Landlord under the Public Health Act 1875 requiring defective drains to be repaired.

Held:

The covenant by the tenant to discharge *"all outgoings imposed on the Landlord in respect of the premises"* had to be construed as being subject to the performance of the Landlord's covenant by him. He covenanted to keep the exterior of the premises in repair and the repairs to the drains were necessary in order to comply with that covenant.

Relief from forfeiture

Inntrepreneur Pub Company (CPC) Ltd. and Another v Langton

The Times 10 November 1999

The tenant who sought relief from forfeiture could not produce evidence of her ability to pay the arrears within a fixed time. All she could produce was evidence of her ability to pay in the event of a successful collateral warranty claim. The court could not be reasonably satisfied that the arrears would be paid within a reasonable time and could not therefore grant relief.

Mrs Justice Arden so held in a reserved judgement in the Chancery Division and allowing the Appeal of Inntrepeneur Pub Company (CPC) Ltd. against an order of Martin Moncaster on August 16 1999 granting to the tenant Sarah Louise Langton relief against forfeiture.

Mesne profits for trespass

Inverugie Investments Ltd v Hackett

Privy Council [1996] 19 EG 124

Trespass – Mesne profits - Specified apartments in hotel - Whether wholesale prices payable by tour operators less expenses resented reasonable rent.

By a lease dated June 5 1970 the plaintiff was granted for a premium of $300,000 a 99-year term of 30 specified apartments in an hotel.. On November 11 1974 the plaintiff was ejected by the defendant owner. Following proceedings to recover possession, the defendants did not give up possession until April 12 1990. For this period of trespass the plaintiff sought mesne profits on the basis of two alternative calculations, one based on published room rates gave $8,164,590 and the other, based on average revenue less expenses, gave $3,373,838. The Court of Appeal of the Bahamas determined the mesne profits at $1,800,000. The defendants appealed.

Held:

The appeal was dismissed. The owner deprived of possession of his property is entitled to be paid by way of mesne profits a reasonable rent for the wrongful use of his property by the trespasser. Applying the user principle derived from *Stoke-on-Trent City Council v W&J Wass Ltd [1988] 1 WLR 1406,* the defendants must pay the going rate for the use of the 30 apartments. It was appropriate to take the wholesale rates paid by tour operators for the period. It was irrelevant that the plaintiff would have been unable to let the apartments to tour operators for 365 days in the year. Deductions should then be made for ground rent and for the cost of maintaining the common areas.

Chattels

Inyoung v Dalgety PLC

(1987) EGLR 116

In this case carpets were held to be chattels.

See also La Salle Recreations v Canadian Camdex Investments (1969) 3DLR (3rd) 549

Forfeiture - Liability of sureties

Ivory Gate Ltd v Spetale and others

Court of Appeal: [1998] EGCS 69

Compromise of lessor's proceedings for forfeiture - Terms discontinuing action and transferring lease to lessor - Lease merging with reversion - Whether sureties liable for rent accruing after date of issue of proceedings and before assignment of lease to lessor

By a lease dated October 30 1981 between the then landlord, four named sureties and IL Ltd as tenant, premises in Princes House and Princes Arcade, Piccadilly, London W1, were demised to IL Ltd for a term of 26 years. The lease provided, inter alia[45], for forfeiture should the tenant fail to observe its covenants, including a covenant not to assign, and for re-entry by the landlord in the event (among other things) that the tenant should "suffer a receiver to be appointed". The landlord gave IL Ltd licence to assign the lease to Capital City Leisure Ltd and an additional surety was joined. Capital City was registered as the proprietor of the lease. In July 1985 Capital City executed a debenture in favour of Lloyds Bank plc. On April 25 1991 Ivory Gate Ltd was registered as the freehold proprietor of the premises. At all material times the reversion was vested in Ivory Gate and the lease in Capital City, the tenant.

In June 1993 Lloyds Bank plc, acting under the terms of the debenture, appointed administrative receivers over the tenant and a notice under section 146 of the Law of Property Act 1925 was served. A writ claiming forfeiture was issued on July 13. On August 24 the tenant, acting by its receivers, served a defence and counterclaim for relief

---

[45] among other things.

following which various meetings were held with a view to reaching a compromise. On September 13 the rent for the current period was determined at £175,000. Shortly thereafter an order was made by consent adding Lloyds Bank as a defendant to the forfeiture action.

Negotiations took place for the settlement of the issues raised resulting in the execution of a deed dated February 18 1994 between (1) Ivory Gate, (2) the receivers, (3) the tenant and (4) Lloyds Bank. The deed, having recited that the bank had on the same day transferred the demised premises to Ivory Gate, provided that Ivory Gate would: (a) take no steps to enforce its rights under the lease against the other parties to the deed; and (b) would retain all its rights and remedies against the sureties. On the same day notice of discontinuation of the forfeiture action was given to the court. On July 25 1994 Ivory Gate issued a writ claiming from the sureties arrears of rent, insurance premiums and service charges due from the tenant up to February 18 1994. The judge concluded (see [1996] PLSCS 90) that Ivory Gate's claim against the sureties failed and Ivory Gate appealed.

Held

The appeal was allowed.

1. The service of a writ claiming forfeiture and possession of demised premises did not by itself bring the lease to an end (dictum of Lord Templeman in *Billson v Residential Apartments Ltd [1992] 1 AC 494* at p535 explained). It operated as an unequivocal election by the landlord to rely on a breach of covenant or condition as a forfeiture: see *Driscoll v Church Commissioners for England [1957] 1 QB 330* per Lord Denning at p340. In the instant case there was no doubt that the lease was not forfeited; it came to an end only by merger when it was acquired by the plaintiff.

2. The deed executed on February 18 1994, discontinuing the forfeiture action and transferring the lease, free from the claim for forfeiture, to the plaintiff, had the effect of ensuring that the liabilities of the sureties, and the additional surety to the plaintiff up to February 18 1994, remained unaffected.

Damages for failure to yield up in good and tenantable repair - Diminution in value of reversion where premises immediately relet

Jaquin v Holland

Court of Appeal [1960] 1 WLR 258

Landlord and Tenant - Repairs - Covenant - Measure of damages for failure to yield up premises in "good and tenantable" repair - Diminution in value of reversion where premises immediately relet - Landlord and Tenant Act, 1927 s. 18 (1).

On the termination of a tenancy containing a covenant to keep and yield up the demised premises "in good and tenantable repair," the landlord spent £19 10s in putting the premises into a lettable condition and the premises were immediately relet at the same rent as in the earlier tenancy. The premises were situated in an area where there was a high demand for houses to let. In an action by the landlord for damages for breach of the repairing covenant, the diminution in value of the reversion under section 18 (1) of the Landlord and Tenant Act, 1927, was found to be £50, this sum being based upon the estimated reduction in selling value of the premises. It would have cost about £100 to put the premises in good and tenantable repair. It was contended for the tenant that in the circumstances the sum of £19 10. represented the true measure of damage since the premises were immediately relet at the same rent subject to the payment of that sum or, alternatively, because the lettable value of the freehold should be taken into consideration:-

Held:

(1) that the test for assessing the measure of damages for breach of a repairing covenant at common law was the amount that was necessary to put the house into a proper condition for letting in accordance with the terms of the covenant, so that it would be taken by a reasonable man wanting a house in reasonable condition, having regard to the nature and type of house involved.

(2) That the damages so assessed would have been over £50, and, applying section 18 (1) of the Act of 1927, £50 - the amount by which the value of the reversion was diminished - was the sum to which the landlord was entitled. Even if one lease immediately succeeded another, there must always be a notional moment of time when the unincumbered freehold estate was vested in the landlord and the value of the reversion was therefore the value of the freehold as it had come back into the hands of the landlord before he let it again

Dictum of Lawrence L.J. in *Hanson v. Newman [1934] Ch. 298, 304; 50 T.L.R. 191, C.A.* applied.

Quaere,[46] whether in determining the diminution in value of the reversion it was right to take into consideration the fact that there was a shortage of houses in the area.

---

[46] question

Landlord's right to enter and repair - Claim in debt –
not in damages

Jervis v Harris

Court of Appeal: [1995] EGCS 177

Underlease - Landlord's right to enter premises and view
state of repair - Remedy want of repair at tenant's expense -
Whether repair clause enforceable without leave of court -
High Court finding in favour of landlord - Court of Appeal
upholding decision - Landlord's claim in debt not damages.

An underlease was granted at a premium of £26,000 and a
rent of £1,000 pa in respect of the entire works at a site at
Adelphi Street, Salford, Greater Manchester. The defendant
became the tenant of part of the site known as the West
Works at an apportioned rent of £80 pa. The benefit of the
term regarding the remainder of the site, together with the
leasehold reversion to the whole, was vested in the
plaintiff. Clause 2(10) of the underlease gave the landlord
the right from time to time during the term to enter on the
demised premises to view the state of repair and to remedy
any want of repair at the tenant's expense. As a preliminary
issue, the High Court held, inter alia[47], that the plaintiff was
entitled to enforce the provisions of clause 2(10) without
obtaining the leave of the court under section 1 of the
Leasehold Property (Repairs) Act 1938. The defendants
appealed.

Section 1(1) of the 1938 Act restricted the landlord's right
to forfeit the lease for want of repair. Under section 1(2)
and (3) a right to damages for breach of a tenant's repairing
covenant was not enforceable by action commenced at a

---

[47] among other things.

time when three or more years of the term were unexpired without the leave of the court.

Held

The appeal was dismissed.

1. The question was whether the landlord's right to enter the property, effect the repairs himself and then claim to recover the cost of doing so from the tenant, was a claim for damages "for breach of a covenant by the tenant to keep or put in repair during the currency of the lease all or any of the property comprise in the lease". McNeill J had answered that question in the affirmative: see *Swallow Securities Ltd v Brand [1981] 2 EGLR 48.*

2. In a later case Vinelott J declined to follow that decision and reached a different conclusion: see *Hamilton v Martell Securities Ltd [1984] Ch 266;* also *Elite Investments Ltd v T I Bainbridge Silencers Ltd [1986] 2 EGLR 43.*

3. The issue thus came before the appeal court for the first time. The tenant's liability to reimburse the landlord for his expenditure on repairs was not a liability in damages for breach of his repairing covenant. The landlord's claim sounded in debt not damages.

4. A clause such as clause 2(10) enabled the landlord to take remedial action himself to avoid any loss consequent on the tenant's failure to repair. Once the landlord carried out the repairs himself, the value of his interest in the property was restored. The work of repair enured to the benefit of the tenant as well as the landlord. The landlord was out of pocket because he carried out repairs, not because the property was in disrepair.

5. It was not the intention of Parliament to put obstacles in the way of a landlord whose object was to secure that necessary repairs were carried out, preferably at the expense of the tenant, but if necessary at his own.

Landlord's failure to repair

Jeune and Others v Queens Cross Properties Ltd.

Chancery Division [1974] Ch 97

Landlord and Tenant - Repairs - Covenant - Specific performance of - Breach of lessor's covenant to repair - Specific work required to remedy breach - Whether order to remedy breach ought to be made

Each of the underleases, under which four tenants were respectively in possession of four flats comprised in the property, contained a covenant by the lessors, the predecessors-in-title of the landlord company, to maintain, repair and renew the structure of the property, including the external walls thereof. The tenants alleged that the landlord, in breach of the repairing covenants, had failed to reinstate a balcony at the front of the property at first floor level in the form in which it existed prior to its partial collapse on May 13, 1972. The balcony was not included in any of the underleases. The tenants issued a writ claiming an order that the landlord should forthwith reinstate the balcony in the form in which it existed prior to its partial collapse. The landlord entered appearance but did not serve a defence.

On motion for judgment in default of defence: -

Held:

That the court had power, which should be carefully exercised, to make an order in an appropriate case against a landlord to do some specific work under a covenant to repair; that, where there had been a plain breach of a covenant to repair and there was no doubt as to what was required to be done to remedy the breach, an order for carrying out the required work ought to be made; and that, accordingly, the landlord should be ordered to reinstate the balcony forthwith.

Breach of repairing covenants - Measure of damages - lessor no worse off than if the defendant's covenant had been performed.

Joyner v Weeks

Court of Appeal [1891] 2 QB 31

Landlord and Tenant - Lease - Breach of Covenant to deliver up Premises in Repair - Measure of Damages.

The general rule with regard to the measure of damages in an action for breach of a covenant by a lessee to deliver up the demised premises in repair is that such damages are the cost of putting the premises into the state of repair required by the covenant.

Such measure of damages is not affected by the fact that, by reason of the terms of a lease granted by the lessor to another lessee from the expiration of the defendant's term, the lessor is at the time of action brought no worse off than he would have been if the defendant's covenant had been performed.

Forfeiture - Reversion purchased but rent arrears assigned back to vendor - New landlord able to forfeit for arrears of rent though they had been assigned to the previous landlord

Kataria v Safeland plc

Court Of Appeal [1998] 05 EG 155

Landlord and tenant - Forfeiture - Assignment of reversion - Assignment back to assignor of right to rent arrears - Whether assignee entitled to forfeit lease - Whether section 141(3) of Law of Property Act 1925 requires assignee to have interest in arrears before effecting a re-entry.

By a lease dated September 29 1983 the respondent tenant held a term of shop premises for 15 years at a rent subject to review. By October 1995 Standard Life Assurance Co Ltd held the reversion; by then the tenant owed over £10,000 in arrears of rent. On November 14 1995 Standard Life sold the reversion, with other properties, to the appellant landlords who assigned back to Standard Life the right to recover all the arrears of rent. Two days later the landlords effected peaceable re-entry of the premises for non-payment of the rent arrears. The landlords appealed the decision of the county court judge who had held that the forfeiture was unlawful.

Held:

The appeal was allowed. Given that the proprietary remedy of re-entry had been unquestionably assigned to the landlords and that the conditions on which the landlords were entitled to re-enter were fulfilled, the landlords were entitled as a matter of law to re-enter. If rent is owing under the lease, albeit to a previous landlord to whom the incoming landlord had assigned a personal right to recover it, the new landlord is entitled to exercise his contractual right to forfeit. Similarly, when under the assignment the right to receive the arrears and all rights of action in relation to the recovery of the arrears were assigned to the new landlord's predecessor in title, that did not carry with it an assignment of the right to re-enter, which is not a right of action within the meaning of the provisions of the assignment. The condition of re-entry was not released in any way by the completion of the sale of the reversion and the assignment back of the right to recover the arrears; for the purposes of section 141(3) of the Law of Property Act 1925 it was not necessary for the assignee of a reversion to have an interest in the arrears himself to be able to rely on the right of re-entry contained in the lease.

Evidence of events occurring after the termination of a tenancy would normally be inadmissible for the purpose of deciding whether section 18 (1) of the Landlord and Tenant Act, 1927 applied

Keats v Graham And Another

Court Of Appeal [1960] 1 WLR 30

Landlord and Tenant Act of 1927 - Repairs - Demolition required by planning authority - Whether premises to be demolished "at or shortly after ... termination of tenancy" - Meaning - Admissibility of evidence of events after tenancy terminated - Landlord and Tenant Act, 1927 s.18 (1).

By section 18 (1) of the Landlord and Tenant Act, 1927:

"Damages for a breach of a covenant ... to leave ... premises in repair at the termination of a lease, ... shall in no case exceed the amount (if any) by which the value of the reversion ... is diminished owing to the breach ... ; and in particular no damage shall be recovered ... if it is shown that the premises, in whatever state of repair they might be, would at or shortly after the termination of the tenancy have been or be pulled down."

A lease in 1952 of premises comprising a building with an extension at the back contained a covenant by the tenants to leave the premises in substantial repair at the termination of the tenancy. The rear extension had been erected on the basis of permission granted by the London County Council under the Town and Country Planning Act, 1947, which had limited the period for which the building could be retained to seven years, and the use to "storage purposes only" (though, in 1953, this was amended to *"stove" enamelling"* after an application had been made by the tenants). The tenants were informed in 1953 that it was unlikely that the period for which permission had been granted would be extended, and an application on behalf of the landlord was, in fact, turned down. When the authorised period expired the council did not take any steps to enforce the condition, but an appeal to the Minister against their refusal to grant any extension was unsuccessful. In December, 1956, the council wrote asking for written assurance that the extension would be removed within 14 days. The letter was sent to the tenants, and soon afterwards they notified the landlord that they would shortly be leaving. They left the premises on March 27, 1957. In defence to a claim by the landlord for damages for breach of the repairing covenant, the tenants said that at the time the tenancy ended the extension was to have been pulled down. This defence was tried as a preliminary issue.

The county court judge admitted as evidence that after the termination of the tenancy the landlord had re-let the premises with the extension for a different industrial use and that, subsequently, he had been successful in obtaining permission to use the building for that purpose or for storage until 1962:-

Held:

That in the circumstances, the probabilities at the relevant time, that is, when the tenants left the premises, were that the rear extension would shortly be pulled down.

(2) That the evidence as to the events after the tenants left was inadmissible.

Salisbury v Gilmore [1942] 2 KB 38; 58 T.L.R. 226; [1942] 1 All ER 457 applied.

Per Lord Evershed M.R. and Sellers L.J. Evidence of events occurring after the termination of a tenancy would normally be inadmissible for the purpose of deciding whether section 18 (1) applied, though rarely they might be used to clarify and explain an ambiguity in what had gone before.

Damages for covenant due to be performed in the year lease came to an end

Kirklinton v Wood

King's Bench Division [1917] 1 KB 332

Landlord and Tenant - Covenant to repair - Covenant to do Specific Repairs in a Particular Year Notice by Lessee to terminate Lease during Currency of Year - Liability of Lessee under the Covenant.

Where a lease contains a covenant to execute specific repairs in a particular year, if the lease shall be then subsisting, the obligation to perform the covenant attaches as soon as the year begins, and the fact that the lease is determined by the lessee by notice expiring before the end of the year does not relieve the lessee of his obligation to perform the covenant.

A lease contained (inter alia[48]) the following covenant by the lessee: *"And will in the year 1909, and also in the year 1916, if this lease shall so long last paint varnish and grain all the inside wood and iron work usually painted varnished or grained of the said demised premises with three coats of good oil and white lead paint in a proper and workmanlike manner."*

The lessee died in 1915, and his executors, under a power in that behalf contained in the lease, gave six months' notice to the lessor to determine the lease on March 1, 1916. On the determination of the term, the covenant not having been performed, the lessor claimed damages for the breach of it:-

---

[48] among other things.

Held:

That the executors were liable.

Damages for inability to claim lease extension - Decision turned on state of repair

Kitney v Greater London Properties Ltd and Another

Chancery Division: [1984] 286 EG 272

Landlord and tenant – Provision in lease entitling lessee to extend term for a further 21 years from date of expiry – Whether on construction of provision and in the events which had happened the lessee was able to claim an extension – Lessee sought by originating summons a decision in his favour – Proceedings were originally brought against both the original lessors and the owners of the reversion at the date of expiry of the term, but the claim against the latter was dropped because the lease had never been registered as an estate contract under the Land Charges Act 1925 and so was void as against them – Claims therefore became a claim for damages against the original lessors because of plaintiff's inability to obtain extension - Defendants resisted claim mainly on the ground that it was a condition precedent that the plaintiff should have complied with all his covenants, and that he had not done so – Covenants included keeping the property in good and substantial repair, painting the outside and painting the inside – This defence depended primarily on fact, but involved also a question of law as to whether anything short of strict and complete observance of the literal terminology of such covenants could constitute compliance with the obligations in the sense required – After reviewing various authorities the judge expressed the opinion that the right to the extension of the lease would not be defeated by merely trifling or trivial breaches – However on an exhaustive review of the evidence he concluded that there were defects of repair which could not be so characterised and that consequently the defendants had had discharged the onus of establishing sufficient non-compliance with the covenants – The plaintiff was not therefore entitled to damages form the defendants for his inability to obtain a 21 year extension.

Statute barred negligence claim for loss due to failure of
plaintiff's surveyors to arrange repairs for which they
had been instructed

Kitney v Jones Lang Wootton

Queens Bench Division: [1988] 20 EG 88

Limitation of action - Preliminary issue – Whether for the
purpose of section 2 of the Limitation Act 1980 the cause
of action arose prior to the period of six years before the
issue of a writ for negligence of six years before the issue
of a writ for negligence – The present proceedings were not
concerned with liability, which was decided, but only with
the date when the cause of action, if any, arose – the
allegation against the defendants was that they were
negligent in carrying out instructions given by the plaintiff
to ensure that certain repair works required to the property
in which the plaintiff had a leasehold interest were properly
carried out – The importance of this was that the plaintiff
was entitled to extend the term of his lease, which was
shortly coming to an end, provided that he had complied
with all the covenants – One of these covenants was a
repairing covenant to be performed during the last year of
the term – Such performance was therefore of critical
importance in securing the plaintiff an extension of 21
years.

The plaintiff met with difficulties when he endeavoured to
exercise his option – A claim against the assignees of his
original lease was dismissed because the option had not
been registered as an estate contract – A claim against the
original landlords for damages for breach of covenant
failed because it was found that the repairing covenant,
performance of which was a condition precedent to the
extension, had not been complied with – The plaintiff now

sued the defendants, a firm of chartered surveyors, seeking under the head of negligence damages representing the loss of the extension of the lease – The preliminary issue was whether the cause of action was statute barred – It was agreed that the cause of action accrued when the plaintiff suffered damage caused by the alleged negligence – Was this on December 25 1974 when the stipulated time for the plaintiff to comply with the repairing covenant expired or was it May 9 1984 when the judge in the previous proceedings held that the covenants had not been complied with, the former date being outside and the latter within the limitation period?

In support of the latter date the plaintiff submitted that the damage only crystallised at the date of the judge's decision – Before that there was no certainty that the plaintiff would fail in his action against the original lessors - The court rejected this submission on the ground that it adopted a subjective assessment of the prospect of success as a criterion for postponing the date of accrual of damage –

The judge's decision merely confirmed that the right to a new lease or damages in lieu had been lost on December 25 1974 – Hence the cause of action was statute barred.

Note :

See also *Kitney v MEPC Ltd. and another 1 WLR 981*

Mr. Kitney also failed against his landlords with his application for a new lease because the option was not registered in the Land Charges Register. Top marks for perserverence.

Tenant's Improvements - Consent unreasonably withheld

Lambert and Another v F. W. Woolworth And Company, Limited.

Same v Same

Court of Appeal [1938] Ch 883

See

Tenants improvements
Consent withheld

F. W. Woolworth and Company, Limited v Lambert

Court of Appeal 1937 Ch 37

Below

Leave to bring forfeiture proceedings

Land Securities Plc v Metropolitan Police Receiver

[1983] 1 WLR 439

This concerned a New Scotland Yard let on a full repairing lease for 99 years. Some of the polished granite cladding panels had cracked and some of the fixings were unsatisfactory. The tenant wished to replace all the granite panels with stainless steel at a cost of £5m whereas the landlord only wanted the defective panels replaced at a cost of £½m. The tenant sued the architect and consulting engineer for negligence and whilst this action was pending, issued an originating summons in July 1982 under the Landlord and Tenant Act !927 against the landlord seeking declarations, among other things:-

- that the removal of the granite and replacement with stainless steel would amount to an improvement under the act;

- that the landlord had unreasonably withheld consent to the improvement; and

- that the tenant was entitled to carry out the work without landlord's consent.

In October 1982 the landlord issued an originating summons under section 1 of the Leasehold Property (Repairs) Act 1938 applying for leave to bring an action for forfeiture of the lease and damages for the tenants breach of repairing covenants. The landlord stated that his reason for applying for leave was a desire for all matters in dispute to be resolved in a binding form by the court; and that an action for forfeiture was the normal way to resolve disputes over repairing covenants, since the tenants application for relief from forfeiture would bring all the matters into issue.

It was held that the landlord merely had to show that one of the matters stated in section 1(5) of the Leasehold Property (Repairs) Act 1938 was satisfied to apply for leave. Since all the matters which the landlord wanted resolved could be more conveniently and cheaply dealt with under the proceedings under the Landlord and Tenant Act 1927 leave was refused

Fixtures and fittings

La Salle Recreations v
Canadian Camdex Investments

(1969) 3DLR (3rd) 549

Held that carpets can be fixtures.

See also Inyoung v Dalgety PLC (1987) EGLR 116

Whether lien or set off against future rents, on property for expenditure

Lee-Parker and Another v Izzet and Others

Chancery Division [1971] 1 WLR 1688

Landlord and Tenant - Repairs - Covenant - Mortgagee's action against mortgagor's tenants - Mortgagor's breach of covenant to repair - Mortgagor's contract to sell to tenants - Repairs done by tenants - Collateral agreement - Whether cost recoverable out of future rents - Whether lien on property for expenditure

In an action for the enforcement of a registered charge on several separate properties the mortgagees claimed, inter alia[49], that contracts made by the mortgagor with the various occupiers for the purchase of the properties were not binding on them (the mortgagees) and for delivery up to them of the relevant properties. The court ruled, on the particular facts, that the occupiers' contracts with the mortgagor were not now enforceable against the mortgagees but that the occupiers were entitled to liens on the properties for deposit money and interest thereon.

On the question whether occupiers having a tenancy had a right of set off or a lien for the cost of repairs which the mortgagor, in breach of his covenant as landlord, had failed to carry out or whether they had a lien based on their relationship with the mortgagor as vendor, for the value of any permanent improvement effected by the repairs: -

---

[49] among other things.

Held:

(1) that irrespective of the rules of set off, the occupiers had a right at common law to recoup themselves out of future rents for the cost of the repairs in so far as those repairs fell within the express or implied covenants of the landlord, provided he was in breach and after due notice given to him.

Dicta[50] in *Taylor v. Beal (1591) Cro.Eliz. 222* applied.

(2) That as against the mortgagees there could be no set off for repairs falling outside the landlord's covenants.
Government of Newfoundland v Newfoundland Railway Co. (1887) 13 App.Cas. 199, P.C. distinguished.

(3) That the occupiers had no claim to a lien on the property based either on the landlord and tenant or vendor and purchaser relationship since they did the repairs to remedy the mortgagor's breach of a purely collateral agreement and, further, they were primarily in possession as tenants and enjoying the benefit of the work they had done.

---

[50] Obiter dicta – non binding opinion

Failure by local authority landlord to repair - Implied covenant under s 32 (1) of the Housing Act 1961 to keep in repair and proper working order the structure and specified installations

Liverpool City Council
Respondents

and

Irwin and Another
Appellants

House of Lords [1976] 2 WLR 562

Lord Wilberforce,
Lord Cross of Chelsea,
Lord Salmon,
Lord Edmund-Davies and
Lord Fraser of Tullybelton

Landlord and Tenant - Repairs - Covenant, implied - Multi-storey council dwellings - Landlords retaining control over common parts - Recurring damage by vandalism - Whether necessary to imply obligation an landlords to keep common parts in repair

Housing - Repair - Implied covenant - Internal defects in demised premises - Installation for sanitation - Water closet cistern overflowing each time closet used - Defective design or unsuitability in situation - Whether in "proper working order" - Housing Act 1961, s. 32 (1) (b) (i)

Liverpool City Council (Respondents) and Irwin and Another (Appellants)

The tenants of a council maisonette on the ninth and tenth floors of a 15 storey tower block withheld their rent as a protest against conditions in the building and in their maisonette. In an action by the council for possession the tenants counterclaimed nominal damages, alleging, inter alia[51], that the council were in breach of their duty to repair and maintain the common parts of the building of which they retained control, including lifts, staircases, rubbish chutes and passages, and were also, in relation to the demised maisonette, in breach of their covenant for quiet enjoyment and of the implied covenant under section 32 (1) of the Housing Act 1961[52] to keep in repair and proper working order the structure and specified installations. The council denied the existence of the duty alleged and denied breach of covenant. There was no formal demise of the maisonette but merely a document described as "conditions of tenancy" with a form attached signed only by the tenants stating that they accepted the tenancy on those conditions, which related to obligations only on the part of the tenants and not on the part of the council. The county court judge viewed the premises and found that lifts were out of action, staircases unlit and the general conditions appalling as a result of, inter alia[53], recurring acts of vandalism, despite the council's efforts, at considerable expense, to deal with the problem. The conditions in the demised premises of which the tenants complained included a water closet cistern which overflowed each time the closet was used and flooded the floor, due probably either to defective design or to the unsuitability of the installation for a high rise block.

---

[51] among other things.

[52] Housing Act 1961, s. 32: "(1) In any lease of a dwelling-house, being a lease to which this section applies, there shall be implied a covenant by the lessor - (a) to keep in repair the structure and exterior of the dwelling-house ... ; and (b) to keep in repair and proper working order the installations in the dwelling-house (i) ... for sanitation (including ... sanitary conveniences ...) . .....

[53] among other things.

The judge held in favour of the tenants that the council were under an implied duty not only to keep the structure in repair but also to keep the common parts in repair and properly lit and that they were in breach of that duty, and that they were also in breach of the obligations imposed by section 32 of the Act of 1961 in relation to defects in the maisonette itself. He awarded the tenants the £10 nominal damages which they claimed. The Court of Appeal (Lord Denning M.R. dissenting in part) allowed an appeal by the council.

On appeal by the tenants: -

Held: allowing the appeal in part

(1) that since the contract of letting between the council and the tenants as represented by the "conditions of tenancy" which the tenants had signed was incomplete in that its terms were of a unilateral nature it had to be established what the complete contract was; that so far as the common parts were concerned there had to be implied an easement for the tenants and their licensees to use the stairs, a right in the nature of an easement to use the lifts and an easement to use the rubbish chutes; that the obligation to be read into the contract on the part of the council was such as the nature of the contract itself implicitly required; that where an essential means of access to units in a building in multiple occupation was retained in the landlord's occupation then unless the obligation to maintain that means of access was placed in a defined manner on the tenants individually or collectively the nature of the contract and the circumstances required that it be placed on the landlord; that the standard of obligation was what was necessary having regard to the circumstances, viz., an obligation to take reasonable care to keep the means of access in reasonable repair and usability with the recognition that the tenants themselves had their responsibilities according to what a reasonable set of tenants would do for themselves; that the obligation applied

to local authority lettings as well as to private lettings and also applied to the lighting of the common parts of the building; but that in the present case it had not been shown that there had been any breach of the obligation

(2) That a water closet cistern which flooded the floor every time it was used could not be said to be in "proper working order" and accordingly the council were in breach of their obligation under section 32 (1) (b) (i) of the Act of 1961; and that the nominal damages to be awarded should be in the sum of £5

Interpretation of repairing covenant - Whether girders formed part of demise

London Underground Ltd v Shell International Petroleum Co Ltd

Chancery Division: [1998] EGCS 97

Underlease of ground floor of building - Upper limit of demised property defined by reference to "underside" of the first floor - Girders supporting first floor in bad disrepair - Each party claiming that other liable to remedy - Question turning on whether girders included in demise.

The defendant (Shell) was the leasehold owner of the building known as the Shell Centre, London SE1, by virtue of a headlease granted in 1963. In 1967 a predecessor of the plaintiff took an underlease of parts of the ground floor and basement for use, inter alia[54], as a ticket hall for a London Underground station. The structural slab floor of the first floor was supported by steel girders which in turn were supported by six concrete columns in the ground floor. The suspended ceiling of the ticket hall was attached by hangers to the slab floor. A schedule to the underlease recited that the upper limit of the station entrance ticket hall was to be "the underside of the structural slab floor of the first floor". The plan made clear that the columns were excluded from the demise.

The issue between the parties arose because the asbestos cladding to the girders and the coating of sealant had deteriorated to the point of posing a danger to public health. It was common ground that, by reason of the wording of the relevant repairing covenants, the question whether the

---

[54] among other things.

responsibility for the remedial work lay on the plaintiff or Shell depended upon whether the girders were included in the demise. For Shell it was argued that they were so included as they were located below the upper limit which was described in terms of the floor. Reliance was also placed by Shell on the presence, in clause 3(10) of the underlease, of a covenant by the plaintiff not to cut or maim the "roofs, main walls, main timbers, stanchions or girders of the Demised Property".

Held:

The girders were not included in the demise. Depending on the context, the words "underside of the ... floor" were capable of extending to supporting members beneath, and should be so interpreted in the present case. A strong indication of such an intention was the express exception of the columns from the demise. Other indications were the lack of any reservation of a right of support from the girders for the benefit of the defendant and an express right, elsewhere in the underlease, for the defendant to enter the demised property to carry out works to parts of the building other than the demised property. The covenant in clause 3(10) provided, if anything, a further indication to the same effect, as certain of the items mentioned could only be found outside the main property.

"repair, uphold, and maintain" - Inherent defect

Lister v Lane & Nesham

Court Of Appeal [1893] 2 QB 212

Landlord and Tenant - Covenant by Lessee to "repair, uphold, and maintain" Demised Premises - Inherent Defect in Premises.

The plaintiffs granted to the defendants a lease of a house in Lambeth, containing a covenant by the lessees that they would *"when and where and as often as occasion shall require, well, sufficiently, and substantially, repair, uphold, sustain, maintain, amend and keep"* the demised premises, and the same "so well and substantially repaired, upheld, sustained, maintained, amended and kept," at the end of the term yield up to the lessors. Before the end of the term one of the walls of the house was bulging out, and after the end of the term the house was condemned by the district surveyor as a dangerous structure and was pulled down. The plaintiffs sought to recover from the defendants the cost of rebuilding the house. The evidence shewed that the foundation of the house was a timber platform, which rested on a boggy or muddy soil. The bulging of the wall was caused by the rotting of the timber. The house was at least 100 years old, and possibly much older. The solid gravel was seventeen feet below the surface of the mud. There was evidence that the wall might have been repaired during the term by means of underpinning:-

Held:

That the defect having been caused by the natural operation of time and the elements upon a house the original construction of which was faulty, the defendants were not under their covenant liable to make it good.

Section 28 Landlord and Tenant Act 1927 - Loss of
reversionary value where liability to freeholder but lease
and underlease terminate on same day - Costs where
superior interest not disclosed and where underlease did
not reserve costs

Lloyds Bank Ltd. v Lake

[1961] 1 WLR 884

A lease to F dated 4th April 1921 for 21 years on internal
repairing obligations, was extended. The freeholder C by
means of a supplementary deed, extended the term for a
further 21 years from 25th March 1942 if F should live so
long, subject to the same covenants in the original lease.

By "lease" dated 31st December 1946 F as "lessor" sub-let
the premises to the defendant and his brother jointly for 14
years from 25th November 1946 on full repairing terms,
provided that on the death of F the term should cease
forthwith and absolutely determine.

F did not disclose that there was a superior interest.

F died 6th August 1957. The executor for the freeholder and
the executors for F the sub-lessee both served notices on
their tenants determining the lease on the 25th December
1957.

The freeholder's executors served a schedule of dilapidations
on F's executors and the matter was settled by a payment of
£715.

F's executors, the plaintiffs in the action served a schedule on
the defendant, the surviving sub-tenant, valued at £1,397 in
respect of breaches in the repairing covenants in the underlease. They limited their claim to £715 being the amount
payable by them to the freeholder under the liabilities in the

head lease. In addition they claimed solicitors and surveyors fees incurred in the claim against the underlessee and those payable to the freeholder under the head lease.

Although the cottage was old, under the principle established in Proudfoot v Hart [1890] 25 QBD 42 the plaintiffs were able to claim for treatment of woodworm because there was a bad infestation which could attack an occupants furniture. The judge accepted that £715 was a fair assessment of the damage suffered by the plaintiff as a result of breaches of repairing covenants by the defendant and this sum did not exceed the diminution in value of the plaintiffs reversion.

The defendant argued that as the reversionary interest expired at the same time as the sub interest, its value was nil and there was no loss of reversionary value. The judge found the argument ingenious and almost attractive but said that, on the contrary, the reversionary value was a negative one because of the liability to the freeholder.

The plaintiffs failed to recover surveyors and solicitors costs in relation to the action by the freeholder because the underlessee did not have notice of the superior interest.

As to the costs on the claim against the underlessee which the plaintiff attempted to recover as damages, these were disallowed because they were not reserved in the underlease. This decision was in accordance with the rule in *Maud v Sanders [1943] 2 All ER 783*

repairing covenant implied by section 32 of the Housing Act 1961 - Claim by tenant for damages for living in a house in disrepair

London Borough of Newham v Patel

Court of Appeal [1978] 13 HLR 77

The Council served a Notice to quit and brought an action for possession. The tenant counter-claimed for breach of the repairing covenant implied by Section 32 of the Housing Act 1961. The Appeal turned on the standard of repair and whether this was affected by the amount of rent charged and the condition of the house. The house, in fact, was very damp and on 7th January 1977 the Public Health Inspector confirmed that the house was unfit due to roof defects, defects to walls, guttering, floors and lack of adequate ventilation. As a result the council decided to re-house Mr. Patel but he was not prepared to move to the houses offered.

The Notice to Quit expired on 5th September 1977 and the council sought possession at Bow County Court. The Landlord had an obligation under Section 32 of The Housing Act 1961, *"(a) to keep in repair the structure and exterior of the dwelling-house (including drains, gutters and external pipes); and (b) to keep in repair and proper working order the installations of the dwelling-house."*

Section 32(3) says *"in determining the standard of repair required by the lessor's repairing covenant, regard should be had to the age, character and prospective life of the dwelling-house and the locality in which it is situated".*

Although the house was in a poor state of repair, the low rent reflected the condition. No calculation as to damages had been given, although the figure of £300 was mentioned no evidence had been offered as to hardships suffered.

The Appeal was dismissed.

"Keep in thorough repair and good condition" - Repair distinguished from giving back something quite different

Lurcott v Wakely & Wheeler

In The Court Of Appeal [1911] 1 KB 905

Landlord and Tenant - Repairs - Lessee's Covenant – "Keep in thorough repair and good condition" - Old Building - Natural Decay - Dangerous Structure Notice - Rebuilding - Liability of Lessee.

A lease of a house in London contained a covenant by the lessee to substantially repair and keep in thorough repair and good condition the demised premises and at the end or sooner determination of the term to deliver up the same to the lessors so repaired and kept. Subsequently the reversion expectant on the lease was assigned to the plaintiff and the lease to the defendants. Shortly before the expiration of the term the London County Council served a notice on the owner and occupiers requiring them to take down the front external wall of the house to the level of the ground floor as being a dangerous structure, and the plaintiff called upon the defendants to comply with this notice, which they failed to do. After the expiration of the term, the plaintiff, in compliance with a demolition order of a police magistrate, took down the wall to the level of the ground floor, and then, in compliance with a further notice of the London County Council, took down, the remainder of the wall and rebuilt it in accordance with modem requirements. The house was very old and the condition of the wall was caused by old age, and the wall could not have been repaired without rebuilding it:-

Held: that the defendants were liable under the covenant to recoup the plaintiff the cost of taking down and rebuilding the wall.

The extent of a tenant's obligation under repairing covenants in a lease considered.

..... under a covenant to repair there may be such a change of circumstances that the covenantor is not liable, on the ground that what he is required to do cannot fairly be called repairs at all, and that it involves giving an entirely new subject-matter. When I look at the facts in *Torrens v. Walker*, when I see that that was a covenant by the landlord simply to repair the outside of the premises, and when I see that the outside walls in question in that case, which were two sides of a triangle, were in such a condition that they could not be repaired and had to be pulled down from top to bottom, I think that that decision was quite right on the facts, and that the change of circumstances in that case was one which could not have been in the contemplation of the parties when the covenant was entered into, and that the covenant must be construed with reference to that limitation. The same thing is true of *Lister v. Lane,* where a house, which was rather an old house, was built upon what is called a timber cill and really had no foundation. The timber was put on the top of 17 feet of mud. That timber had rotted. The house could not be repaired. Nothing could be done but to remove it, to pull it down, or to underpin it to a depth of 17 feet, and to build some brick or other structure from the gravel or chalk up to the house. It was there held by the Court of Appeal, and I see no reason to quarrel with their decision, that the change of circumstances which had arisen could not have been in the contemplation of the parties and that it would not be reasonable to construe the covenant to repair as applicable to that change of circumstances. But then when I come to what I should have thought was everyday experience in cases of this kind, when I come to consider what is to happen when by reason of the elements acting on an old building, say, a chimney stack is blown down, is it possible for the tenant to say he is not liable to put that up because the collapse was due merely to age and the elements? I am astonished to hear that such a contention can be raised. So, if a tenant under a repairing lease finds that a floor has become so rotten that it cannot be patched up, that it is in such a condition that it cannot bear the weight of human beings or of furniture upon it, can it be said that the tenant is exempt from the liability of replacing that floor, and repairing it in the only way in which it can be repaired in order to make the house habitable, merely because the state of the floor is due to time and the elements? I am entirely unable to follow that argument. *Proudfoot v. Hart* seems to lay down a perfectly sound and intelligible proposition on this point, namely, that in such a case it is the duty of the tenant, if he cannot patch up the floor so as to make it a floor, to replace that which is no longer a floor by something which is a floor.

That being so, it seems to me that we are driven to ask in this particular case, and in every case of this kind, Is what has happened of such a nature that it can fairly be said that the character of the subject-matter of the demise, or part of the demise, in question has been changed? Is it something which goes to the whole, or substantially the whole, or is it simply an injury to a portion, a subsidiary portion, to use Buckley L.J.'s phrase, of the demised property? In this case the view taken by the official referee and the Divisional Court is the view which commends itself to me, that this portion of the wall, 24 feet in front, is merely a subsidiary portion of the demised premises, the restoration of this wall leaving the rest of the building, which goes back more than 100 feet, untouched........

Housing Act, 1936 section 2 - Landlord's obligation to repair provided he has notice of disrepair

McCarrick v Liverpool Corporation

House Of Lords [1947] AC 219

Landlord and tenant - Dwelling-house - Want of repair - No express notice - Landlord's obligation Housing Act, 1936 s. 2.

By s. 2 of the Housing Act, 1936: *"(1.) In any contract for letting for human habitation a house at a rent not exceeding (a) in the case of a house situate in the administrative county of London, forty pounds; (b) in the case of a house situate elsewhere, twenty-six pounds; there shall, notwithstanding any stipulation to the contrary, be implied a condition that the house is at the commencement of the tenancy, and an undertaking that the house will be kept by the landlord during the tenancy, in all respects reasonably fit for human habitation*

.... (2) The landlord, or any person authorized by him in writing, may at reasonable times of the day, on giving twenty-four hours' notice in writing to the tenant or occupier, enter any premises to which this section applies for the purpose of viewing the state and condition thereof."

The undertaking implied by the section that a dwelling-house will be kept in all respects reasonably fit for human habitation is subject to an implied term that the obligation on the landlord to repair any defect does not arise until he has notice of it.

Morgan v Liverpool Corporation [1927] 2 KB 131, approved.

Decision of the Court of Appeal affirmed.

Landlord's failure to repair - Dampness - Damages

McCoy and Company v Clark

[1982] 13 HLR 87 Court of Appeal

The tenant of a second floor flat complained from 1977 about dampness. This was due to the leaking roof which the Landlord took no action to repair until 1981. The Landlord sued for rent arrears and the tenant counter claimed for damages for diminution in value of his flat, for damage to property, for damage to health resulting in pain and his admission to hospital with pneumonia for nine days and feeling ill for a period of five to six weeks afterwards and for the Landlord's behaviour which was tantamount to a nuisance.

Held:

1.   There was dampness due to a leaky roof. A complaint had been made, but he noted that the flat was of minimal important to the defendant tenant who used it only as a place to sleep. Damages would be calculated at 10% of the rent for the first two years of dampness and 20% for the second two years with an additional £10 for damage to property.

2.   It was held that the defendant's illness was partly his own fault and that he had been comfortable in hospital. £100 damages were awarded reduced by 50%.

3.   Finally there had been a nuisance which was not deminimis so it was too small for damages to be awarded. The tenant appealed.

Held on Appeal:

1. The roof leak was the main cause of dampness. The measure of the damages should be based on a proportional reduction of the comfort for which the tenant was paying and should not be reduced because was not important to him.   The Award would be doubled.

2. It was not correct to reduce the damages to the tenant because he had been comfortable in hospital.   The £100 would be doubled, but again reduced by 50%.

3. The nuisance went beyond de minimis and £5 damages ought to be awarded.

"in single occupation" - Interpretation of covenant

McDonnell v Griffey and another

Chancery Division: [1998] EGCS 70

Lessee covenanting to use flat solely as a private residence "in single occupation" - Lessor declaring that he would apply restrictive interpretation should flat be sold for occupation by friends or unmarried couple - Lessee seeking declaration showing lessor to be in error - Whether court engaged in purely hypothetical exercise - Declaratory relief refused.

The plaintiff and the defendant were respectively lessor and lessee under a 99-year lease, granted in 1972, of a flat in a converted house in London W5. The defendant lived in one of the other two flats in the same house and was anxious that the house should not become, in his words, "a house in multi-occupation". Clause 2(20) of the lease contained a covenant by the lessee "not to use or suffer to be used the flat otherwise than as a private residence in single occupation". Over a period of 18 months the defendant, knowing that the plaintiff was anxious to sell her flat, wrote a number of letters (the correspondence) to the plaintiff and the plaintiff's solicitors intimating that "in single occupation" should be narrowly construed, and that he would make his views known and pass copies of the correspondence to any prospective purchaser of the defendant's flat. In particular he asserted that he would treat occupation by a childless, unmarried couple as a breach of the covenant unless they had executed a binding agreement containing mutual obligations of a marital nature.

Over the period of the correspondence the plaintiff tried unsuccessfully to sell her flat and was able to cite a particular instance of a sale going off after the buyer had learned of the defendant's attitude. Having failed to persuade the defendant that his interpretation of the covenant was wrong, the plaintiff sought a declaration that upon its true construction the clause restricted the lessee to use the premises "as a private residence in the occupation of a single household unit, that is by any persons living together as a family or as friends without any subletting or assignment or parting with possession of any part of the demised premises as between themselves". In the alternative the plaintiff invited the court to make a series of declarations, directed to such of the of the defendant's assertions as were plainly wrong.

Held:

The plaintiff was not entitled to declaratory relief.

1. Though there was a dearth of authority on the words in issue, the defendant was plainly wrong in asserting that occupation by an unmarried couple or two or more friends would inevitably amount to a breach of the covenant. However, that did not assist the plaintiff, because in each case of alleged breach the question would be one of fact and degree: see *Segal Securities v Thoseby [1963] 1 QB 887,* in which the phrase "in the occupation of one household only" was considered. The court could not grant relief in the terms sought without purporting to legislate in advance for all possible circumstances. Such a hypothetical exercise was not permissible: see *Re Barnato Dec'd [1949] 1 Ch 258; Re Clay [1919] 1 Ch 66; Naylor v Wrotham Park Settled Estates [1987] NPC 25.*

2. The same objections applied to the alternative claim for relief, which the court could not accede to without making a series of academic assertions.

3. No order would be made as to costs.

Housing Act 1961, sections 32 and 33 - Damages for failure to repair - Betterment considered

McGreal v Wake

Court of Appeal [1984] 269 EG 1254

Landlord and tenant - Housing Act 1961, sections 32 and 33 House in bad condition - Tenant's claim for damages - importance of giving landlord notice of defects - "The golden rule is 'tell your landlord about the defects' – "Unfortunate" decision in *O'Brien v Robinson* (but established law) that liability under the implied covenant in sction 32 arises only when landlord learns, or perhaps is put o inquiry, that there is a need for repairs - County court judge in present case dismissed the tenant's claim, holding that the court was precluded by authority from attributing any liability to the landlord.

Court of Appeal, while accepting that liability under section 32 did not arise until the landlord had knowledge of the defects, held that the judge was in error in dismissing the claim for damages, which he should have considered in detail - The landlord was eventually put on notice of the defects when the local authority, after a complaint by the tenant, required the landlord to execute remedial works - He did not do so and the local authority decided to carry out the works at the landlord's expense - In order to facilitate the authority's operations the tenant moved out and paid for temporary accommodation, incurring storage charges for her furniture.

Held by Court of Appeal:

- That the tenant had a valid claim for having to live in an unrepaired house for some months after it should have been repaired;

- that the tenant was entitled to compensation for the work of clearing debris and cleaning up after the authority had completed their operations;

- that she was entitled to recovery of reasonable expenditure on redecoration; and

- entitled to the costs of storing furniture and providing herself with temporary alternative accommodation

- *Green v Eales* considered in the light of comments in *Calabar Properties Ltd v Stitcher* - Tenant must, of course, establish that her expenditure flowed from the landlord's breach of covenant - No deduction for "betterment" justifiable - Appeal allowed and case remitted to the judge to assess damages in the light of this judgment

**Tenant liable for rent of damaged premises -
Warranty of fitness - Notice of defect - Waste**

Manchester Bonded Warehouse Company Limited v Carr

[1880] 5 CPD 507

A multi-storey warehouse was let to a tenant who covenanted *"to repair maintain and keep the inside of the premises in good and tenantable repair and condition and deliver them up at the end of the term damaged by fire storm or tempest or other inevitable accident and reasonable wear and tear only accepted"*.

The Landlord covenanted to *"keep the walls roof and main timbers of the premises in good and substantial repair and condition"*.

There was assessor of rent clause if the premises were burnt down, damaged by fire, storm or tempest.

The floors were overloaded by a sub-tenant of the defendant and, as a result, the building collapsed. The Head Landlord rebuilt it and proceeded against his immediate tenant, who denied liability and counter claimed for damages from the Landlord.

Held:

1. Even though the premises were damaged, the tenant was liable to continue to pay rent.

2. The Landlord had not warranted the building fit for the purpose for which it was let.

3. The Landlord was not liable to keep the walls, roof and main timbers of the building in repair until he had notice of a defect.

4. That the tenant was not liable to pay damages for waste if it was using them in the way they were intended to be used.

5. As the damage did not fall within the exceptions in the repairing covenant, the tenant was liable for the cost of reinstating floors and fixtures and fittings and leaving the premises in good and tenantable repair.

Temporary Repair

Manor House Drive, Ltd. v Shahbazian

Court of Appeal
(Before Lord Denning, M.R., Lord Justice Danckwerts And Lord Justice Winn)
[1965] 195 EG 283

Landlord's liability to repair structure - Tenants to pay proportions of cost - Whether temporary or permanent repair reasonable-Surveyor's advice followed – Landlord's appeal allowed

This was an appeal by landlords, Manor House Drive, Ltd., from an order of Judge Baxter at West London County Court on February 25 rejecting their claim against Mr. Henry Shahbazian, shipping executive, the tenant of an upper maisonnette at 94, Philbeach Gardens, Kensington, London, SW., for £143 8s. 4d., the tenant's share of certain expenditure required by the terms of the lease.

Giving judgment, Lord Denning said that the maisonnette in question was let to the tenant on April 14, 1960, on a 99-year lease at a premium of £3,700 and rent of £50 a year. The landlords covenanted to "maintain, repair and decorate the main structure and roof of the building," and the tenant was under an obligation to pay a proportion of the cost of works. In the winter of 1961-62 there was a great deal of trouble with the roof and water came through, damaging some of the tenant's belongings. The landlords took advice from a surveyor, Mr. Frank Swain, who said that certain zinc below a covering of canvas and bitumen was old and had defects. He advised the removal of the existing temporary coverings and the old zinc, and replacement by new zinc. If the work was carried out as soon as possible there should be no further trouble for another 25 to 30 years, but temporary treatment would be a waste of money and not likely to be effective for more than a few months. On the advice of this qualified surveyor the landlords employed builders to put in a new zinc roof at a cost of £401 11 s. 6d. They then called on the tenants to pay their proportions of the cost of the works. The respondent tenant disputed the claim, and evidence was given at the County Court that instead of the new zinc roof, first-aid repair could have been done of a further coat of heavy bitumen or Aquaseal at a cost of £100. This would last only three years, and would have to be replaced by bitumen every two years at a cost of £25; however, such work would cost only about £300 every. 20 years as against the £400 for the new zinc roof. In argument it was put to the judge that it might have been reasonable in a sense to put in a zinc roof, but that it was not really necessary. The judge accepted this and held it was not necessary to do all the repair work with zinc, and he rejected the landlords' claim altogether.

He (his Lordship) agreed with the judge up to a point. However, the repair that was done was not just renewal or improvement; it was a repair to the entire structure. It was part of the work of maintaining the roof, and was reasonable, and a proper fulfilment of the repairing covenant. On the evidence before the judge there was only one finding, that it was a reasonable and proper way of maintaining the roof to put in zinc as advised. Patching up by bitumen or Aquaseal was not reasonable or even proper in view of the surveyor's advice. If water had come through after temporary repair there would have been no possible answer to a claim by the tenant that the work had not been done properly. Acordingly, the appeal should be allowed and judgment entered for the amount claimed.

Danckwerts, L.J., agreeing, said that even the alternative method of temporary repair would not make a great saving over a period of 20 years. The landlords' method of repair was reasonable and proper. Winn, L.J., also agreeing, said that he could not help wondering, if temporary repair had been done, whether at the end of 30 years the roof would have been able to withstand the weight of 16 layers of bitumen.

The appeal was accordingly allowed with costs and judgment entered for the landlords for the amount claimed.

Damages under lease for loss of value due to landlord's failure to repair

Marenco v Jacramel Co. Ltd.

Court Of Appeal |1964| |1964| EGD 349

Landlords' breach of repairing covenant - Damages for diminution of value of underlease - Tenant one of twelve in block of flats - Amount of damages based on repair cost for whole block - Wrong to divide by twelve - Landlords may he liable in same sum to all tenants - Tenant's appeal allowed

This was an appeal by Mrs. Matilde Marenco, of 10, Chasewood Court, Hale Lane, Mill Hill, London, N.W., from the dismissal by Deputy Judge Glanville-Slack at Willesden County Court on March 17 of her claim for £384 3s. Od. damages from her landlords, Jacramel Co., Ltd., of Ling House, Dominion Street, London, E.C., for breach of covenant to maintain and repair Chasewood Court, resulting in a diminution of the value of her underlease.

Mrs. Marenco[55] appeared in person. Mr. J. E. S. Ricardo (instructed by Messrs. Kanter Jules & Co.) represented the respondent landlords.

Giving judgment, DANCKWERTS, L.J., said that Mrs. Marenco bought an underlease of flat 10, Chasewood Court, Mill Hill, dated May 29, 1962, for a term of 90 years, less 10 days, from December 25, 1955, at a cost of £2,450, and held simply on a ground rent of £18 a year. The landlords covenanted to "keep and maintain the exterior of the flat and the building of which it forms part ... entrances, passageways, staircases, roads, ways, paths . . .

---

[55] Litigants in person are not often successful. Well done Mrs. Marenco.

gardens, structures and fences ... in good repair and condition and properly maintained and. . . to paint all outside woodwork and ironwork . . ." For her part, Mrs. Marenco agreed to pay by way of further rent a proportion of the costs of insuring the building and a fair proportion of the cost of keeping clean and lighting the entrance hall and staircase, and to contribute a rateable or due proportion of the expense of making, repairing, maintaining, rebuilding and cleansing and lighting the exterior of the flat and the building of which it formed part, including fences, etc.

By notice in writing of October 2, 1963, Mrs. Marenco required the landlords within 21 days to repair or restore the light in the entrance hall and staircase; maintain the fences bordering the building in good repair; render and repair the concrete drive, and clear the beds of the gardens of nettles and weeds and otherwise maintain the same in a neat and tidy condition. By a letter of October 23, 1963, the landlords said that they were not prepared to carry out the works until the other underlessees had contributed to the cost of previous works and given security for future contributions. Mrs. Marenco was ready, willing and able to pay a fair proportion of the cost of the works and asked the landlords what was her share, but the landlords failed or neglected to tell her. There were eleven other underlessees in the blocks of flats.

At the trial, the landlords called no evidence and submitted no case. The trial judge had correctly found that the landlords were in breach of their covenant, and that the sum of £384 odd estimated by Mrs. Marenco based on estimates obtained, was a reasonable cost of carrying out the work. However, the trial judge had gone on to say that if this were a single house and Mrs. Marenco the only tenant, then she would be entitled to claim the full cost of the repairs; she would have established that the property had diminished in value, and the cost of repairs would be an indication of the diminution; but that as she was only one of 12 tenants in two blocks of flats and the amenities were enjoyed by the other 11 tenants, the whole of the £384 could not be attributable to her flat. All the flats were equally affected by the breaches, and a fair assessment of the diminution was one twelfth of £384, which was £32. And as in addition to the landlords' covenant the underlease contained corresponding obligations on the tenant to pay a proportion of the cost of carrying out the services and repairs, which, in Mrs. Marenco's case, was one-twelfth, or £32, she had lost nothing. Therefore, concluded the trial judge, she had not established any damage and the action failed, and the landlords must have their costs.

That approach was wrong. Mrs. Marenco had an interest in the whole covenant and was not really interested in what happened to the other tenants. Her covenant was for the landlords to repair. Her contribution could occur only after the landlords had repaired the premises. The measure of diminution was what had been the effect of the failure of the landlords to carry out repairs upon the value of Mrs. Marenco's flat, and not upon the value of any other flat. It was simply her flat in which she was specifically interested. The repairs had not yet been done. The appeal should be allowed and judgment entered for £384 3s., less the amount of her contribution towards the repairs, which meant that she would succeed as to £352 2s. 9d.

Agreeing, WILLMER, L.J., said that where the trial judge went wrong was in taking the view that the diminution of value was to be divided by 12 because Mrs. Marenco was a tenant of only one of the 12 flats. The landlords had covenanted with Mrs. Marenco, and no doubt with the other tenants equally, although the court did not know, to keep the whole of the exterior, garden and roadways and not one-twelfth of them. Mrs. Marenco's property had been diminished in value by the whole cost of the repair, and not by one-twelfth of it. Any other view would mean that the landlords would be able to break their covenant with complete impunity. On the basis of the trial judge's judgment, no tenant would have any right to enforce the covenants into which the landlords had entered. That could not be right, but it was the conclusion to which one was driven by the erroneous process of dividing by 12 the damage Mrs. Marenco had sustained. It was quite right that the landlords might be equally liable to the other 11 tenants. Be it so, if that was right. he (Willmer, L.J.) did not shrink from it. It might be that the other 11 tenants had suffered damage to the same extent. The Court did not know the terms of their leases, but in any case, if the landlords were fearful that that might be the result, they could put it right at any time by executing the necessary repairs to comply with their covenant. In those circumstances Mrs. Marenco was entitled to the full amount claimed, subject to the agreement to pay one-twelfth of the sum as her proper contribution.

DAVIES, L.J.. agreed, and the appeal was allowed with costs.

Implied Obligations   to use in tenantlike manner   -
Limitation Act, 1623

Marsden v Edward Heyes, Limited

In The Court Of Appeal [1927] 2 KB

Landlord and Tenant - Yearly Tenancy - Alteration of Premises - Waste - Implied Obligations - To use in tenantlike Manner - To yield up Premises - Continuing Obligations - Limitation Act, 1623

A tenant from year to year is under an implied obligation to use the demised premises in a tenantlike manner and to yield them up so used at the end of the tenancy. The obligation continues as long as he continues tenant. If he alters the character of the premises he commits a breach of the obligation and is liable in damages for the injury to the reversion.

In 1914 the plaintiff became the owner of the reversion in certain premises consisting of a dwelling-house and shop let to the defendants on an oral tenancy from year to year. In the same year the defendants removed a partition wall, staircase and fireplaces, and converted the premises into one large shop. In 1923 they assigned their tenancy to third persons. In 1925 the plaintiff brought an action against the defendants for waste and for breach of obligations which, as she contended, were implied by law to use the premises in a tenantlike and proper manner, and having so used them to yield them up at the end of the term. The defendants pleaded the Statute of Limitations:-

Held:

That the defendants were under an implied obligation to use the premises in a tenantlike manner; that they had committed a breach of this obligation; that the breach was continuing in 1923, and that the plaintiff was entitled to damages for injury to the reversion.

Repairing covenant - landlord liable for foreseeable
consequences of his failure to repair

Marshall v Rubypoint Ltd

Court Of Appeal [1997] 25 EG 142

Landlord and tenant - Covenant to repair - Disrepair of
front door - Whether landlord liable for loss following
entry of burglar.

In 1993 the plaintiff acquired a 99-year lease of a flat in a
building converted into flats with internal front doors
sharing the use of common parts including the main front
door; the defendant held the reversion. Under the lease the
landlord covenanted to maintain, repair, redecorate and
renew, inter alia[56], the common parts. On August 17,
September 10 and 23 1993 the flat was burgled. The
plaintiffs claim against the defendant landlord, for breach
of repair of the front door, was allowed in the court below
and he was awarded damages and interest of £6,123.19.
The defendant appealed.

Held:

The appeal was dismissed. The disrepair of the front door,
and the breach of covenant by the defendant, was causative
of the burglary. It would have been in the contemplation of
the parties at the date of the lease in 1983 that if the front
door fell into disrepair and did not provide any real
obstacle to a would-be intruder, a burglary was not
unlikely. The damages for the burglary were not too
remote. Where loss results partly from a breach of contract
and partly from an intervening act of a third party, the party

---

[56] among other things.

in breach will be liable for the loss if the intervening act was reasonably foreseeable by the parties at the time of the contract. The breach by the defendant was a substantial cause of the loss to the plaintiff. The doctrine of novus actus interveniens did not apply.

Landlord and Tenant Act 1985 - Section 20 notice - Maintenance work

Martin v Maryland Estates Ltd; Seale v Maryland Estates Ltd

Court of Appeal [1999] EGCS 63

Landlord serving section 20 notice specifying works - Landlord commencing works and discovering need for additional works - Additional works carried out without further notice to tenants - Whether landlord acted reasonably in executing additional works without consulting tenants - Landlord and Tenant Act 1985, section 20 - Appeal dismissed.

The claimants, S and M, were tenants of a property comprising a number of flats of which the defendant was the landlord. In July 1994 the landlord's surveyor wrote to the tenants enclosing a specification of proposed works and inviting observations. A notice under section 20 of the Landlord and Tenant Act 1985, with accompanying estimates, was subsequently served on the tenants, and the landlord's managing agent asked the landlord's surveyor to commence works. Meanwhile, M's solicitors suggested putting the work on hold because the tenants proposed to acquire the freehold under the Leasehold Reform, Housing and Urban Development Act 1993, and that any works would be attended to by them after the acquisition of the freehold. On 21 March 1995 the landlord commenced the works, during the course of which the need for additional works was identified. These were executed alongside the original works identified in the section 20 notice. A service charge was duly prepared by the landlord in respect of the cost of both the original and additional works. The tenants claimed that the landlord was entitled to recover the costs of the works identified in the section 20 notice only, but not the costs of the additional works, since no notice of such works had been given.

The recorder declined to grant the landlord the necessary dispensation under section 20(9) of the Act in order to recover the costs of the additional works, holding that the landlord had not acted reasonably in failing to inform the tenants of the need for the additional works. The landlord appealed, contending that he had acted reasonably for the purposes of section 20(9). It was further contended that, in any event, the landlord was entitled, under section 20(I) of the Act, to the sum of £1,000 towards the cost of the additional works.

Held:

The appeal was dismissed.

1. The works would have cost the tenants almost twice the amount estimated in the section 20 notice. Although it had not been practical for the landlord to comply with all the requirements because of the attitude of the tenants to the works, it did not justify a total dismissal of the requirement that the tenants be informed of the additional works. Accordingly, the recorder had been entitled to conclude that the landlord had not acted reasonably.

2. A commonsense approach was required as to how one batch of "qualifying works" was to be divided from another for the purposes of section 20(1) of the Act. The legislative purpose of the £1,000 was to provide a threshold, rather than to build a margin of error into every contract.

Accordingly, the recorder had been correct to hold that the landlord was not entitled to recover, through the service charge, the sum contended for.

Section 18 of the Landlord and Tenant Act 1927 -
Relevance of Landlords' intentions

Mather and Others v Barclays Bank Plc

Chancery Division [1987] 2 EGLR 254

Landlord and Tenant Act 1927, section 18(1) - Claim by
landlords for damages for breach of covenant to repair and
deliver up in repair - Tenants' liability to repair and the cost
of carrying out repairs were admitted - Issue was as to the
impact on damages of section 18(1) - The lease in question
was for 13 years expiring on June 24 1982 and tenants had
given notice under section 26 of the Landlord and Tenant
Act 1954 requesting a new tenancy - Landlords did not
oppose and an application to the court by the tenant was
duly made, so that the tenancy continued pending the final
determination of the proceedings - The complications and
delay which arose in the present case were due partly to
initial doubts as to whether the tenants, a bank, would
decide to give up their premises, facing a substantial bill for
dilapidations, or continue as tenants at a much increased
rent - Tenants eventually decided to give up the tenancy
and they did so on June 1 1984 - Landlords found new
tenants, a leading building society which, in consideration
of a reduction in rent during the first four years of the new
lease, covenanted to carry out repairs and to introduce
improvements on a 'Substantial scale - The improvements
cost more than twice what the repairs by themselves would
have cost and there was no practicable way by which the
premises could have been first repaired without any
improvement and then improved without any element of
repair - No attempt was made by evidence to identify pure
repairs which could have been carried out before the
building society began operations and which would have
survived such operations - The investment value of the
landlords' reversion following the letting to the building
society, capitalising the cash flow and taking a 7 per cent

yield, produced a valuation well above that for the property repaired but unimproved - The judge held that the landlords' claim failed under the first limb of section 18(1), the value of the reversion not having been diminished by the breach of covenant - As regards the alternative ground under the second limb of section 18(1) (the question whether structural alterations rendered valueless repairs covered by the covenant), the judge was restricted by an order made by Knox J to making a decision only on the issue whether there was an intention at the material date by the landlords or the building society to make alterations to the demised premises According to Knox J's order the effect of any such alterations was a matter to be tried separately - Judge Paul Baker decided that the relevant intention had been established - Landlords' claim dismissed - Judgment includes detailed consideration of rival valuations

Set-off - unliquidated damages against rent and cost of repairs

Melville and Another v Grapelodge Developments Ltd

Queen's Bench Division [1978] 254 EG 1193

Landlord and tenant - Whether obligation under lease to pay rent and obligation under an undertaking by landlords to carry out repairs were dependent or separate - Whether a claim for unliquidated damages for breach of the undertaking was capable of being set oft against a claim for rent.

Held:

That the obligation of the tenants under the lease to pay the rent and the obligation of the landlords to carry out repairs were separate, albeit closely linked, obligations

Held also:

That the claim for unliquidated damages was capable of being set off against the claim for rent in view of the close connection between the two claims - Authorities on equitable set-off considered - Further development of the principle.

Claim under lease covenants for debt - Section 2 of the Leasehold Property Repairs Act 1938 and Section 146(3) of The Law of Property Act 1925 did not apply

Middlegate Properties Limited v Gidlow-Jackson[57]

Court of Appeal [1977] 34 P & CR 4

The Landlord served Notice under Section 146 of The Law of Property Act 1925. The tenant claimed protection under the Leasehold Property (Repairs) Act 1938. The landlords did not obtain leave to bring proceedings.

The tenant covenanted in the lease to pay legal costs and Surveyors' fees incurred by the landlords of, and incidental to, the preparation and service of Notice under Section 146 of The Law of Property Act 1925.

On appeal, it was Held:

Section 2 of The Leasehold Property Repairs Act 1938 did not apply as it would only come into effect if the lessor was claiming benefit of Section 146(3) of The Law of Property Act 1925. In this particular case, the landlords were claiming under Clause 7 of the lease as follows:- *"That the lessee will permit the estate trustees and the agent and the surveyor with or without workmen and others at all reasonable times in the daytime to enter upon the demised premises and take particulars of additions improvements fixtures and fittings thereto or therein and to view and examine the state and condition of the demised premises or any part thereof and the reparation of the same and of all defects decays and wants of reparation found in breach of the covenants herein contained to make and give or leave*

---

[57] Mrs. Gidlow- Jackson represented herself: a courageous and foolish thing to do. Few litigants in person succeed. It is often said that anyone who represents himself in court has a fool for a client.

notice in writing at or upon the demised premises to or for the lessee who will with all proper despatch and in any case within three months then next following well and sufficiently repair and amend the premises accordingly. And will pay and discharge on demand all costs charges and expenses (including legal costs and any fees payable to a surveyor) incurred by the estate trustees of and incident to the preparation and service of such notice or of any statutory notice relating to any breach of covenant. "

Section 13 of The Leasehold Property Repairs Act 1938 only applied to a claim for damages and in this particular case the Landlord was ciaiming for debt under the lease. Leave was not required and the appeal was dismissed.

Leasehold Property Repairs Act 1938 - Service of notice

Middlegate Properties Ltd. v Messimeris

(Lord Denning MR) [1973] 1 WLR 168

A notice was served under subsection 1 of section 146 of the Law of Property Act 1925.

Section 1(4) of the Leasehold Property (Repairs) Act 1938 says that the notice shall not be valid unless it contains a statement in characters not less conspicuous than those used on any other part of the notice to the effect that the lessee is entitled to serve a counter notice claiming the benefit of the Act, and a statement in like characters specifying the time within which and the manner in which, under the Act, a counter notice may be served and specifying the name and address for service by the lessor.

1:      It was held that a form which was filled in by a typewriter with a larger typeface than the type in the standard form was equally readable and was good.

2:      It was held that the fact that the notice only specified registered post for service of the counter notice and made no mention of recorded delivery which would be equally valid for service, did not invalidate the notice. It was sufficient to specify one good method of service.

3:      The notice must specify 'the name and address for service on the lessor'. The name and address of the lessor's solicitor was held to be sufficient to discharge this requirement.

Damages for disrepair - Lands Clauses Consolidation
Act 1845

Mills v Guardians of the Poor of the East London Union

[1872] LR 8CP 79

A 21 year lease was granted to the defendant tenants on
15th June 1859. There were mutual break clauses at the
7th and 14th year allowing either the Landlord or the tenant
to determine the lease.

A Notice to Treat was served on the tenants by a railway
company in February 1866, almost seven years after the
commencement of the term. Their powers stemmed from
the Lands Clauses Consolidation Act 1845. Compensation
was assessed by an Arbitrator and on 29th July 1870 the
premises were transferred.

Notice to Treat was served on the Lessors on 19th June
1868. They made a claim but nothing came of it because
the railway line for which the land was being acquired was
abandoned.

The Landlord brought an action against the former tenants
for breaches of their repairing covenants both before and
after they assigned their interest.

Held:

Full damages were recoverable between the time of the
Notice to Treat but before the tenants' interests had been
assigned to the railway company. The measure of damage
was loss of reversionary value at the date of assignment.

Repairs and renewal distinguished - Repairing
covenants

Minja Properties Ltd v Cussins Property
Group plc
and others

Chancery Division: [1998] EGCS 23

Landlord refurbishing entire commercial building seeking
access to demised office to replace rusting window frames
with double-glazing units - Tenant contending that work
did not involve "repair" Whether mandatory wording of
access clause precluded grant of interlocutory relief

The defendants occupied the upper three floors of a nine
floor office block in Newcastle upon Tyne under two
leases, one expiring in June 1998 and the other in March
1999. The remaining floors were let to a government
department. The landlord company was in receivership and
the building was in poor condition. In particular the steel
window frames, each holding a single pane, were corroded
because of inadequate rust-proofing during installation.
Anxious to sell, the receiver had been advised that sale was
not possible without major refurbishment. Each of the three
leases provided: (i) that the landlord would keep the
structure (including the window frames) in good and
tenantable repair; (ii) that the tenant should bear the cost of
such repair as a service charge item; and (iii) that the tenant
should permit the landlord at all reasonable times to enter
"to effect repairs to the building" (the access covenant). In
1995 the receiver, announcing a general refurbishment
programme, estimated to cost about £400,000, stated that
the frames would be replaced with double glazing-units at
an additional cost of £6,400.

The lessee government department was willing to afford access for this purpose, but the defendant tenants objected on the ground that the proposed work did not amount to "repairs" within the meaning of the access covenant. In 1996 the receiver awarded the refurbishment contract, which included the intended window replacements, to a firm of builders. Faced with the defendants' continuing objections, the receiver sued, inter alia[58], for a declaration that he was entitled to access, and moved for an interlocutory order that access be afforded forthwith.

Held :

The receiver's motion was allowed.

1. The intended works could not be described as renewal rather than repair, it being well established that repair consisted of renewal of parts of the entirety: see *Lurcott v Wakely and Wheeler [1911] 1 KB 905*. Furthermore, since damage by corrosion had in fact occurred, such works amounted to repair notwithstanding a consequent improvement to the original design: see *Quick v Taff-Ely Borough Council [1986] 2 EGLR 50; Elmeroft Developments Ltd v Tankersley-Sawyer [1984] 1 EGLR 47.* For that reason the tenants could not rely on *Post Office v Aquarius Properties Lid [1987] 1 EGLR 40 (CA)*, which turned on the exceptional finding that dysfunctional components (porous bricks) had not in fact been damaged by the flooding complained of.

2. Although the courts were reluctant to make interlocutory orders of a mandatory nature, such considerations barely applied to the access covenant which, though semantically mandatory, obliged the tenant to do little more than open the door.

---

[58] among other things.

3. There were no serious discretionary factors weighing against the order seeing that the defendants: (a) would not be badly inconvenienced; and (b) would only bear one-third of what was in any case a minute fraction of the entire refurbishment cost. Accordingly, the receiver could not he criticised for engaging the builder while the dispute was unresolved.

Fixtures and Fittings

Monti v Barnes

(1901) 1 CH 523

Held that gas fires, if part of the overall design of the room, were fixtures.

"improvement" or "repair" - Rent and Mortgage Interest (Restrictions) Act, 1920 s. 2 (1) (a)

Morcom v Campbell-Johnson And Others

[1956] 1 QB 106 Court Of Appeal

Landlord and Tenant - Rent restriction - Standard rent - Increase – "Improvement" - Old drainage and cold-water systems replaced by new - Defective area level adjoining building lowered Whether "improvement" or "repair" - Test applicable - Improvement from tenant's point of view Increase of Rent and Mortgage Interest (Restrictions) Act, 1920 s. 2 (1) (a) - Rent and Mortgage Interest Restrictions Act, 1939

The landlords of a 60-year-old block of flats incurred expenditure of some £10,000 on replacing the original old and worn water-borne drainage and cold-water systems by more efficient modem equivalents, and on lowering the area adjacent to the building which had been defective from its origin. On their application to the court for declarations that they were entitled to increase the standard rent of the tenants by an apportioned amount of eight per cent. of the sum expended, as "expenditure on the improvement ... of the dwelling-house (not including expenditure on ... repairs)" within section 2 (1) (a) of the Increase of Rent and Mortgage Interest (Restrictions) Act, 1920, as amended:-

Held:

That an "improvement of the dwelling-house" within section 2 (1) (a) meant the provision of something new which was beneficial, judged objectively from the point of view of the reasonable tenant; that (i) the replacement of the old drainage and cold-water systems by their modem equivalents, although resulting in making the dwelling-house better than it was before, were not much improvements but repairs only; and (ii) lowering the area, though an improvement per se, was not, in the circumstances, an improvement of any dwelling-house or flat; and that the landlords accordingly were not entitled to increase the rent under the section.

Covenant to pay fixed sum on repairs or to lessors not subject to s 18(1) of the Landlord and Tenant Act, 1927

Moss' Empires Limited   Appellants;

and

Olympia (Liverpool), Limited, and
Another   Respondents.

House Of Lords [1939] AC 544

Landlord and tenant - Lease - Covenant to expend specific sum each year on repairs - Breach Whether debt or damages - Landlord and Tenant Act, 1927 (17 & 18 Geo. 5, c. 36), s. 18, sub-s. 1.

A lease, of which the respondents were assignees, contained a covenant by them *"to expend during each year of the said term on .... repairs and decoration a sum of five hundred pounds and at the end of each year of the said term to produce to the lessors evidence of such expenditure or to pay to them at the end of each such year a sum equal to the difference between the amount so expended and five hundred pounds...."*

Held:

That the obligation created a debt, and was not a covenant to pay damages for breach of covenant to repair within s. 18, sub-s. 1, of the Landlord and Tenant Act, 1927, the stipulated sum being payable whether or not there was a breach of covenant.

Myers v Oldschool

Reasonable time for repairs to be done

Myers v Oldschool

[1928] EGD 167 Divisional Court

The defendant tenant took an assignment of a lease of some slum properties in 1924. They were houses divided into upper and lower floors and let to weekly tenants.

On 3rd December 1926 the Plaintiff ground Landlord wrote to the defendant tenant complaining of disrepair in the houses and subsequently on 10th January 1927 served a Notice of Forfeiture under Section 146 of The Law of Property Act 1925 for breach of the repairing covenant. The Notice gave three months to comply with about 2000 items of disrepair. Amongst these were taking off and renewing roofs of houses during the months of January through to April. The houses were occupied by tenants under The Rent Restriction Act and this prevented them being disturbed.

After the three months Notice had expired the Landlord took judgement and was granted it subject to relief on the basis that the repairs must be done to the satisfaction of a Surveyor. Costs, mesne profits and two guineas damages also to be paid by the defendant tenant to the Landlord. In considering whether a reasonable time had elapsed for the repairs to be done, all the circumstances had to be taken into account.

Tenant's Improvements

National Electric Theatres, Limited v Eudgell

Chancery Division [1939] Ch 553

Landlord and Tenant – Demolition and rebuilding – *"Improvement"* – *"Reasonable and suitable to character"* of holding - Landlord and Tenant Act, 1927, s. 3, sub-s. 1,

At the date of this action the plaintiffs were the assignees of two leases, executed respectively in 1911 and 1918, demising for ninety-nine years from June 24, 1910, certain land with a cinema thereon. The defendant, at the date of the action, was the freeholder. In both leases were covenants not without the lessor's written consent to use the holding or permit its use except as a hall licensed for entertainments and meetings, such consent not to be unreasonably withheld, and in the lease of 1918 there was also a lessee's covenant not to erect or permit the erection of anything on or near the south-west corner of the land so as to prevent access to the windows of the lessor's shop and premises adjoining the land on its south side, or to interfere with the access and use of light and air to and for such windows. Until March 31, 1938, the building had always been used as a cinema. The licence for its use was not then renewed, and the plaintiffs were told that they would not be given a licence to use for public entertainment any building on the land not conforming to certain requirements. In 1937 the plaintiffs had submitted to the defendant a plan and specification for shops with flats above, to be built on the land after demolishing the cinema. They now wished to proceed with the demolition and building. They had not served on the defendant, in accordance with s. 3, sub-s.1, of the Landlord and Tenant Act, 1927 (1), notice of intention to make the improvement.

(1) Sect. 3, sub-s. 1: *"Where a tenant of a holding to which this Part of this Act applies proposes to make an improvement on his holding, he shall serve on his landlord notice of his intention to make such improvement, together with a specification and plan showing the proposed improvement and the part of the existing premises affected thereby, and if the landlord, within three months after the service of the notice, serves on the tenant notice of objection, the tenant may, in the prescribed manner, apply to the tribunal, and the tribunal may, ... if satisfied that the improvement - (a) is of such a nature as to be calculated to add to the letting value of the holding at the termination of the tenancy; and (b) is reasonable and suitable to the character thereof, and (c) will not diminish the value of any other property belonging to the same landlord, or to any superior landlord from whom the immediate landlord of the tenant directly or indirectly holds; ....certify in the prescribed manner that the improvement is a proper improvement: ......"*

Sub-s. 2: *"In considering whether the improvement is reasonable and suitable to the character of the holding, the tribunal shall have regard to any evidence brought before it by the landlord or any superior landlord (but not any other person) that the improvement is calculated to injure the amenity or convenience of the neighbourhood."*

Sect. 21, sub-s. 1, provides that the tribunal to whom application is to be made under s. 3, sub-s. 1, shall be the county court, unless all persons affected agree that the claim or application should be heard by the High Court, or the matter is transferred to the High Court under the County Courts Act, 1888, s. 126. By Order LIII.D of the Rules of the Supreme Court the proceedings are assigned to the King's Bench Division.

The defendant admitted that the proposed works would enable the holding to be used profitably and increase its value for letting purposes and otherwise, but contended that works involving the entire demolition of all the buildings could not be an *"improvement"* within the meaning of the Act.

The plaintiffs claimed a declaration that the proposed works would constitute an improvement within the meaning of s. 3 of the Act, a declaration that they would constitute an improvement reasonable and suitable to the character of the holding within s. 3, sub-s. 1, and a declaration specifying, on the construction of the lease of 1918, the windows protected by the covenant in that lease:-

Held: (1.) that the proposed works would be an improvement on the holding in any ordinary use of the word *"improvement,"* and would constitute an *"improvement"* within the meaning of s. 3;

(2.) that s. 3, sub-s. 1, did not refer only to alterations of buildings, for, if it did, the erection of a new building on unoccupied land could not be an improvement, and it was clearly intended that it might be an improvement;

(3.) that the provision in the sub-section that there should be served on the landlord notice of the intention to make the improvement *"together with a specification and plan showing the proposed improvement and the part of the existing premises affected thereby"* was not inconsistent with the view that improvement could include demolition and rebuilding;

(4.) that the provisions of the Act did not necessitate that a rebuilding of business premises after demolition should, in order to constitute an *"improvement,"* be a rebuilding for the purpose of the same business;

(5.) that the question whether the proposed demolition and rebuilding would constitute an improvement "suitable to the character of the holding" within the meaning of s. 3, sub-s. 1, was hypothetical, since the tenant had not served on the landlord notice of intention to make the improvement, and, since it would therefore have to be assumed that the landlord had objected to the improvement, and that the Court was the proper tribunal, which in fact it was not: the Court would not answer the question.

F. W. Woolworth & Co., Ld. v. Lambert [1937] Ch. 37 and Lambert v F. W. Woolworth & Co., Ld. [1938] Ch. 883, considered and distinguished.

Recovery of Landlord's costs under S 146 (3) of the Law
of Property Act 1925

Nind v Nineteenth Century Building Society

[1984] 2 QB 226

In 1884 the plaintiff's predecessor in title let eleven houses
under eleven separate leases to separate lessees on repairing
leases each with proviso for re-entry on breach of covenant.
The interests of the lessees became vested in Henry Hall who
mortgaged them by way of underlease to the defendants.
The plaintiff discovered the houses were in a state of
disrepair and employed a surveyor to prepare a schedule of
repairs and a solicitor to serve notice under S 14 (1) of the
Conveyancing and Law of Property Act 1881. These were
served by leaving them at the respective houses.   The
defendants complied with the notices and repaired the
houses.

The plaintiff then brought an action to recover costs of £50
incurred in preparing and serving the notices. There was no
written evidence of waiver by the plaintiff of right of re-entry
or forfeiture and no request from the defendant for the lessor
to waive this right. The Judge gave judgement for the
plaintiff and this was confirmed on appeal to the Divisional
Court.

The Court of Appeal reversed these decisions. The found:-

1:        An underlessee is not, as between himself and the
original lessor, a "lessee" within the meaning of the
Conveyancing and Law of Property Act 1892, s 2 (1), and
therefore such a lessor cannot recover from him the costs and
expenses mentioned in that subsection. The word "lessee"
has the same construction as it has in s 14 of the
Conveyancing and Law of Property Act 1881,

2:      A lessee complying with a notice under s 14 (1) of the   Conveyancing and Law of Property Act 1881, prevents a right of forfeiture becoming enforceable, is not "relieved" of forfeiture within the meaning of S 2 (1) Conveyancing and Law of Property Act 1881. prevents a right of forfeiture from becoming enforceable, is not "relieved" from forfeiture within the meaning of S 2 (1), of the Conveyancing and Law of Property Act 1892.

Lessor under no obligation to repair defect until he has notice

O'Brien and Another v Robinson

House of Lords [1973] 1 All ER 583

Section 32(1) of The Housing Act 1961 provides: *"in any lease of a dwelling – house, being a lease to which this section applies, there shall be implied a covenant by the lessor – (a) to keep in repair the structure ... of the dwelling-house ...."*

In this particular case the ceiling fell down. The tenant was not aware that the ceiling was defective and had not told the Landlord because of this. The Landlord had no prior knowledge of the defect.

Held:

The lessor has no obligation to repair defects until he had notice of it. As this was a latent defect the lessor could not be held liable for damages suffered by the Plaintiff.

Illegal assignment - forfeiture proceedings - cross claim by "illegal assignee"

Old Grovebury Manor Farm Ltd. v W. Seymour Plant Sales & Hire Ltd. and Another

Chancery Division [1979] WLR 263

Practice - Possession of land - Interim payment for use and occupation - Counterclaim by defendant for amount exceeding interim payment claimed - Whether precluding claim for interim payment R.S.C., Ord. 29, r. 18'

The lessee of land used as a garage and petrol filling station purported to assign the lease to the defendant company without the consent of the lessor, the plaintiff company, as required by a covenant in the lease. The plaintiff company issued a writ for forfeiture of the lease alleging breach of the covenant. The lease was due to expire on January 1, 1978, but the defendant company claimed that it had exercised an option to renew it under a provision in the lease or, alternatively, that the term continued under the Landlord and Tenant Act 1954 as a business tenancy. There had been no payment of rent to the plaintiff company by the defendant company, though it had been offered. The defendant company counterclaimed in the proceedings for £20,000 damages for harassment by the plaintiff company resulting in a reduction in petrol sales.

On the plaintiff company's summons seeking an interim payment of £11,400 under R.S.C., Ord. 29, r. 18-

Held: dismissing the application,

That although a plaintiff claiming possession of premises was prima facie[59] entitled to an interim payment in respect of rent or mesne profits by virtue of R.S.C., Ord. 29, r. 18, by analogy with the practice under R.S.C., Ord. 14, r. 3 (2) it would not be proper to make such an order where the defendant company raised a bona fide cross-claim for damages for a sum in excess of that claimed by the Plaintiff company.

---

[59] On the face of it – as things seem.

Disrepair - licence to assign refused

Orlando Investments Ltd v Grosvenor Estate Belgravia

Chancery Division [1989] 49 EG 85

Landlord and tenant - Assignment of long lease - Complaint by tenants that consent to assignment had been unreasonably withheld - House in bad condition on the Grosvenor Estate - Plaintiff tenants had taken an assignment from predecessors who had failed to carry out repairs - Plaintiffs had not entered into a covenant to observe the terms of the lease but were, of course, liable while the lease was vested in them - Plaintiffs prepared a scheme of works which was approved by defendant landlords, but before the scheme could he implemented plaintiffs entered into an agreement to assign to a neighbouring proprietor who was interested in the possibility of combining the two houses – As time went on, the defendants were becoming concerned about the delay in carrying out repairs and it was evident that the proposed assignee did not want to carry out the plaintiffs' scheme – In reply to the plaintiffs' pressure for the completion of the licence to assign the defendants laid down as conditions of the a strict timetable for the completion of the works and requirements to guarantee the security of the proposed assignees' financial position - Eventually the present originating summons was issued.

The defendant landlords referred to the propositions set out by Balcombe LJ in *International Drilling Fluids v Louisville Investments (Uxbridge) Ltd* and claimed that, in view of the ruinous state of the premises and the failures of the plaintiffs and predecessors in title, they were entitled to be satisfied that a prospective assignee was ready, willing and able to put the house good repair within a reasonable time - They were not so satisfied because the prospective assignee (1) had not agreed to a timetable for the works, (2) had broken promises to execute some urgent works, (3) had been balked by the estate of his plan to join the two houses and might now wish only to find another purchaser and sell at a profit, and (4) had not satisfied the financial conditions required by the estate.

The judge considered that these reasons formed the basis of a decision to refuse consent to which the defendants might reasonably have come - He rejected a number of objections put forward by the plaintiffs, including a suggestion that the refusal imposed a burden on them disproportionate to the benefit to the defendants - Plaintiffs' summons dismissed.

Tenant's improvements - Compensation claim - No compensation for work done *"in pursuance of a contract"*

Owen Owen Estate Ltd. v. Livett And Others

Chancery Division |1955| 3 WLR 1

Landlord and Tenant - Act of 1927 - Improvement - Claim for compensation by tenant - Objection by landlord that improvement made *"in pursuance of a contract"* Meaning of *"contract"* Practice - Procedure for testing question - R.S. C., Ord. 54A, r. 1A Landlord and Tenant Act, 1927 ss. 2 (1) (b), 3 (1).

The expression *"contract"* in section 2 (1) (b) of the Landlord and Tenant Act, 19271 (which provides that a tenant shall not be entitled to compensation for any improvement made *"in pursuance of a contract"*), is to be interpreted literally, and is not restricted to a contract made between a landlord and a tenant.

The tenants of certain shop premises served on the landlord notice of a proposal to make improvements on the premises in the way of improved lavatory accommodation. The landlords served notice of objection, not on the merits, but on the ground that the tenants were under an obligation to make the said improvements pursuant to a covenant in a sublease which they had executed, and that such sublease was a *"contract"* within the meaning of the subsection.

The tenants applied by summons to the court as the tribunal under the Act for a certificate that the improvements were proper improvements for which they were entitled to be compensated on the expiration of their tenancy, and contended that a *"contract"* within the subsection was limited to one made between a landlord and a tenant or their successors in title:-

Held:

That there was nothing in the context of the subsection to cut down the meaning of the perfectly general words there to be found, or to limit their literal interpretation; so that the covenant in the sublease fell within the mischief of the subsection, and the tenants were precluded from claiming compensation.

Held also:

That as the dispute between the parties was one concerning the construction of the Act, the proceedings were not in proper form; and that a pro forma summons should be taken out under Ord. 54A, r. 1 A.

----

1 Landlord and Tenant Act, 1927, s. 1: *"(1) ... a tenant ... shall, if a claim for the purpose is made in the prescribed manner - ... be entitled, at the termination of the tenancy, on quitting his holding, to be paid by his landlord compensation in respect of any improvement ... made by him ... which at the termination of the tenancy adds to the letting value of the holding: ... (3) In the absence of agreement between the parties, all questions as to the right to compensation under this section, or as to the amount thereof, shall be determined by the tribunal hereinafter mentioned ..."*

S. 2: *"(1) A tenant shall not be entitled to compensation ... (b) in respect of any improvement ... which the tenant or his predecessors in title were under an obligation to make in pursuance of a contract entered into ... for valuable consideration, including a building lease; ..."*

S. 3: *"(1) Where a tenant of a holding to which this Part of this Act applies proposes to make an improvement on his holding, he shall serve on his landlord notice of his intention to make such improvement ... and if the landlord ... serves on the tenant notice of objection, the tenant may, in the prescribed manner, apply to the tribunal, and the tribunal may ... certify in the prescribed manner that the improvement is a proper improvement: ..."*

Notice of disrepair - Bad parts of notice did not invalidate it

Pannell v City of London Brewery Company

[1900] 1 Ch 496

A notice under section 14 of the Conveyancing Act, 1881 listing a number of clearly defined breaches of covenant was not invalidated because although some of the alleged breaches had never occurred, others had.

The notice required among other things, for the premises to be painted, although this work had been done. The judge said that if one breach could invalidate a notice, a separate notice would have to be served for every alleged breach and this was absurd. In the event, the action was dismissed with costs because the judge found no breaches upon which the plaintiff could rely.

Whether Housing Act 1961, sections. 32 (1), 33 (1) (2)[60] applied to lease because of option to determine, relieving tenant of liability for repairs

Parker v O'Connor

Court Of Appeal [1974] 1 WLR 1160

Landlord and Tenant - Lease - Option to determine - 90 years' lease with full repairing covenants - Provision for determination at option of either party on death of landlord - Whether determinable at option of landlord within seven years of commencement of term - Whether tenant liable for repairs - Housing Act 1961, ss. 32 (1), 33 (1) (2)

A landlord let a dwelling house for a term of 90 years from June 24, 1970, at a rent of £546 a year for the first seven years with increases thereafter in accordance with a schedule. The lease contained full repairing covenants by the tenant who also covenanted to execute all works required by the local authority under any Act of Parliament. The landlord had a right to enter to inspect the state of repair. Clause 16 provided that if, in the event of the death of the landlord, either party should desire to determine the term and within six months of the death should give three months' notice in writing the lease should cease and be void.

60

[60] Housing Act 1957 s. 111: *"(1) The general management, regulation and control of houses provided by a local authority under this Part of this Act shall be vested in and exercised by the authority, and the authority may make such reasonable charges for the tenancy or occupation of the houses as they may determine..."*

See also Supreme Court Act 1981, s. 37(1)

In March 1973 the landlord served a notice under section 146 (1) of the Law of Property Act 1925 requiring the tenant to carry out repairs, mainly to the roof and walls, required by the local authority pursuant to a notice served under the Housing Acts 1957-1969. The tenant failed to carry out the work and served a counter-notice claiming the benefit of the Leasehold Property (Repairs) Act 1938. The landlord applied for leave to commence proceedings for re-entry and/or forfeiture and/or damages on the grounds set out in section 1 (5) (a), (b) and (d) of the Act of 1938'. The tenant opposed the application and contended that the option to determine in clause 16 brought the lease within section 32 (1) of the Housing Act 1961 and in those circumstances he was not liable for repairs. The county court judge upheld that contention and refused the landlord leave to proceed.

On appeal by the landlord: -

Held:

Allowing the appeal, that though the lease might be determinable under clause 16 in the circumstances there set out, the landlord had no unfettered option thereunder to determine the lease before the expiration of seven years from the commencement of the term and therefore it could not be treated as a lease for less than seven years within the meaning of section 33 (1) of the Housing Act 1961; that accordingly, section 32 (1) of the Act did not apply, the tenant was liable to remedy the state of disrepair under his covenant in the lease, and the landlord was entitled to the leave she sought.

Landlord and Tenant Act 1927 section 1 as amended by Landlord and Tenant Act 1954 section 47 - Compensation for tenant's improvements

Pelosi and another v Newcastle Arms Brewery Ltd

Court of Appeal
[1981] 2 EGLR 36, (1981) 259 EG 247

Landlord and Tenant Act 1927 - Compensation for improvements - Whether improvements had been made by tenants' "predecessors in title" so as to entitle tenants to compensation - Tenants had been assignees of the sublessees who had carried out the improvements but the tenants subsequently acquired the reversionary interest immediately expectant on the sublease - It was argued that by acquiring the reversion on their sublease the sublessees had destroyed their right to compensation, as their predecessors in title then became the reversioners in whose interest their sublease had merged

Held:

Allowing appeal from county court judge's decision, that the tenants derived their title as tenants in possession not merely from the assignment of the reversion but also from the original assignment of the sublease - The improvements had therefore been carried out by their "predecessors in title" and their claim to compensation under the Act of 1927 was good

Dampness in Buildings

Pembery v Lamdin

Court of Appeal [1940] 2 All ER 435

A lessor of some old premises which lacked a damp proof course and damp proof membrane covenanted to keep the external part of the demised premises, other than the shop front, in good and tenantable repair and condition. The tenant claimed that this made the landlord liable to waterproof the outside walls and thus make the place dry.

Held:

     1: The obligation on the landlord was only to keep the premises in repair in the condition in which they were when let. As the premises were old this meant the landlord only had to point the brickwork.

     2: An external wall is one forming part of the enclosure of the premises, and is not necessarily exposed to the atmosphere, but may adjoin another building.

Costs - If the recipient of a Calderbank offer is in doubt about its effect, he has a duty to seek clarification.

Phyllis Trading Ltd v 86 Lordship Road Ltd

Court of Appeal
19 February 2001

[2001] EWCA Civ 350
[2001] 28 EG 147

Lands Tribunal - Costs - Calderbank offer to settle - Lands Tribunal allowing landlord's appeal from leasehold valuation tribunal - Award of tribunal exceeding determination of leasehold valuation tribunal - Nominee purchaser's Calderbank offer exceeding award - Calderbank offer omitting reference to costs - Tribunal awarding costs to landlord - Whether Calderbank offer should deal with costs - Whether tribunal entitled to award costs to landlord

The appellant nominee purchaser was appointed by qualifying tenants in respect of the exercise of their rights of collective enfranchisement of premises containing their flats. The respondent landlord appealed to the Lands Tribunal against the leasehold valuation tribunal's determination of the purchase price of £3,300. By a Calderbank letter dated 6 October 1999, the purchaser offered £4,000 for the freehold interest to settle the appeal "without prejudice save as to costs". The letter made no reference to the parties' costs. The Lands Tribunal allowed the appeal and determined the purchase price at £3,610. The tribunal accepted the landlord's submissions that there were still grounds for dispute as regards costs in relation to the purchaser's Calderbank offer, as the offer was too uncertain to be accepted, and awarded costs to the landlord. The purchaser appealed

Held: The appeal was allowed.

The tribunal was wrong to take the view that the offer was too uncertain to be capable of acceptance. The Calderbank offer was plainly made on the basis that, if accepted, the proceedings before the tribunal would determine, and that neither side would be entitled to any costs. Alternatively, the tribunal was wrong not to have addressed the question of whether it was reasonable for the landlord to reject the offer without attempting to ascertain the position regarding costs. A reasonable offer by a purchaser ought to be accepted, notwithstanding that the offer does not make provision for costs, in circumstances where, as in the present case, it was made at an early stage. If the recipient of a Calderbank offer is in doubt about its effect, he has a duty to seek clarification.

Set Off

Platt and Others –v- London Underground Limited

Chancery Division   The Times 13th March 2001

Two kiosks, at Goodge Street Station, were let to the same tenant under separate leases. One of the kiosks was used as a Bureau de Change and the other sold food and drinks. The Landlord, London Underground Limited arranged passenger movements so that passengers could enter both entrances but could exit from only one of them.

The tenant complained that this was a derogation from grant in respect of the lease of one of the kiosks, which had adversely affected trade. This was accepted by the Court but it was also held that as a result of the increased flow through one of the exits the trade to the second kiosk increased and this increase could be used to offset any damages due from the derogation from grant.

Repairs - Service Charge

Postel Properties Ltd and another v Boots the Chemist

Queen's Bench Division [1996] 41 EG 164

Landlord and tenant - Repairs - Service charge Whether proposals by landlord to recover roofs and repair windows of large shopping mall within covenant to keep premises in good and substantial repair and condition - Whether recoverable under service charge.

The plaintiff landlords are the owners of the Milton Keynes shopping centre, the largest such building in Europe. In 1991 they carried out repairs to the low-level roofs and upper windows. The defendant, a representative tenant, contended that the cost of the work was not recoverable under the service charge provisions of the leases. The flat low-level roofs, which were constructed in 1975 and 1976 with a maximum life expectancy of 20 years, were recovered under a phased programme. The tenants argued that the replacement of the roof covering was premature and the specification was increased to a point where there was an irrecoverable excess, and that the work to the windows was due to rust which could have been contained with timeous maintenance.

Held:

The landlords were entitled to recover all the cost claimed, save for 45p per M^2 for the priming of certain roof troughs. The repairs to the roof were repairs which a reasonably minded building owner might undertake and they did not amount to giving back to the landlord something different from that which existed before. It was reasonable to commence them when the landlord did, notwithstanding that some parts yet to be recovered had not yet failed. It was reasonable to accept the recommendations of the experts on certain improvements to the specification. However, no useful purpose was served by priming the galvanised roof troughs which showed no evidence of deterioration. The works to the windows and cladding were repairs, and, in so far as the landlord may have been guilty of delay in carrying out such works, that was more than balanced by the saved costs of earlier repaintings.

Structural alterations distinguished from repairs

Post Office v Aquarius Properties Ltd.

[1985] 2 EGLR 105
(1985) 276 EG 923

The basement of an office building flooded due to a rise in the water table and faults in the construction of the joint between the floor and the walls. Between 1979 and 1984 there had been several inches of water in the basement. After 1984 the water table had dropped and the basement had been dry. Remedial measures required substantial structural additions to the basement.

Held:

The works fell outside the repairing covenants because they involved structural alterations and improvements to the basement.

"Good and Tenantable Repair" defined

Proudfoot v Hart

Court Of Appeal   25 QBD 42

Landlord and Tenant - Lease - Covenant – "Good Tenantable Repair, " What is.

Under an agreement to keep a house in "good tenantable repair," and so leave the same at the expiration of the term, the tenant's obligation is to put and keep the premises in such repair as, having regard to the age, character, and locality of the house, would make it reasonably fit for the occupation of a tenant of the class who would be likely to take it.

Implied liability to keep in repair Section 32 of Housing
Act 1961 - Cure of inherent defects

Quick v Taff-Ely Borough Council

Court of Appeal [1985] 276 EG 452

Landlord and tenant - Section 32 of Housing Act 1961
Implied liability to keep in repair the structure and exterior
of the dwelling-house - Appeal by local authority landlords
from county court decision in favour of tenant - Case of
importance on scope of liability - Tenant's claims were
under headings of condensation and water penetration, but
appeal related only to the former, the landlords accepting
the judge's findings and decision on the latter - It was not
disputed that in respect of section 32 of the 1961 Act, a
local authority was in, the same position as a private
landlord - The windows in the house in question were
single-glazed with metal frames set in wooden window
surrounds and concrete lintels above the windows with no
facing of insulating material - There was a central-beating
system based on warm-air ducts - There was evidence of
very severe condensation due to the warm air of the rooms
reaching the cold surfaces of the building - By modern
standards the house in the winter, when the condensation
was most severe, was virtually unsuitable for human
habitation - Furniture and fabrics had become rotten and
tenant and wife hardly used the living-room, where a three-
piece suite had been ruined by damp and had to be
jettisoned - However, evidence of physical damage to the
structure was confined to rot in the wooden surrounds of
some windows and the perishing of plaster in a bedroom -
The county court judge held that the landlords were in
breach of section 32 in respect of the condensation,
awarded damages and made an order for the specific
performance of the repairing covenant, requiring the
landlords to replace the metal frame windows with warmer
material, such as timber or PVC, and face the lintels with

insulating material – The judge accepted a broad principle that anything defective or inherently inefficient for living in or incapable of providing the conditions of ordinary habitation was in disrepair.

Held:

After reviewing the authorities, that this principle went beyond the scope of section 32 of the 1961 Act, which was confined to disrepair in relation to physical condition - There must be some damage to structure which had to be made good - In some cases this could involve curing an inherent defect, thus improving the property to some extent, if that was the only way to make good the damage to the subject-matter of the implied covenant - But in the present case the repair work to the wooden surrounds and the replacement of plaster did not require in any realistic sense the replacement of the metal windows by wooden-framed windows or windows with PVC frames.

Appeal allowed and case remitted to reassess the damages in the light of the judgments - As the tenant had been rehoused, there had in any case been no issue as to specific performance

Repairs - Specific performance

Rainbow Estates Ltd v Tokenhold Ltd and another

Chancery Division [1998] 24 EG 123

Landlord and tenant - Repairs - Covenant - Whether specific performance of tenant's repairing covenant can be granted

In 1976 the second defendant and his brother bought a Grade 11 listed building and later transferred the freehold to V, a company owned by the brothers. In 1993, when a bank came to enforce its charge on the property, the brothers revealed the existence of two leases of the property dated December 15 1987, each granted by V. The leases, of separate parts of the property, were granted to the first and second defendants respectively. Each lease contained a covenant by the tenant to repair the property demised. Following an appointment of a liquidator, the freehold was ultimately acquired by the plaintiff. On December 10 1997 the recorder held that the defendants were responsible under the leases for repairs. The defendants applied to amend their defence to seek rectification of the repairing covenants. The plaintiff landlord sought specific performance of the repairing covenants.

Held:

The applications to amend the defence were refused. An order for specific performance of the repairing covenants was granted. A modern law of remedies requires specific performance of a tenant's repairing covenant to be available in appropriate circumstances and there are no constraints of principle or binding authority against the availability of the remedy.

First, even if want of mutuality were any longer a decisive factor (which it is not), the availability of the remedy against the tenant would restore mutuality as against the landlord.

Second, the problems of defining the work and the need for supervision can be overcome by ensuring that there is sufficient definition of which has to be done in order to comply with the order of the court.

Third, the court should not be constrained by the supposed rule that the court will not enforce the defendants' obligation in part.

Subject to the overriding need to avoid injustice or oppression. it will be appropriate for the remedy to be available when damages are not an adequate remedy or, in the more modern formulation, when specific performance is the appropriate remedy. It follows that not only is there a need for great caution in granting the remedy against a tenant, but also that it will be a rare case in which the remedy of specific performance will be the appropriate one: in the case of commercial leases. the landlord will normally have the right to forfeit or to enter and do the repairs at the expense of the tenant; in residential leases, the landlord will normally have the right to forfeit in appropriate cases. The lack of any serious alternative remedy, the absence of any real dispute about the repairs required, the scope of the repairs and the deterioration of the state of the property and the notices served by the district council together strongly point to specific performance being the appropriate remedy.

Repair distinguished from improvement

Ravenseft Properties Ltd v Davstone (Holdings) Ltd

Queen's Bench Division [1978] 249 EG 51

Landlord and tenant - Important decision on repairing liability - Judge's review of authorities on doctrine of "inherent defect" - *Lister v Lane* considered - *Collins v Flynn* doubted - Inherent defect not as such a defence to tenant on repairing covenant - True test a matter of degree - Whether what tenant is asked to do is properly described as repair or whether it involves giving landlord a wholly different thing from that which was demised - Tenants liable under repairing covenant in present case for remedial works caused by stone cladding on concrete frame of maisonettes and flats becoming loose and dangerous - Inclusion of expansion joints not building practice at date of construction

Disrepair of roof - Lessors had not reserved right of access to repair if tenants defaulted

Regional Properties Ltd v City Of London Real Property Co Ltd

Sedgwick Forbes Bland Payne Group Ltd v Regional Properties Ltd

Chancery Division [1981] 257 EG 64

Landlord and tenant - Problem of repairing a leaking roof - Interesting questions of landlord and tenant law canvassed in the course of interlocutory proceedings in two interrelated actions – Motions for injunction in first action by tenants of parts of an office block, including. the roof, against the freeholders - Injunction sought to restrain freeholders, who had already obtained a judgment for damages against these tenants, from entering to repair the roof - These tenants were in breach of their covenant to repair roof but freeholders had reserved no right of entry to repair it – Motion for injunction in second action by tenants of other parts of the block against the tenants whose demise included the roof - The tenants of these other parts, who were not themselves in occupation, wished to protect their subtenants against damage caused by the penetration of water from the leaking roof - Hence they wished to carry out repairs themselves to the roof and sought an injunction to prevent the *"tenants of the roof"* from obstructing access for this purpose

Held:

on the first motion that the tenants of the roof were entitled
to an injunction, but in view of mutual undertakings an
order was unnecessary - The unusual relief sought in the
second motion by the tenants of the other parts was refused
after consideration of various submissions and taking
account of the undertaking given by the tenants of the roof
which satisfied the freeholders in the first action.

"Fair wear and tear"

Regis Property Co. Ltd.   Appellant;

And

Dudley   Respondent.

House Of Lords [1959] AC 370

Viscount Simonds,
Lord Morton Of Henryton,
Lord Tucker,
Lord Keith Of Avonholm And
Lord Denning.

Landlord and Tenant - Rent restriction - Rent limit - Appropriate factor - Tenant's liability for repairs under terms of tenancy - Concurrent liability at common law – "Fair wear and tear" - Services - Rent Act, 1957, ss. 1, 2, Sch. I, para. 1 (1) (2) and (3).
Landlord and Tenant - Repairs - Covenant – "Fair wear and tear" - Meaning.

By section 1 (1) of the Rent Act, 1957, *"the rent recoverable for any rental period from the tenant under a controlled tenancy shall not exceed ... a rent of which the annual rate is equal to the 1956 gross value of the dwelling multiplied by two (or, if the responsibility for repairs is such as is specified in Part 1 of the First Schedule to this Act, by the appropriate factor specified in the said Part I) .*
.....

By Part 1 of Schedule 1: " 1 - (1) The following provisions shall have effect in ascertaining the rent limit by reference to the 1956 gross value. (2) If under the terms of the tenancy the tenant is responsible for all repairs, the appropriate factor shall be four-thirds. (3) If under the terms of the tenancy the tenant is responsible for some, but not all, repairs, the appropriate factor shall be such number less than two but greater than four-thirds as may be ... determined by the county court."

The landlords of a block of flats in London applied to the county court to determine the increase of rent permissible under the Act in respect of one of the flats let unfurnished at an inclusive rent of £139 16s 9d a year, which, owing to an increase of rates, had been increased to £145 12s 5d. The tenant's obligations to repair under the lease were to keep the interior of the flat in good and substantial repair and clean sanitary condition, fair wear and tear and damage by accidental fire excepted. The judge fixed the appropriate factor at $1^{2/}_3$, holding that the liability of the landlords and of the tenant for repairs was about equal:-

Held:

(Lord Keith of Avonholm and Lord Denning dissenting)

that the judge had not erred in principle in fixing the appropriate factor. Even though some items of repair might be made necessary by the act of the tenant for which he could be made liable at common law, yet, if he was also liable for it under the terms of the tenancy, he was to be regarded as responsible for it for the purpose of determining the appropriate factor, since the court was concerned only with his responsibility expressed by the terms of the tenancy. For the purpose of the determination a hypothetical tenant was to be assumed who was reasonably careful in his user of the premises, but that did not import a tenant who was never guilty of any act of negligence.

Held, further, unanimously,

that the judge did not err in crediting the tenant with more than a nominal amount in respect of his liability to repair, in view of the "fair wear and tear" exception. The exemption covered no more than the remedying of things which wear out in the course of reasonable use; it did not cover other damage which flowed from the wear and tear.

Relief from forfeiture - Immoral use

Ropemaker Properties Ltd v Noonhaven Ltd

Chancery Division [1989] 34 EG 39

Landlord and tenant - Forfeiture - Clubs used for purposes of prostitution - Scale of activities known to all concerned in the running of the clubs - Relief against forfeiture - Reasons why relief given despite breaches "of the utmost gravity" - Possession claimed by owners of West End premises after investigations into conduct of two night clubs occupying parts of premises, one of them by an underlease and the other by licence granted by the defendants, lessees for a term of 25 years from October 28 1982 at a rent of £75,000 pa with provision for rent review - User clause in the lease, in addition to prohibiting m any illegal or immoral purpose, forbade the use of the parts underlet "for any purpose other than as a high-class restaurant/night club" ; and both underlease and licence prohibited use for any illegal or immoral purpose.

There was "overwhelming evidence" that both clubs were used for the purpose of prostitution - The hostesses were not paid by the club but were required to negotiate a "hostess fee" with clients, not the usual arrangement at a reputable night club – Most, if not virtually all, the hostesses were prostitutes - At one of the clubs, if not at both, a customer was expected or required to buy two bottles of champagne (at a wholly extortionate price) and a meal in order to enable the hostess to leave the club with him ("the two bottle rule")

There were clear breaches of the user covenants and the scale of the prostitutes' activities made it impossible to believe that anyone involved in the actual day-to-day management and running was unaware of what was going on - The defendants, the lessees of the premises, were a private company owned and controlled by a sole director, a man of 64, said to suffer from a us heart condition - He strongly denied knowledge of the conduct complained of and said that he had confidence in his managers, who were experienced night club operators - The judge's assessment of him was that if he did not know, for example, as a fact that the hostesses were engaged in prostitution, it was because he took care not to know - He distanced himself from the actual running of the dubs - The concluded that, whether or not he had actual knowledge of what was going on, he must he taken to have known of it - That was sufficient to fix the defendants, as distinct from the managers and staff, with knowledge, so that breach of the covenants against knowingly permitting immoral user was established – The managers and staff, of course, had actual knowledge of the breaches.

The main importance of the decision lies in the reasons given by the judge for granting relief against forfeiture of the lease, despite the admittedly grave character of the misconduct disclosed - After reaffirming that it was only in the rarest and most exceptional circumstances that the court would grant relief in such a case, he listed the considerations which had influenced him as follows:

1: the substantial value of the lease;

2: financial loss to the defendants out of proportion to their offence or to any conceivable damage to the plaintiffs;

3: immoral use had been ended and was unlikely to be renewed (the defendants, inter alia[61], would enter into a deed of of variation banning hostesses from the premises);

4: any "stigma" attaching to the premises would be short lived and might already have disappeared;

---

[61] among other things.

5: getting rid of the defendants would not help to remove any remaining stigma - those who ran the clubs had already gone

6: the grant of relief would not saddle the plaintiffs with unacceptable tenants, as in all respects save the one complained of in this action the defendants had been excellent tenants;

7: the director of the defendant company was in seriously poor health and had been thinking of retiring and disposing of the lease; he had offered to use his best endeavours to find purchaser within some appropriate time-scale if relief were granted (The judge did nor require an undertaking, but was satisfied that the intention to dispose of the lease was genuine)

Landlord's interference with tenant's right to park on forecourt

Saeed v Plustrade Ltd

Court of Appeal [2002] 02 EG 102 (CS)

Respondent lessee parking car on forecourt of block of flats - Appellant lessor carrying out refurbishment works - Lessee unable to park - Lessor reducing number of parking spaces - Whether substantial interference with lessee's right to park - Appeal dismissed

The claimant was the lessee under a long lease of a flat. The defendant was her lessor. The second schedule to the lease conferred on the lessee, by para 7: *"The right... in common with all other persons entitled to the like right to park his private motor car on such part of the Retained Property as may from time to time be specified by the lessor as reserved for car parking when space is available and subject to such regulations as the lessor may make from time to time"*.

The forecourt to the premises had a designated parking area with space for 13 cars in unmarked bays. The defendant decided to refurbish the parking area and define the parking bays. No parking was possible during the period of refurbishment, and posts subsequently delineated the parking spaces, reducing the number to 12. Between May 1997 and August 2000, the forecourt could not be used for parking because the area was required for the defendant's contractors, who were refurbishing the building. In August 2000 the defendant informed the claimant that it would honour an informal agreement with the planning authority and provide four marked spaces for the lessees.

The claimant issued proceedings seeking an order that the defendant permit her to park in the specified area in which she had been permitted to park until 1997. She also claimed damages. She contended that she had a right, in the nature of an casement, to park on the forecourt, and that, from 1997 to 2000, the interference with that right had been total. The judge held, inter alia[62], that para 7 of the lease the claimant gave an casement to park in the spaces on the forecourt to the extent that space was available from time to time, subject to the lessor's right to specify alternative spaces from time to time. He concluded that the defendant had substantially interfered with that right from 1997 to date. He concluded that the defendant's scheme to restrict parking to four car-parking spaces would similarly constitute a substantial interference with her right. The defendant appealed.

Held:

The appeal was dismissed.

1. In the circumstances of the instant case, it did not matter whether the claimant's legal rights of parking could be categorised as easements. The purported complete determination by the defendant of the claimant's right to park, between May 1997 and August 2000, was a clear derogation from the right to park to which the claimant was entitled under the lease. It entirely frustrated the purpose for which right this had been given to her by para 7, a purpose that must have been in the contemplation of both parties to the lease at the time of the original grant. The right had never been varied or determined. The claimant's right had been infringed, and her claim to damages for that period was established.

2. In relation to the defendant's scheme, the relevant date for determining whether there was substantial interference with the claimant's right was the date of the interference. It

---

[62] 'among other things'

was not necessary to compare the position with the parking situation when the claimant had taken over the lease. Before the interference, she had been able to park on some 12 or 13 spaces, in competition with other lessees. She was now restricted to three or four spaces, but with the same level of competition. That constituted substantial interference with the enjoyment of her right.

Intention to demolish changed after expiry of the lease due to onset of war. Intention at the date of determination is crucial. Afterwards the tenant is unable to fulfil his covenant

Salisbury and Another v Gilmore and Marcel

[1942] 2 KB 38

A landlord sued his tenant for damages for failure to deliver up in repair in accordance with his lease covenants when the lease expired on 29th September 1939. From 1937, the landlord had intended to demolish and rebuild the premises at the expiration of the term but changed his mind due to the onset of the war. On December 5th 1939, following the expiry of the lease, a letter was sent to the former tenant giving the first notification of the change of intention by the landlord to demolish the building.

The tenant contended that this case fell within section 18(1) of the Landlord and Tenant Act 1927 and that since the landlord's change of intention had not been communicated before the termination of the lease, there was no liability under the covenant to repair.

On appeal it was held that:-

(i)   the crucial date is the determination of the lease since, after that date has passed, the tenant is no longer in a position to fulfil his covenant, and if it shown that before that date arrives the landlord has decided to pull down the building and that this intention is still subsisting at that date, the requirements of the subsection are satisfied. In the present case, therefore, the tenant was entitled to the relief which the subsection gives.

(ii)   there is no need to transpose or to add any words in order to construe the Landlord and Tenant Act, 1927 section 18(1). The explanation of the apparent difficulty is that two points of time have to be considered.

The fate of the building has to be considered at the termination of the lease, but the tenant has to prove the intended fate of the building at the hearing of the action.

(iii) since it was agreed that the premises at the termination of the lease, had only a site value, there could be no diminution of the value of the reversion, and, for this reason, the action failed.

Liability for damp penetration of flat

Samuels v Abbints Investments Ltd.

High Court Of Justice Chancery Division
[1963] 188 EG 689

Leasehold flat - Landlords' liability to repair main structure - Dry rot caused within flat by saturated wall - Judgment for plaintiff tenant

In this action Miss Mary Sarnuels, of Flat 19, 16-25, Kings Gardens, West End Lane, Hampstead, N.W., claimed damages from her landlords, Abbints Investments Ltd., of 16, Wimpole Street, W., for breach of a covenant binding them to keep the main structure of the building in repair.

The plaintiff claimed £118 for work she had had done to remove dry rot, due, she said, to water coming through the outside walls of the building, mainly from defective outside plumbing. The lease was dated February 21, 1962, and was for 99 years, at £50 a year, and it included a covenant by the landlords binding them

... to keep the main structure of the block in tenantable repair provided nevertheless that the landlords shall not be liable for any breach of this covenant unless the landlords shall fail to take reasonable steps to remedy such breach after written notice thereof is given to the landlords by the tenant."

Before entering into her contract, the plaintiff obtained a surveyors' report, and this referred to evidence of dampness and rot in parts of the flat. When the matter was referred to the defendants' solicitors they replied that defects in the flat would be the plaintiff's responsibility. The plaintiff accepted this. The position therefore was that the plaintiff had taken over the flat knowing that there had been damp and rot there. She had disclaimed any claim in respect of rot existing before the lease was granted, and the liability for repairs clearly was governed by the lease.

In September 1962 the defendants' surveyors informed the plaintiff that under the terms of the lease she was responsible for the eradication of the dry rot. The plaintiff instructed a firm to deal with the dry rot, and her solicitors wrote to the defendants' surveyors claiming that the dry rot had been caused by defects in the building's structure, and stating that the plaintiff would hold the defendants responsible for the repair. There was substantial agreement among the expert witnesses about the cause of the rot. As a result of a defective waste pipe the external wall had become wet, resulting in the removal of mortar, infiltration of water through the brickwork, and dry rot. This dry rot had been dealt with, and had not reappeared. The evidence clearly established that defective pointing of itself, apart from its association with the leaking pipe, had not caused dry rot in the interior wall of the flat, and he (his Lordship) was also satisfied that although from time to time water had come out of the overflow pipes against the wall it had not caused the trouble complained of. Any trouble subsequent to the lease being granted must have been due to the wet condition of the walls when the lease was granted.

The next question was liability for that state of disrepair-the saturation of the wall resulting in dry rot spreading-under the provision of the lease. At the date of the lease the plaintiff became liable for the state of disrepair of the flat under the lessee's covenant, however the disrepair was caused. Therefore she was liable for the dry rot in the flat at that date, and for any dry rot resulting from that which existed at that date. The defendants, however, were liable for the disrepair of the main structure and, also, apart from considerations of notice and the construction of the covenant, for the saturation of the wall and for making good any damage by dry rot due to saturation of the wall after the date of the lease. The question was how far under the landlords' repair covenant the defendants were liable for the saturation of the external brick wall as it existed after the granting of the lease. If on the true construction of the lease the flat was defined to include - as prima facie[63] it would - the external walls, and if the walls were specifically mentioned, there would be a very strong case for giving these words a meaning that would prevail over the prima facie meaning of "main structure" in the covenant.

The, first schedule to the lease defined the flat as including "the internal and external walls . . . *but excluding the outside brick, steel or concrete work.*" It seemed to his Lordship that *"but excluding the outside brick, steel or concrete work"* applied to the external walls, so that the outside bricks of the external walls would not come within the definition of the flat for which the plaintiff was responsible. If that were so, the outside bricks would come within *"the main structure of the block."* The position therefore was that the plaintiff was responsible for the inside part of the external walls and the defendant for the external part. This might seem an odd arrangement, but the evidence was that there was a recognisable distinction between the two parts.

So subject to the question of notice, the defendants' responsibility was limited to the outside bricks and any damage resulting from them, and to dry rot which had spread from the outside bricks since the date of the lease.

On the facts, Ungoed-Thomas, J. had come to the conclusion that proper and adequate. notice of the saturation had been given by the plaintiff by letter. The defendants' liability dated from that notice. However, before even that degree of liability could operate, it was provided in the covenant that the landlord should not be

---

[63] On the face of it – as things seem

liable for any breach unless he had failed to take reasonable steps to remedy such breach. It had been suggested that it had not been possible to take reasonable steps. What reasonable steps could have been taken? The judge had been told that although heat treatment could dry the inside of the wall it would not be effective in the outside part. But it would have been possible to dispose of the saturation by taking out the bricks and treating or replacing them, and in his opinion the defendants were liable for damage resulting from their failure to take those or other appropriate steps.

That left the question of damages, limited to damage caused after the receipt of the notice. The firm employed by the plaintiff had treated the inside of the flat with a fluid, the effect of which was to put down a toxic barrier that shut out the possibility of dry rot damage being caused by reason of the wet condition of the outside walls. That seemed to his Lordship to have been a proper course to have taken in mitigation of any damage that might have occurred, and presumably was cheaper than having the bricks replaced. It was an expense for which the defendants were liable, and to that limited extent, therefore, the plaintiff succeeded.

"Good repair and condition" - Cesser of rent during repairs

Saner v Bilton

Chancery Division [1876] 7 Ch D 815

Landlord and Tenant - Waste - Reasonable Use of Demised Premises - Covenant by Landlord to keep in Repair - Construction - Implied License to enter - Proviso for Cesser or Abatement of Rent – "Inevitable Accident."

Semble[64], that an injury to or the destruction of demised premises, resulting from the use of them by the tenant in a reasonable and proper manner, having regard to the class of tenement to which they belong, is not waste.

In a lease of a newly constructed grain warehouse there was a covenant by the lessor that he would during the term *"keep the main walls and main timbers of the warehouse in good repair and condition"* The lessee entered under the lease and stored grain in it, in (as the Court held upon the evidence) a reasonable and proper way. After a short time a beam which supported one of the floors broke, and ultimately the external walls sank and bulged outwards, and the lessor spent a large sum in repairing the premises. In an action by the lessor to recover from the lessee what he had thus expended:-

Held:

that the lessee had not been guilty of waste:

Held, also,

that the lessor was bound under his covenant to put the walls and main timbers in good repair, having regard to the

---

[64] It appears

class of buildings to which the warehouse belonged, and not merely to the condition of the particular building:

Held, also,

that the covenant implied a license by the tenant to the landlord to enter upon the premises for a reasonable time for the purpose of executing the necessary repairs.

The lease contained a proviso that, in case the warehouse, or any part thereof, should at any time during the term *"be destroyed or damaged by fire, flood, storm, tempest, or other inevitable accident,"* the rent, or a just proportion thereof, should cease or abate so long as the premises should continue wholly or partly untenantable or unfit for use or occupation in consequence of such destruction or damage. During the period in which the lessor was executing the repairs the lessee was excluded from the use and occupation of the whole or a part of the premises, and he claimed an abatement of rent under the proviso:-

Held,

that the words inevitable accident imported something ejusdem generis[65] with what had been previously mentioned, and did not apply to that which, though not avoidable so far as the lessee was concerned, was not in its nature inevitable, but resulted from the default of the lessor, and that the lessee was not entitled to an abatement of rent.

---

[65] Applying to things of a particular class

Illegal subtenancy created assignment - S 146 of the Law of Property Act 1925 - Breach of covenant not to assign incapable of remedy - Relief from forfeiture granted

Scala House & District Property Co. Ltd. v Forbes and Others

Court Of Appeal [1974] 575 Q.B.

Landlord and Tenant - Forfeiture of lease - Relief from forfeiture - Breach of covenant not to assign lease - Whether breach capable of remedy - Whether reasonable time to remedy breach - Law of Property Act 1925, s. 146 (1)

By a lease dated February 8, 1968, the lessees covenanted not to assign underlet or part with the possession of the demised premises without the landlords' consent. The lease was assigned to the first defendant with the landlords' consent and he used the premises as a restaurant. He intended to enter into an agreement with the second and third defendants to manage the restaurant but the written agreement, in fact, created a subtenancy and, therefore, he was in breach of covenant. The plaintiff, who had acquired the reversion of the lease, served on the defendants a notice under section 146 of the Law of Property Act 1925 requiring them to remedy the breach and, after 14 days, issued a writ for possession of the premises. Nield J. held that the breach was capable of remedy and, since 14 days between the notice and the issue of the writ was too short a time for the defendants to remedy the breach, he dismissed the action.

On appeal by the plaintiff.. -

Held:

Allowing the appeal but granting relief from forfeiture, that a breach of covenant not to assign underlet or part with possession was not a breach capable of remedy within the meaning of section 146(1) of the Law of Property Act, 1925 and, therefore 14 days was a sufficient time to elapse between the service of the notice under the section and the date of the writ.

"so often as need should require well and sufficiently to repair uphold sustain paint glaze cleanse scour the premises (with all needful reparations and cleansings) and to leave the premises in such repair, reasonable wear and tear excepted."

Scales v Lawrence

[1860] 2 F & F 289

In 1852 a tenant took a lease for a term of seven years, of a house comprising three sitting rooms, four bedrooms, stables, outhouses and a garden. The tenant covenanted *"so often as need should require well and sufficiently to repair uphold sustain paint glaze cleanse scour the premises (with all needful reparations and cleansings) and to leave the premises in such repair, reasonable wear and tear excepted."*

Held:

That if the tenant had carried out reasonable repairs during the course of the term he did not have to repaint, but merely clean it down. If anything was actually broken he had to repair it.

Service charge - "reasonably and properly expended or incurred"

Scottish Mutual Assurance plc v Jardine Public Relations Ltd

Technology and Construction Court [1999] EGCS 43

Plaintiff landlord granting defendant three-year lease Plaintiff landlord carrying out long-term roofing works towards end of lease - Whether defendant liable to pay service charges in respect of works – Plaintiff's claim failed

On 14 October 1992 the plaintiff landlord granted the defendant tenant a lease of premises that formed part of second-floor offices at Waynflete House, Esher. The lease expired on 29 September 1995. By clause 4 of the lease the defendant was to contribute towards expenditure incurred "in respect of the services, particulars of which are set out in the Third Schedule". These services included "Maintaining, repairing and (if necessary) renewing... the structure of the building". In 1995roofing works were carried out. It was common ground that the roof was in a state of disrepair. The plaintiff claimed £30,173.77 in service charges under the lease.

The defendant disputed liability to contribute towards the cost of the works on two grounds. Notably, it said that a number of requirements that would need to be established before liability for service charges arose were not satisfied.

First, it was submitted that the roofing works did not fall within the ambit of schedule 3. The defendant submitted, inter alia[66], that the works constituted "renewal" of the roof, and part I of schedule 3 provided that renewal was only justified if "necessary". Further, the defendant submitted that renewal was not "necessary" for the adequate performance of the roof over the remainder of its term.

Second, it said that its liability was limited to expenditure that was "reasonably and properly expended", and the roofing works did not constitute reasonable and proper expenditure.

Held:

The plaintiff's claim failed.

1. Whether works, including works to remedy an inherent defect, went beyond "repair" and amounted to "renewal" was a question of fact and degree in every case: *Ravenseft Properties Ltd v Davstone (Holdings) Ltd [1979] 1 EGLR 54* and *McDougall v Easington District Council [1989] 1 EGLR 93* applied. The roof was in a state of disrepair prior to the execution of the works.

Neither the works necessary to overcome the effect of the inherent defect nor the totality of the works went beyond "repair". The roofing works fell within the terms of Schedule 3.

2. The lease did not entitle the plaintiff to charge the defendant for the cost of carrying out works that would fulfil its obligations over a period of 20 years or more, when such works were not necessary to fulfil those obligations over the shorter period of defendant's lease. The works had been executed not for the purpose of fulfilling the plaintiff's obligation to the defendant but for the

---

[66] among other things.

purpose of satisfying the requirements of a prospective tenant. Considerable moneys had recently been expended on short-term repairs, and there was no evidence that those works had been ineffective. There was therefore no pressing need to commence long-term repairs prior to the end of the defendant's term, which was imminent. The total amounts expended by the plaintiff were not "reasonably and properly expended or incurred".

3. It was, however, reasonable for the plaintiff to expend money on short-term repairs, as the roof was in a state of disrepair and had the potential to leak. Therefore, in respect of those items or elements of the works, the defendant was liable to make a contribution of 40%.

Leasehold Property (Repairs) Act 1938 - Landlord
doing repairs after tenant's default

S.E.D.A.C. Investments Ltd. v Tanner and others

[1982] 1 WLR 1342

The lessor had the right under the general repairing covenant
of the lease to call upon the tenant to carry out repairs but if
the tenant failed to do so, the lessor could enter upon the
premises and carry out the work. On April 25th, 1980 the
lessees informed the lessor that there was loose stonework on
the front wall and that pieces were falling to the pavement.
They inquired whether there was adequate insurance cover
for claims of injury from passers by.

The lessors inspected and realising that work had to be
carried out urgently for the safety of the public, had the
works started on May 1st and completed on May 9th at a
cost of about £3,000.

No claim to recoup the expenditure was made under the
terms of the lease but on 5th January, 1981 solicitors for the
landlord served notice on the tenant under section 146(1) of
the Law of Property Act 1925. The notice claimed breach of
covenant to repair and required compensation of the sum
expended. The lessee served a counter notice under the
Leasehold Property (Repairs) Act 1938 without prejudice to
their contention that the lessor's notice was void.

The lessor's summons for leave under section 1(2) of the
Leasehold Property (Repairs) Act 1938 to commence an
action for damages for breach of the repairing covenants of
the lease was dismissed. Section 1(2) of the Leasehold
Property (Repairs) Act 1938 clearly contemplated a breach

which had not yet been remedied. Therefore the lessor's section 146 notice was ineffective. Having themselves remedied the breach they were unable to give the lessee information referred to in section 146(1)(a) (b) and (c). Since section 1 of the 1838 Act depended on serving of "such notice as is specified" in section 146(1) and the lessors had failed to comply with it, the lessees had been deprived of their right to serve a counter notice under section 1(2) of the 1938 Act. The court could not therefore exercise its power under section 1(3) giving the lessors leave to bring proceedings.

By summons, the lessors applied to Maidstone District Registry for leave to bring proceedings for damages against the lessees for breaches of covenant to repair contained in their 14 year lease which had about 7 years unexpired. The district registrar was prepared to give leave under section 1(5)(e) of the Leasehold Property (Repairs) Act 1938 but adjourned the summons into court at the request of the lessees.

Held:

Having done the work, the lessor could not serve a valid section 146 notice and so the procedure laid down in the 1938 Act could not occur and the court could not grant leave to bring an action for forfeiture or damages for breach of the repairing covenants.

The judge commented that once the lease had less than three years unexpired, the lessor could bring a claim for damages without leave and that in this particular case, fortuitously, it would not be statute barred. The lessors could have protected their interests in other ways. They might have called upon the lessees to remedy the breach under the appropriate lease clause and they could have reinforced this by seeking or threatening to seek a mandatory injunction on the lessees to undertake the necessary remedial work. Alternatively they could have served a notice under section 146 in whatever terms they could stating that in view of the urgency works should be commenced within 48 hours. However none of these measure would be practical in a real emergency. Had the judge had jurisdiction, he would unhesitatingly have exercised it in favour of the lessors.

See Jervis v Harris Court of Appeal: [1995] EGCS 177 which reverses this decision

Possession - Sections 83 and 85 of the Housing Act
1985 - Court has unfettered discretion to hear new
evidence

Sheffield City Council v Hopkins

Court of Appeal

[2001] 26 EG 163 (CS)

Landlords issuing proceedings for possession on ground of
non-payment of rent - Judge granting possession order
suspended on terms requiring tenant to pay arrears - Tenant
not complying with terms - Tenant seeking suspension of
warrant for possession - Landlords opposing suspension
and seeking to adduce evidence of nuisance - Whether
court entitled to consider matters other than those relied
upon in possession proceedings

The defendant tenant was granted a secure tenancy of 571
Martin Street, Sheffield, on 30 August 1999. After the
tenant moved in, complaints were made about her conduct
and the keeping of animals at the property, and the claimant
council were sent written warnings concerning those
complaints in October, November and December 1999. In
February 2000 the council issued a summons for
possession of the property. Attached to the particulars of
claim was a schedule of the tenant's account history; which
showed that no payments had been made. On 3 July 2000
the district judge made an order for possession suspended
on terms that required the tenant either to make payment by
10 July 2000 or give up possession by 31 July 2000. The
terms were not complied with and a request for a warrant of
possession was issued by the council in August 2000.

The tenant then issued an application seeking suspension of
the warrant for possession and indicating that her non-
compliance was due to illness and depression. At the

hearing of the application, the council adduced evidence of nuisance on the part of the defendant, and the tenant raised arguments concerning the discretion permitted to the court by section 85 of the Housing Act 1985. A preliminary hearing was ordered to decide whether matters other than the non-payment of rent could be raised in the proceedings. The district judge ordered that arguments on matters other than rent were not to be raised upon an application to suspend a warrant for possession. The council appealed, contending that the discretion under section 85 was unfettered in regard to the arguments that could be raised, and that all relevant matters should be considered.

Held: The appeal was allowed.

1. Legislation did not confine the court's discretion in the possession proceedings to the ground relied upon initially by a landlord when giving notice under section 83 of the Act. It would be unfair if matters that arose after the possession order, which made it clear that it would be wrong to suspend or stay the order for possession, could not be taken into account. However, there could be circumstances in which it would be wrong to allow a landlord to rely upon different matters when opposing a suspension order or a stay of execution.

2. In situations where a landlord might rely upon additional grounds, the landlord should give notice to the tenant that, although certain conduct was not being relied upon as a ground for seeking possession, if an application for a suspension or stay were to be made, it might ask the court to impose a condition to prevent such conduct from taking place thereafter. That would be particularly appropriate where the conduct feared was a nuisance. However, the condition should be sufficiently specified and clear so that the tenant would be in no doubt as to what would constitute a breach of the condition.

The Housing Act 1961, Section 32 (1) - Implied obligation on Council to repair

Sheldon v West Bromwich Corporation

Court of Appeal [1973] 25 P & CR 360

An old water tank burst and the Landlords had prior knowledge that the tank was discoloured, although not weeping. They were on notice that it needed repair or renewal. The Housing Act 1961, Section 32 (1) placed an implied obligation on the council to keep the installation for the supply of water in repair. The tank burst causing damage and the action alleged breach of the implied covenant.

Held on tenant's appeal:

That the Landlords had notice of the discolouration and should have replaced the tank at that point.

Repairing Covenants - Diminution in value - Negative
equity

Shortlands Investments Ltd v Cargill plc

Official Referees' Business: [1994] EGCS 198

Landlords claiming for dilapidations - Tenants admitting
some want of repair - Diminution of value of reversion -
Property having negative equity - Whether tenants liable -
Judgment for the landlords in part

The plaintiff landlords took an assignment of an underlease
of 3 Shortlands Road, Hammersmith, a substantial 10-floor
office block, which had been leased in 1981 for 99 years.
The defendant tenants were subunderlessees of two floors,
together with a wing of another floor, which they let. In
1990, they exercised a break option to bring their personal
occupation to an end. The defendants had covenanted to
keep the interior in good and tenantable repair, as well as to
decorate it and to yield up the premises in accordance with
those covenants. When the defendants exercised their break
options almost half the building was empty. The landlords
had to compete for tenants with owners of brand new
buildings while having to negotiate a rent revision on the
underlease.

Three leases were subsequently granted to an incoming
tenant, which comprised the defendants' two floors plus one
other floor for the residue of the term. The incoming tenant
was paid £690,000 plus VAT, to bring the premises up to
"landlords' basic standard". The defendants admitted
repairs at a figure of £56,386.77, but stated that they were
not liable to pay anything because: (a) no one could have
been expected to foresee such a lavish refit so it rendered
the claimed repairs unnecessary; and (b) the landlords'
premises, which had a negative equity, could not therefore

suffer diminution in value. The landlords claimed £304,599 plus interest.

Held:

Judgment for the landlords.

The landlords had argued that if the value of the premises was somewhat negative in value in repair, then it was yet more negative out of repair. The court accepted that view. It was plain that the plaintiffs had suffered damage.

2. The worse negative value was evidenced by subsequent events when the landlords had to offer a very large sum specifically related to the condition of the premises.

3. It would he unfair to the tenants to have to pay the whole of the sum paid to the incoming tenants in respect of disrepair. Damages were assessed on the basis: (a) of the cost of repairs; and (b) as at the end of the lease, to take into account in valuing the reversion in its actual state, the consideration that any incoming tenant would demand money related to the disrepair. That sum of money would be related to the disrepair as viewed by the incoming tenant, not to breaches of the outgoing tenant's covenants.

4. Thus, the actual disrepairs in the present case were greater than those for which the outgoing tenant was responsible, so that the only way of assessing that part of the difference in value of the reversion for which the tenant was responsible was by examining the cost of repairs and then applying to that the "cap" imposed by section 18(1) of the Landlord and Tenant Act 1927. That imposed a limit on the common law measure, but did not alter the method of its assessment.

5. Judgment for the plaintiffs for £295,321.37. Interest to he assessed from end of September 1991.

Validity of Notice and Service

Silvester v Ostrowska

[1959] 1 WLR 1060

A lease for a term of 31 years from 25th December 1931 contained a repairing covenant and gave the landlord a right of entry if the tenant failed to pay damages and costs awarded for breach of this covenant three months after judgment.

The landlord served a notice under section 146 of the Law of Property Act 1925 and section 1 of the Leasehold Property (Repairs) Act 1938 alleging breaches of the covenant to repair specified in a schedule of dilapidations, and breach of a covenant against sub-letting, though there was no such covenant in the lease.

Held:

No particular form of notice was provided by the Law of Property Act 1925. The reference to a non existent covenant did not invalidate the good parts of the notice. This is distinguished from Guillemard v Silverthorne 1908 99 L.T. 584 because this was a claim for damages and not for forfeiture and the judge could approach the matter 'res integra' (A point governed by no decision or rule of law and to be decided upon in principle)

Tenant required to deliver up premises in good and tenantable repair but prohibited from doing repairs without Landlord's consent in writing - Landlord had notice of defect - No implied term landlords must keep premises fit for human habitation

Sleafer v Lambeth Borough Council

Court Of Appeal [1960] 1 QB 43

Landlord and Tenant - Repairs - Weekly tenancy - Implied term - Express conditions of tenancy restricting tenant from doing work to demised premises without consent and reserving to landlords right to enter and do repairs - Tenant required to deliver up premises in good and tenantable repair - Practice of council to do repairs - Tenant of council flat injured by defect in demised premises - Whether term to be implied that landlords must keep premises fit for human habitation - Whether any duty in landlords independent of contract to guard against foreseeable dangers from defect in demised premises of which they have notice.

Contract - Implied term - Landlord and tenant.

The printed conditions of a weekly tenancy of a borough council flat required, inter alia[67], that the tenant should *"reside in the dwelling,"* and that he should at the end of the tenancy deliver up the dwelling in good and tenantable repair and condition. By clause 9: *"The tenant shall not do nor allow to be done any decorative or other work to any part of the dwelling without consent in writing. ..."* By clause 11 the council was to be at liberty to enter the dwelling to inspect the state of repair and execute repairs therein. No express term in the agreement placed on either party liability for repairs, but it was the practice of the council to do all the repairs, within certain limits.

---

[67] among other things.

On November 30, 1955, the tenant was leaving his flat by the front door when, owing to a long-standing defect in the door which caused it to jam, he had to use force to close it by pulling on the only external handle, the letter-box knocker. The knocker came off and he fell backwards against an iron balustrade and suffered injury to his back.

The tenant brought an action against the council claiming damages, first, for breach of contract, contending that having regard to the express terms of the agreement, there must be implied a term that the landlords would make and keep the demised premises in all respects reasonably fit for habitation; and secondly, for breach of duty in that, having had notice of the defect in the demised premises, the landlords had allowed it to continue in that condition to the possible danger of the user. It was found by the trial judge that notice of the defect had been given:-

Held:

That there was here no breach of duty by the landlords either under or independently of the contract. Nothing in the express terms of this contract required that as a matter of business efficacy there should be implied a term, contrary to the general law of landlord and tenant, obligating the landlords to keep the demised premises in a fit state for human habitation. The express terms, and in particular the prohibition on the tenant doing repairs without consent, were explicable on other grounds in the context of this agreement and could not by implication make the landlords liable to do repairs.

Repair distinguished from improvement

Smedley v Chumley & Hawke Ltd (Warrell, Third Party)

Court Of Appeal [1982] 261 EG 775

Landlord and tenant - Action by tenant of restaurant forming part of motel complex against landlords in respect of damage caused by alleged breach of landlords' covenant in lease - Tenant covenanted to repair interior and exterior of the demised premises, but landlords covenanted to keep the main walls and roof in good structural repair and condition throughout the tenancy - A few years after the commencement of the tenant's lease it became evident that the foundations of the restaurant were defective - There were no piles under part of the concrete raft on which the building was constructed, with the result that the raft tilted, causing damage to walls and roof - The action by the tenant concerned the liability of the landlords under their covenant - Landlords submitted that the judge was wrong in holding that, as the walls of the restaurant had become unstable owing to subsidence, the landlords were in breach of their covenant to keep the walls and roof in good structural repair and condition - The landlords argued that the imposition of such a liability amounted to requiring the premises to be improved, thus rendering them different from the premises demised - Authorities reviewed

Held:

that the landlords were liable - The only way to put the walls and roof into a safe structural condition was to carry out such major works to the foundations as were necessary to give the walls a stable base - Appeal dismissed

Damages

Smiley v Townsend

[1950] 2KB 311 Court of Appeal

The defendant took an assignment of a fag-end lease with only two years still to run. The premises which had been requisitioned, were still requisitioned at the time the lease terminated. The Landlord sued for breach of covenant to repair.

Held:

1.   Damages were the difference in value of the reversion at the time the lease terminated with the premises in repair and in an actual state of disrepair.

2.   The fact that the requisitioning authority might pay for repairs in the future could not be taken into account.

3.   Because the Landlord was unlikely to carry out the repairs, the cost of the repairs was no use in deciding the diminution in value of the reversion. This, in any event, would be nominal. The nub was the value of the loss of reversion.

S 4(4) of The Defective Premises Act 1972 - Landlord obliged to repair on notice unless defect due to tenant's contractual failure - "premises" means entire premises let

Smith (Arthur) v Bradford Metropolitan Council

Court of Appeal [1982] P & CR 171

Section 4 Defective Premises Act 1972 - Council liable to carry out repairs upon Notice under terms of tenancy agreement.

Smith was a tenant of a council house which was defective and the council had notice of the disrepair. The council house and yard were let on a weekly tenancy under which Condition 6 provided, amongst other things, *"the tenant shall... (ii)g give the council officers, agents, contractors and workmen reasonable facilities for inspecting the premises and their state of repair and for carrying out repairs."*

Condition 9 defined the premises as *"the dwelling-house or flat let to the tenant and where the context so admits shall include any garage, outbuilding, garden or yard let to the tenant."*

In 1979 the patio became so dangerous that the Plaintiff made complaints to the council. On 26th June 1979, whilst hanging out the washing, he slipped due to crumbling concrete and broke his right leg. He sued for damages for his injury. Whilst the Judge found that his injury had been caused by the dangerous condition of the patio, he found that the council were not liable under Section 4(4) of The

Defective Premises Act 1972 because it was not liable for personal injuries. The Plaintiff appealed.

Held:

1. The Appeal was granted. The term of the tenancy placed a duty on the Landlord to carry out repairs upon Notice unless the defect was due to the tenant's failure to carry out his obligations under the contract.

It was held that "premises" meant the whole of the premises let. The land and the buildings. In order to restrict the meaning, clear language would have to be used to make clear that it was not included. Accordingly the appeal was allowed.

Forfeiture - equitable jurisdiction of court to grant relief

Smith v Metropolitan City Properties Ltd

Chancery Division [1986] 277 EG 753-754

Landlord and tenant - Forfeiture of lease - Attempt of former tenant, against whom forfeiture proceedings had been completed and landlords had re-entered, to reopen the question of relief against forfeiture by invoking the ancient equitable jurisdiction of the court - Notice of motion by defendant owners, under RSC Order 18, rule 19, or under the inherent jurisdiction of the court, to dismiss the summons as frivolous or vexatious or an abuse of the process of the court - It had been argued that, although the statutory jurisdiction under section 146(2) of the Law of Properly Act 1925 could not be relied on, the court still had an equitable jurisdiction to grant relief in any circumstances in which the statutory jurisdiction was not available.

Held:

that it was clear from the speech of Lord Wilberforce in *Shiloh Spinners Ltd v Harding*, as explained by Dillon J in *Official Custodian for Charities v Parway Estates Developments*, that such a submission was not sustainable - Decision of Nicholls J in *Abbey National Building Society v Maybeech Ltd* not followed - Lord Wilberforce's reference to equitable jurisdiction not being ousted concerned cases outside the area of leases and underleases covered by s 146 - Originating summons dismissed as an abuse of the process of the court

Dangerous structure notice - Inadequate foundations

Sotheby v Grundy

[1947] 2 All ER 761

In 1861 a 99 year lease was granted for a new house. The tenant covenanted to *"repair, uphold, support, maintain.....*" the premises *"with all necessary reparations and amendments whatsoever".*

In 1944 the house was in a dangerous condition with bulging walls and the London County Council served a Dangerous Structure Notice under The Building Acts and the house was demolished. The Landlord sued for damages.

Held::

The house was built on inadequate foundations and on made up ground. It therefore had an inherent defect and this did not come within the terms of the Repairing Covenant. The Landlord failed to recover damages.

Section 11 of Landlord and Tenant Act 1985 - Damp – Condensation - Landlord had no duty to advise on proper use of cupboard

Southwark London Borough Council v McIntosh

Chancery Division [2001] 47 EG 145 (CS)

Section 11 of Landlord and Tenant Act 1985 - Council tenant persistently complaining of damp - Council contending that various aspects of causation neither pleaded nor established - Trial judge holding that causation inferred from council's failure to respond to complaints - Council appealing against £7,500 damages award -Appeal allowed

In October 1992 the appellant council (the landlords) granted to the respondent (the tenant) a tenancy of a four-bedroom maisonette on the Gloucester Grove Estate in Peckham. The tenant became aware of a pervading atmosphere of damp, which became progressively worse. Mould appeared in various places and the main bedroom ceased to be usable as such. In 1994 the tenant reported the matter to the landlords after water began to leak through the kitchen ceiling. Despite repeated complaints by the tenant, no remedial steps were taken before 1999.

The tenant took county court proceedings alleging that the landlords had, over a period of five years, been in breach of their covenant, implied by section ii of the Landlord and Tenant Act 1985, to keep in repair the structure and exterior and installations for sanitation and for the supply of water. The claim particularised various items of damage alleged to have been caused by damp. Fuller particulars were subsequently given in an expert report, which concluded with an opinion that the landlords were in breach of the covenant relied upon by reason of their failure "to keep in repair the property including inter alia entrance doors; fire protection; water leaks... WC pan; flushpipe; corroded water tank". It was established at the trial that a significant cause of the damp was the tenant's practice of using a cupboard designed for storing dry goods for the purpose of drying (recently washed) clothes.

Awarding the tenant damages Of £7,500 in respect of discomfort, the judge held that the landlords were responsible for the misuse of the cupboard because they had failed to advise the tenant against such use. The judge further rejected the landlords' contention that the tenant had failed to plead and establish that the damage was attributable to physical damage to the structure or exterior of the property; on the ground that the landlords could not raise a causation issue when they had effectively done nothing over a period of five years in response to the tenant's complaints. The landlords appealed to the High Court.

Held: The appeal was allowed.

1. There was no pleaded duty to advise on the proper use of the cupboard, and no such duty upon the landlords could arise under the covenant.

2. The alleged failure of the council to investigate the complaints had no bearing on the issue of causation. No such duty was pleaded, nor could such a duty arise unless the damp was in fact caused by relevant physical damage. Such a lacuna in the particulars of claim could not be filled by an expert report: *Quick v Taff-Ely Borough Council [1985] 2 EGLR 50* applied.

Noise nuisance

Southwark London Borough Council v Mills and Others

Court of Appeal: [1998] EGCS 132

Occupiers of badly soundproofed council flats disturbed by slightest noise from neighbouring flats - Council appealing from arbitrator's ruling that council in breach of express covenant not to disturb tenants' quiet occupation - Whether covenant capable of being broken where neighbours' activity otherwise unobjectionable

The respondent tenants occupied flats in a council-owned block in London SE24, on tenancies providing for the determination of contractual disputes by the Southwark Arbitration Tribunal (the tribunal). In each agreement the council had expressly covenanted not to interfere with the tenant's right to enjoy the quiet occupation of the flat. At a hearing conducted in or about July 1997, the tribunal accepted that the tenants had good reason to complain that the soundproofing of the flats was so inadequate that they could hear all the private and most intimate moments of their neighbours' lives, including the switching on of every light and the opening or closing of every door.

By an award made on August 1 1997 the tribunal declared that the council were obliged to carry out effective soundproofing and made specific directions with regard to 19 of the flats. The council appealed against the award, contending that, since the noise arose from ordinary domestic use by neighbours, the tribunal had wrongly widened a covenant for quiet possession into what was effectively a covenant to improve the flats to meet modern building standards, thus imposing an obligation more onerous than the repairing covenant given by the council. The award was upheld at first instance on the ground that the court was bound to follow the Court of Appeal decisions in *Sampson v Hodson-Pressinger [1982] 1 EGLR 50* and *Baxter v Camden London Borough Council [1998] 22 EG 150*. The council appealed. It was common ground that the tribunal could not and did not consider the possibility of a claim in nuisance.

Held :

The appeal was allowed.

1. Necessary preliminary observations were that the essence of the tenants' complaint was not the noise, but the council's failure to shield them from it, and that nuisance was not a precondition to an action for breach of covenant even though the acts complained of might coincidentally support an action in tort. As a matter of principle, therefore, the tribunal's award was open to the objections that:

(i) the council had not, by an act or omission after the grant of the tenancy, "interrupted" or "interfered with" the tenants' quiet enjoyment;

(ii) (as argued below) the obligation imposed by the tribunal was more onerous than the obligation to repair;

(iii) the primary purpose of the covenant was to ensure that the tenant got what he appeared to be getting, in this case a poorly soundproofed flat, which the landlords were free to offer at a corresponding rent; and

(iv) a tenant, who would not expect to be sued for living a normal life in his flat, could hardly expect to be able to sue his landlords if other tenants led normal lives.

2. Neither the court below, nor the Court of Appeal in *Baxter* (supra), had been invited to consider *Duke of Westminster v Guild [1983] 2 EGLR 37*, which was fully consistent with the restrictive view of the covenant taken

by the older authorities cited by the council. The tenants' case, on the other hand, derived full support from *Baxter* (supra) and considerable support from *Sampson* (supra) and *Sanderson v Mayor of Berwick-on-Tweed (1884) 13 QBD 547*. The court was accordingly free (applying *Young v Bristol Aeroplane Co Ltd [1944] 1 KB 718)* to decide which of the two conflicting lines to follow. For the reasons stated, those relied on by the council were to he preferred.

3. Per Peter Gibson J dissenting:

A breach occurred where, as a matter of fact, the tenants' quiet enjoyment had been substantially interfered with by the acts of the landlords or by the authorised acts of those claiming under them, it being immaterial whether the interference was caused by normal and reasonable use. The covenant did not in terms oblige the landlords to effect improvements. If they wished to avoid future claims, it was for them to decide whether to improve the neighbouring premises or keep them empty.

4. The tenants were granted leave to appeal to the House of Lords.

Damages for want of repair not rent

Standard Life Company Ltd v Greycoat Devonshire Square Ltd

Chancery Division   The Times 10 April 2000

A lease contained a clause that the tenant would pay the landlord a 2.4069% of the "gross rent" in excess of £644,800 which was received by the tenant from sub-tenants. "Gross rents" was defined as the "aggregate of all rents, fees and other moneys from whatever source payable to the tenant...directly or indirectly by virtue of its estate or interest in the demised premises, payable to the tenant...in respect of occupation."

A payment to the tenant from the sub-tenant for dilapidations was not "gross rents" so defined, but rather compensation to the tenant for damage to its estate. It would be anomalous for Greycoat to have to pay the freeholder a percentage of the damages because Greycoat were themselves obliged to keep the premises in repair under the terms of the head lease

Notice to repair

Starrokate Limited v Burry

[1982] 265 EG 871 Court of Appeal

The respondent tenants had a lease of seven years under which they covenanted *"at all times during the said term well and substantially to repair, decorate, cleanse, maintain, amend and keep the interior of the demised premises and the windows thereof and all additions made thereto and the fixtures and fittings therein and all interior walls and appurtenances thereof and the sewers, drains and services serving only the demised premises with all necessary reparations cleansings and amendments whatsoever (damage by fire only excepted)"*. The Landlord served a Section 146 Notice on the tenants requiring repairs and the tenants carried out the works required.

About six months later the landlord served a further Section 146 Notice alleging thirteen further breaches of covenant, including, amongst other things, the unhygienic condition of a toilet contrary to the requirements of the Public Health Authority. The Landlord's real concern was that the premises were being used as an Amusement Arcade instead of as a restaurant and this was causing annoyance to adjoining traders.

Held:

1.   The alleged breaches were not breaches of a covenant to keep or put in repair within section 1(1) of the Leasehold Property (Repairs) Act 1938.

2.   The Notice was not invalid under Section 1(4) of the 1938 Act

section 18 Landlord and Tenant Act 1927 - Valuation of dilapidations - Landlord suffering no loss - Tenant's state of mind in applying for new lease

Sun Life Assurance PLC v Racal Tracs Limited

[2000] 1 QB 138

The tenant occupied a site under two leases. The lease of one expired in December 1998.

Racal, became aware as early as 1996 that it would need to expand. It also knew that an adjoining site was due to be marketed. Racal knew that if it could keep its longer lease, the new site would be sufficient for its needs. If Racal could purchase the land it would vacate the premises held under the expiring lease.

In parallel, the Landlord, Sun Life Assurance PLC, was keen to redevelop the site and it, too, wanted to acquire the adjoining land and it would also need the land occupied under the expiring lease.

If the tenant failed to renew the existing lease it knew that it would face a terminal schedule of dilapidations. If the Landlord opposed the grant of a new lease, it would become liable for compensation under the 1954 Landlord and Tenant Act and would lose its claim for terminal dilapidations because of Section 18 of the 1927 Landlord and Tenant Act.

The tenant, Racal, secretly purchased the adjacent land in November 1997. In January 1998 it served a Section 26 Notice under the Landlord and Tenant Act 1958 seeking the renewal of its lease.

The Landlord was not aware that Racal had purchased the site or that the site had been sold. It therefore responded with a counter-notice indicating it would oppose renewal on the basis of paragraph (f). Racal withdrew its application for a new tenancy at about the time that the Landlord learned that Racal had acquired the site it was keen to have. The Landlord therefore withdrew its opposition to renewal.

Racal vacated and the premises were re-let in October 1999 after competition from rival self-storage firms. As a result the Landlord obtained a higher rent than he otherwise would have.

The tenant argued that the reversion should be valued, taking into account hope value, for use as self-storage units. The Landlord argued its case on the basis of industrial use.

Held:

The Section 26 Notice served by Racal was not valid because the tenant had misrepresented its intention to renew. No compensation was therefore payable to the tenant. The Judge felt this was a rare case where the tenant had found alternative premises and it could be shown with certainty that it did not wish to renew when it served its Notice.

However the Tenant won on Section 18 of 1927 Landlord and Tenant Act point in as much as it was able to rely on the higher valuation and therefore did not have to pay damages based on an industrial valuation.

Court of Appeal decision

The case was appealed - See Sun Life Assurance Plc v Thales Tracs Ltd. (formerly Racal Tracs Ltd.) and another reported Monday June 25th 2001 in The Times. The Court of Appeal held that the true intention of a tenant when he made a request for a new lease under section 26(3) of the Landlord and Tenant Act 1954 was irrelevant and evidence of its state of mind was inadmissible.

The application for a new lease should be treated at face value and the tenant being refused a new tenancy should be entitled to compensation.

Leasehold Property (Repairs) Act 1938 -   Cost of repairs claimed as debt

Swallow Securities Ltd v Brand

Queen's Bench Division [1983] 260 EG 63

Landlord and tenant - Leasehold Property (Repairs) Act 1938 - Landlords' action to recover a sum expended by them on carrying out works of repair and replacement for which the tenant was liable under covenants in the lease - Landlords had not served any notice and had not sought the leave of the court as required by the 1938 Act - Landlords submitted that the sum claimed did not consist of damages for breach of covenant within the meaning of section 1(2) of the Act, but was an ascertained sum in the nature of a debt and thus not affected by the Act - Cases on distinction between debt and damages cited.

Held:

that the debt cases were distinguishable from the present, that the sum claimed here and put forward as debt was in truth a claim for damages for breach of covenant and so offended against section 1(3) of the Act - Appeal from master, who had struck out the landlords' statement of claim as void, dismissed.

See Jervis v Harris Court of Appeal: [1995] EGCS 177

Defective Premises Act 1972 s4 - Duty of care - Carbon Monoxide poisoning - Contributory negligence

Sykes v Harry and another

Court of Appeal [2001] 17 EG 221

Landlord and tenant - Repairs - Section 4 of Defective Premises Act 1972 - Duty of care - Defective gas fire Whether landlord liable for carbon monoxide poisoning Whether breach of duty of care - Whether necessity for notice of defect - Whether tenant contributorily negligent

The claimant and his wife held a shorthold tenancy of premises owned by the first defendant landlord. Shortly before the grant of the tenancy, the landlord installed a gas fire to replace a previously defective one. The landlord did not enter into any service agreement relating to the fire. In February 1994 the claimant was taken to hospital, where he was later diagnosed as suffering from carbon monoxide poisoning. The claimant brought proceedings against the landlord, alleging breach of his obligations, implied by section II of the Landlord and Tenant Act 1985, to keep in repair the fire, and for breach of the duty of care owed by the landlord under section 4 of the Defective Premises Act 1972. At the trial, it was admitted that the claimant's poisoning was caused by carbon monoxide emitted from the fire. It was held that the defects in the fire would have been apparent on routine servicing, but that the landlord was not liable under section it of the 1985 Act or under section 4 of the 1972 Act, as the latter Act did not impose liability in the absence of the landlord's knowledge of the defect. The claimant appealed.

Held:

The appeal was allowed. The purpose of the 1972 Act was to break away from the historic limitations placed by the common law upon the duty/liability owed by a landlord to persons injured as a result of defects in the condition of premises owned by him. Section 4(3) of the Act, in defining a "relevant defect" was designed to make clear that a landlord's broad duty of care under subsection (1) was responsibility only for such defects as fall within the scope of those repairing obligations as expressed or implied in the tease. A person suing under section 4 would be relieved of the obligation to show that the landlord had notice of the defect. Such a claim merely has to show a failure on the part of the landlord "to take such care as is reasonable in all the circumstances" to see that the claimant is reasonably safe from personal injury. The trial judge's assessment, that the claimant was 80% contributory negligent, was upheld. A tenant in occupation, and in immediate control of the premises, is in the best position either to effect the necessary repairs or to bring them to the attention of the landlord, where the burden of repair rests with him.

Relief from forfeiture - Mortgagee in possession

Target Home Loans Ltd v Iza Ltd

Central London County [2000] 02 EG 117

Mortgage - Mortgage of leasehold interest - Mortgagee in possession - Landlord and tenant - Forfeiture - Relief Terms of relief - Whether mortgagee in possession entitled to serve counter notice under section 1 of Leasehold Property (Repairs) Act 1938 - Whether landlord estopped from relying on time-limit for relief from forfeiture under section 139 of the County Courts Act 1984

The applicant mortgagee held a charge by way of a legal mortgage over a 99-year lease of a maisonette, the reversion to which was owned by the respondent landlord. The lease had been granted in 1986 at a premium of £150,000 and the mortgagee had loaned £135,000 to the lessee. In 1990 the mortgagee obtained a possession order against the lessee for arrears of mortgage instalments; the mortgagee finally obtained possession in October 1996 of part of the premises and in October 1997 of the remaining part. On 5 March 1997 the landlord's solicitor served a notice under section 146 of the Law of Property Act 1925 requiring repairs to be carried out. On 11 March 1997 the mortgagee's solicitor served a counter notice under section 1 of the Leasehold (Repairs) Act 1938. The landlord failed to provide keys to the outer door of the premises despite requests on behalf of the mortgagee from April 1997. In February 1998 the landlord claimed to have forfeited the lease by peaceable re-entry in May 1997, relying on a failure to pay ground rent and service charges and to comply with the section 146 notice. At the hearing of the application for relief, the mortgagee accepted that the landlord was entitled to forfeit for the failure to pay a half year's ground rent, and that it should pay the service charge arrears as a condition of obtaining relief from forfeiture, but contended that the counternotice under the 1938 Act was effective to prevent a forfeiture in respect of the disrepairs.

Held:

The mortgagee was entitled to relief from forfeiture upon payment of the arrears of rent and service charges. The landlord was not entitled to forfeit the lease for the disrepairs for the following alternative reasons.

(1) Where a mortgagee has taken possession of leasehold premises, service of a section 146 notice on the lessee would be pointless because he could not lawfully enter the premises and do anything to remedy the breach. The only person who can remedy, and hence the only person the landlord can require to remedy, the breach is the mortgagee in possession. The mortgagee had an interest in receiving the section 146 notice and taking the benefit of the 1938 Act; the counternotice under section 1 of the 1938 Act was effective: *Church Commissioners for England v Ve-Ri-Best Manufacturing Co Ltd [1957] 1 QB 238* distinguished as in that case the mortgagee was out of possession.

(2) Because the landlord had failed to provide the mortgagee with a key to the outer door of the premises, a reasonable time for effecting the repairs had not elapsed by May 1997. If the forfeiture for the failure to carry out the repairs had been lawful, the mortgagee would not have been required, as a condition of obtaining relief, to do the works in the section 146 notice. The time-limits under section 139 of the County Courts Act 1984 were procedural and the landlord was estopped from relying on these for the purposes of relief from forfeiture in respect of the arrears of rent.

Validity of notices under section 146(1) Law of Property
Act 1925 and section 1(4) of the Leasehold Property
(Repairs) Act 1938

Tarrokate Ltd v Burry and Another

Court of Appeal [1983] 265 EG 871

Landlord and tenant - Leasehold Property (Repairs) Act
1938 and section 146(1) of Law of Property Act 1925 -
Appeal from decision of county court judge holding that a
notice under section 146(1) was invalid because of non
compliance with the 1938 Act - County court judge held
that the notice related to a breach of covenant to repair and
that it failed to contain the statement required by section
1(4) of the 1938 Act to the lessee's entitlement to serve a
counternotice claiming the benefit of that Act - The lessors'
notice recited a number of covenants, which included a
repairing covenant, and alleged 13 breaches, one of which
was the unhygienic condition of a toilet contrary to the
requirements of the public health authority - The complaint
was substantially that the premises, instead of being used as
a restaurant in accordance with the user covenant, were
used for the operation of amusement machines, causing a
nuisance to adjoining occupiers

Held:

that the breaches alleged in the lessors' notice were not breaches of a "covenant or agreement to keep or put in repair" within the meaning of section 1(1) of the 1938 Act and that the notice was not invalid under section 1(4) of that Act - Question raised but not answered by May LJ as to whether a notice specifying both breaches of covenant to repair and of other covenants could be severed and held good in part and bad in part - Practice mentioned of serving two separate notices in such cases - Appeal allowed

Damages for landlord's failure to repair

Taylor v Knowsley Borough Council

[1985] 17 HLR 316 Court of Appeal

The Plaintiff tenant rented a flat at Halewood in Liverpool for £15 per week plus rates.

There was a burst pipe in 1982 and the hot water system no longer worked. This was brought to the attention of the landlords in January 1982 but took five months until June for the repair to be carried out, during which time he had no hot water. The burst pipe also caused the light in the living room to fail and this was unusable for three months. In addition there was a leak from the bathroom ceiling which continued for a period of eight months, until about January 1984.

The tenant was single and managed by bathing in relatives' homes and doing his laundry in a local launderette and later, because of the cost, at the home of a nearby relative.

Damages for loss of hot water and the lack of a ceiling light were assessed at £100, including £68 for the cost of the launderette and some was paid to relatives for the use of their laundry and bathroom facilities. He was also awarded £59 for the dripping in the bathroom.

He appealed on the grounds that these figures were too low.

Held on Appeal:

In the absence of evidence of severe inconvenience, the damages were not so low as to be obviously wrong.

"Fair wear and tear"

Taylor v Webb

Court Of Appeal [1937] 2 KB 283

Landlord and tenant - Lease of dwelling-house - Covenant to repair - Landlord's covenant to keep outside walls and roofs in good and tenantable repair, fair wear and tear excepted - Disrepair due to natural causes, including wind, rain and decay - Liability of landlord under covenant.

The under-lease of a house contained a covenant by the under-lessors to *"keep the outside walls and roofs in good and tenantable repair as and so far only as is required to be done by them under the head-lease."* By the head-lease the lessees (predecessors in title to the sub-lessors) covenanted to keep the premises *"in good and tenantable repair (destruction or damage by fire and fair wear and tear excepted)"*:-

Held:

That the exception from the covenant of fair wear and tear included damage to the outside walls and roofs of the house caused by natural agencies such as rain, wind and decay, and also consequential damage to the interior of the house caused by the same agencies.

Damages for dilapidations payable on basis of immediately due reversion – not on reversion of lease with term commencing after expiration of the earlier lease

Terroni and Necchi v Corsini

Chancery Division [1931] 1 Ch 515

Lease - Covenant to repair - Partnership Business on Premises - Reversionary Lease granted to Partners - Agreement for Dissolution and for Sale of Assets to Partners - Date for Completion of Sale - Damages then Recoverable for Breach of Covenant to repair - Law of Property Act, 1925 s. 149 - Landlord and Tenant Act, 1927 s. 18, sub-s. 1.

The plaintiffs and the defendant were partners. One of the partnership assets was the lease of the premises on which the business was carried on, expiring on March 25, 1930. On October 7, 1929, the landlord granted to the three partners a reversionary lease for fourteen years from March 25, 1930, at an increased rent. On October 29, 1929, by an agreement made between the parties for dissolution of the partnership, it was provided that the partnership assets should be sold to the highest bidder of the three partners and proceeds divided, the defendant's share being one-half, also, that the date for completion should be November 18, 1929, and that the defendant should out of his share make certain payments, and should pay the rent under the lease, all rates, taxes and outgoings in respect of the premises, and *"all trade debts and other liabilities whatsoever in respect of the said premises and business"* down to the date fixed for completion, making these payments out of his share of the proceeds of sale. The agreement came before the Court for construction, and it was declared that the phrase, *"other liabilities whatsoever in respect of the said premises"* included the liability in respect of damages which the landlord could, on November 18, 1929, have recovered for breach of the repairing covenants in the lease. On an application for a decision whether at that date the damages recoverable by him in respect of non-repair were to be estimated on the basis of the depreciation in market value of the reversion expectant on the determination of the lease, or of that expectant on the determination of the reversionary lease:-

Held:

That the "reversion" was the immediate reversion expectant on the lease, and that the fact that a reversionary lease had been granted, to take effect at a date after the date for the assessment of damages, was immaterial.

"Good and substantial Repair" Lessor's failure to repair 200 year old house which had become so worn by time that demolition and reconstruction were the only possible course

Torrens v Walker

Chancery Division [1906] 2 Ch 166

Landlord and Tenant - Lease - Lessor's Covenant - Construction - Good and substantial Repair Old Building - Natural Decay - Extent of Obligation.

A covenant by a lessor to keep the outside walls of the demised premises in repair will be construed as a covenant to repair on notice, and there can be no breach of such a covenant until the lessor has notice of want of repair.

The principles of construction which have been applied to lessees' covenants to repair apply equally to similar covenants by lessors. Regard must be had to the age and condition of the buildings to which the covenant refers. A lessor is not bound by such a covenant to rebuild during the term of the lease premises which have at the date at which he receives notice become worn out by age, and, merely from the action of time on the materials used, been reduced to a state in which repair is impossible.

In 1890 the three upper storeys of a house in London were demised to the lessee for a term of eighteen years from March 25, 1890, at a rent of £150. The lessor covenanted to keep the outside of the demised premises in good and substantial repair. The lessee covenanted to keep the inside in repair, to permit the lessor to enter and view the state of repair, and to use the premises for the business of a private hotel-keeper. In 1905 the plaintiff was the assignee of this lease and the defendant was the owner of the reversion. On

July 13, 1905, the London County Council served on the premises a notice requiring the owner to take down the front and back walls of the house as being dangerous structures. The plaintiff at once communicated this notice to the defendant and required him to repair the walls. The defendant did nothing, and the London County Council themselves took down the walls from the first floor upwards, propped up the floors with timber, and left the place uninhabitable.

The plaintiff brought this action against the defendant for breach of the covenant to keep the outside in repair. The defendant had no notice before July 13, 1905, of any want of repair. At that date the house, which was about 200 years old, had by the natural effect of time become so worn out and decayed that it was impossible to repair it except by taking it down and rebuilding:-

Held:

that there had been no breach of the lessor's covenant to repair.

Fixtures and fittings - Chattels

TSB Bank v Botham

Court of Appeal (1996) EGCS 149

This was a dispute where the carpets, light fittings, curtains, blinds, bathroom and kitchen fittings, gas fires and electrical white goods, including a dishwasher, freezer and cooker with oven, hob and extractor fan, were fixtures and fittings. The bank sought to retain them as mortgagees. The Court of Appeal held only the kitchen units and bath fittings to be fixtures and fittings. All others were chattels.

Damages for failure to repair - Building sold and
redeveloped - Landlord's loss not proven

Ultraworth Ltd v General Accident Fire and
Life Assurance Corporation plc and another

Technology and Construction Court [2000] EGCS 19

Substantial office building let on long full-repairing lease -
Claim for terminal dilapidations - Whether tenant required
to replace ageing heating system - Tenant relying on
section 18(1) of Landlord and Tenant Act 1927 - Whether
disrepair had caused diminution in value of reversion -
Landlord failing to establish loss

In 1973 a 25-year, full-repairing lease was granted of a
five-storey office building, Enterprise House, in Station
Road, New Barnet. By subsequent assignments the
reversion and the lease became vested in the claimant
landlord and the defendant tenant respectively. Following
the expiry of the lease on 4 July 1998, the landlord, having
taken various steps to market the freehold, sold it on 24
March 1999 to a developer (B Ltd) for £1m. Thereafter, B
Ltd. obtained planning permission to convert all the
building, save for the ground floor, into residential flats.

On the question of terminal dilapidations, the parties agreed
that the building was not in the state of repair required by
the covenant, but fell into dispute over the extent of the
tenant's liability for the poor state of the combined. heating
and air-conditioning system. The system consisted Of 150
units, of a type no longer manufactured, that drew and
returned water from and to heating and cooling apparatus
located on the roof of the building. The landlord
maintained that the covenant could only be performed by
substantially replacing the entire system at an estimated
cost Of £420,500. The tenant claimed that the units were

capable of being reconditioned and argued for a figure not exceeding £100,000. The tenant further argued that, in view of the subsequent disposal of the freehold, even the lower figure was irrecoverable as the disrepair had not brought about a diminution in the value of the reversion within the meaning of section 18 of the Landlord and Tenant Act 1927.

In proceedings brought by the landlord, the judge preferred both the technical and the marketing evidence given by experts called for the tenant.

Held:

No loss had been sustained by the landlord.

1. The landlord was correct in so far as it alleged that the required works were works of repair as distinct from renewal. It was well established that repair could consist of renewal of parts and that the court should consider, inter alia[68], the nature, extent and cost of the proposed remedial works, the value of the building and its expected lifespan; the ultimate question being one of degree: *see Holding & Management Ltd v Property Holding & Investment Trust plc and others [1990] 1 EGLR 65*.

2. However, the landlord had failed to establish that the work proposed by the tenant would be futile. It was sufficient if the repaired system worked substantially as well as the original system, and there was no requirement that it should require as little maintenance as the new system: *Emcroft Developments Ltd v Tankersley-Sawyer [1984] 1 EGLR 47* and *Stent v Monmouth District Council [1987] 1 EGLR 59* distinguished.

---

[68] among other things.

3. The court was satisfied on the evidence that, even if the system had been repaired: (i) the property would not have attracted a potential occupier or investor; (ii) no higher price would have been obtained from B Ltd, whose scheme required a different system altogether. In those circumstances, no loss had been proved.

Landlord's obligation to repair - Occupant injured by
defect of which landlord had no notice

Uniproducts (Manchester) Ltd. v Rose Furnishers Ltd.

Manchester Assizes [1956] 1 WLR. 45

Landlord and Tenant - Repairs - Covenant - Breach -
Notice - Covenant to keep structure in repair - Breach
existing at date of lease - Implied condition of notice of
want of repair.

Landlords covenanted to keep in good tenantable repair the
roof, main structure and outside walls of a shop leased to
the plaintiffs in February, 1953, for a term of five years. In
June, 1953, the plaintiffs themselves carried out limited
repairs to make safe the floorboards of a store room on the
ground floor at the request of the local authority. On
November 10, 1953, while the shop manager was standing
on this floor it gave way and he was precipitated therefrom
into the basement whereby he sustained serious injuries for
which he was compensated by the plaintiffs. No notice of
want of repair had been given to the landlords. In an action
by the plaintiffs for breach of covenant in which they
claimed an indemnity from the landlords to cover the
compensation and the costs which they had paid to the shop
manager:-

Held:

that although the landlords' covenant to keep in repair included a duty to repair any defect that existed when the premises were let, such obligation did not arise until they had notice thereof; and that as the landlords had not been given notice of the defect and the plaintiffs had not proved that they had actual knowledge of it, they were not in breach of their covenant.

Dicta of Lord Buckmaster and Lord Sumner in *Murphy v. Hurly [1922] 1 A.C. 369; 38 T.L.R. 386* applied.

Quaere[69] whether the landlords would have been liable if they had had actual knowledge at the time of letting.

---

[69] Question.

Repair or improvement - Implied obligation under section 32 of Housing Act 1961

Wainwright v Leeds City Council

Court of Appeal [1984] 270 EG 1289

Landlord and tenant - Section 32 of Housing Act 1961 - Appeal from county court - Scope of covenant to repair implied by section 32 - Application to tenancies from local authorities - Rising damp in council house let to appellant caused by absence of damp-course - Old back-to-back terraced house - Appellant claimed that the implied covenant to repair under section 32 imposed on the landlord authority a duty to provide a damp-course so as to eradicate the damp

Held:

Upholding decision given in the county court, that the implied obligation did not extend to providing the tenant with a new and different thing, namely, a house with a dampcourse in place of a house without one - The position under section 32 was the same as under a covenant to repair at common law, as illustrated by *Pembery v Lamdin* - The extent of the implied obligation under section 32 was the same for local authority as for private tenancies

Appeal dismissed.

Damages for failure to repair

Wallace v Manchester City Council

Court of Appeal: [1998] EGCS 114

Council landlords in breach of statutory repairing obligations - County court judge awarding general damages for discomfort and inconvenience but refusing to make separate assessment of diminution in value of tenant's interest in property - Tenant's appeal dismissed.

In proceedings brought in Manchester County Court the appellant council tenant established that the respondent council had, over the period between October 1994 to July 1997, been in breach of their repairing obligations both under section 11 of the Landlord and Tenant Act 1985 and section 4 of the Defective Premises Act 1972. The defects complained of included a partially collapsed external wall, rotting window frames, inadequate damp-proofing and poor drainage leading to rat infestation. At all material times the tenant remained in the house with her two children. Having awarded each child a sum of £2,000, and having made an award of £780 in respect of damage to curtains, carpets and furniture, the judge proceeded to award the tenant a sum of £3,500 as general damages to compensate her for the discomfort and distress suffered as a result of the defects and for the further discomfort while remedial works were being carried out. In making that award, the judge expressly refrained from including, under the head of general damages, a sum to reflect a diminution (as a result of the disrepair) in the value of the tenancy. The tenant appealed, contending that the diminution element had been wrongly excluded.

Held The appeal was dismissed.

1. For the period during which a tenant remained in occupation, notwithstanding the landlord's breach, the loss to him requiring compensation was the loss of comfort and convenience which resulted; and the expression "difference in value to the tenant of the premises" (as used by Bankes W in Hewitt v Rowlands (1924) 93 LJKB 1080, at pp 1082) was to be understood accordingly: see per Stephenson and Griffiths LJJ in Calabar Properties Ltd v Stitcher [1983] 2 EGLR 46, at pp 48-50. The sum could be ascertained In terms of a notional reduction of rent, or as a global figure for discomfort and inconvenience, or as a mixture of the two elements; but the courts were not bound to make separate assessments under each head, nor was it appropriate to adduce expert valuation evidence.

2. A judge seeking to assess the monetary compensation to be awarded for discomfort and inconvenience on a global basis would he well advised to cross-check his prospective award, by reference to the rent payable for the relevant period, in order to avoid over or under assessments through failure to give proper consideration to the period of the landlord's breach or the nature of the property.

3. Different considerations arose where the tenant was forced by the landlord's breach to sell or sublet, in which case the tenant could recover for the resulting diminution of the price or recoverable rent: see Calabar.

Repairs - Flat roof replaced with pitched roof - Metal windows with uPVC

Wandsworth London Borough Council v Griffin and another

Lands Tribunal [2000] 26 EG 147

Landlord and tenant - Service charges - Section 19 of Landlord and Tenant Act 1985 - Replacement of flat roof with pitched roof - Replacement of metal-framed windows with uPVC double-glazed units - Whether replacements were repairs - Whether costs reasonably incurred - Whether cost-in-use calculations relevant Whether costs reasonably incurred on matters resulting from past neglect.

The appellant council were the owners of an estate consisting of blocks of flats. The buildings were constructed with flat roofs and had metal-framed windows. The roofs and windows fell into disrepair. The council replaced the flat roofs with pitched roofs and the windows with uPVC double-glazed units. In deciding to make the replacements, the council relied on cost-in-use calculations that indicated that such works offered better value for money over the life of the buildings. Two-thirds of the flats were held under long leases acquired under the right-to-buy provisions of the Housing Act 1985. The long leases imposed a service charge on the tenants in relation to such matters as repairs to roofs and windows.

On an application by two of the tenants, the leasehold valuation tribunal decided that the decision to carry out the works was unreasonable, and that the additional costs incurred thereby were not reasonably incurred in accordance with section 19 of the Landlord and Tenant Act 1985. The council appealed.

Decision:

The appeal was allowed. The costs of the new roofs and windows were based on the lowest of six tenders; the costs of carrying out the disputed items were reasonable. The works did not go beyond works of repair within the meaning of the council's repairing obligations in the leases; the works constituted repairs, as they were cheaper than the alternatives taking into account both initial and future costs. The council were entitled to use a cost-in-use exercise. The decision to replace the roofs with pitched roofs and the windows with uPVC double-glazed units was a reasonable one; the costs incurred were reasonably incurred for the purposes of section 19(1)(a) of the Landlord and Tenant Act 1985.

"wind and water tight" - **"to use premises in a tenantlike manner"**

Warren v Keen

Court of Appeal [1954] 1 QB 15

Landlord and Tenant - Repairs - Weekly tenancy - Duty of tenant - Keeping premises "wind and water tight" - Duty "to use premises in a tenantlike manner" - Permissive waste - Tenant from year to year.

A weekly tenant is not under a general covenant to put and keep the premises in repair. His only duty is to use the premises in a husbandlike or tenantlike manner. If the house falls into disrepair through fair wear and tear or lapse of time, or for any reason not caused by him, he is not liable to repair it.

Per Somervell L.J.: Whether there is an additional obligation on a tenant from year to year to keep the buildings wind and water tight, as stated by Swinfen Eady L.J. in *Wedd v. Porter [1916] 2 K.B. 91, 100*, remains at any rate in a state of some doubt.

Per Denning L.J.: It was suggested in argument that an action lies against a weekly tenant for permissive waste. I do not think that that is so.

Repairs distinguished from improvement or structural alteration

Wates v Rowland

Court of Appeal [1952] 2 QB 12

The water table had risen and water had seeped between the concrete foundations, on which were laid floor joists, and the floor itself causing it to rot. The sanitary inspector served a notice requiring the nuisance to be abated. The landlord laid concrete on the original foundation raising the surface by nine inches and on that he laid a tiled floor. The house was protected by Rent Restriction Acts and when the works were complete, the landlord served a notice on the tenant raising the rent by 8% of the cost of the works less the cost of the flooring.

The tenant refused to pay the increase, arguing that the though the work might be an "improvement" or "structural alteration" they were "repairs" and the landlord could not therefore increase the rent under the powers contained in section 2 (1)(a) of the Increase of Rent and Mortgage Interest (Restrictions) Act, 1920, as amended by the Rent and Mortgage Interest Restrictions Act, 1939. The county court judge found for the tenant.

On appeal it was held:

1: That work required to make a dwelling house fit for habitation was not necessarily "repairs" within the meaning of the section. It might be an "improvement" or "structural alteration" expenditure on which ranked for increased rent under section 2 (1)(a) of the Act of 1920. It was a matter of degree whether such expenditure constituted and "improvement" or "structural alteration"

2:       The expenditure by the landlord on an additional nine inches of concrete was prima facie[70] an "improvement", since the house was better than before.   There was no sufficient ground to exclude this expenditure as being a "repair".   The landlord had done more than provide a new floor. He had made a structural alteration.

---

[70] On the face of it – as things seem.

Condensation - Meaning of "Good repair <u>and</u> Condition"

Welsh v Greenwich London Borough Council

Court of Appeal [2000] EGCS 84

Local authority letting property - Property suffering from condensation and damp - Whether local authority in breach of covenant to maintain dwelling in good condition" - Judge awarding tenant damages - Appeal dismissed.

By a written agreement dated 7 August 1990, and with effect from 13 August 1990, the defendant council granted the claimant and her husband a secure tenancy of a ground-floor flat at 100 Barnfield Gardens, Plumstead Gardens, Greenwich. Clause 2.1 of the tenancy agreement stated: "The Council hereby agrees: To maintain the dwelling in good condition and repair, except for such items of repair which are the responsibility of the tenant". Clause 3.2 stated: "The tenant hereby agrees: To carry out those minor repairs which are the tenant's responsibility and to keep the dwelling clean, in good condition and to prevent damage". The flat had three external walls and did not have thermal insulation.

In 1993 the husband left and the claimant became the sole tenant until she was rehoused in 1994. Throughout the four years of her tenancy, the flat had suffered from damp and condensation as a result of a lack of proper insulation. This had caused severe black spot and mould growth around the windows, on the walls, on soft furnishing and under the carpets. The claimant issued proceedings against the council seeking damages. The judge concluded that, in the circumstances, the uninsulated character of the claimant's flat and the consequence of excessive condensation constituted the "condition" of the dwelling for the purposes of clause 2.1. On that basis, the judge concluded that the council had been in breach of their covenant to keep the flat in "good conditiod", and awarded the claimant £9,000 damages.

The council appealed, contending that the obligation to "maintain in good condition and repair" required only that the existing physical elements of the dwelling were kept in good condition and repair. It was submitted that as it was common ground that the structure of the building had not been damaged by the condensation, the judge had erred in concluding that the council had been in breach of the covenant contained in clause 2.1.

Held:

The appeal was dismissed.

The tenancy agreement had been in a very short and simple form. This was suitable, since the council were letting the property as providers of social housing, and it was unlikely that the tenant would have taken legal advice. Accordingly, the agreement was to be given the meaning that an ordinary person in the street would give to it. The reference to "good condition" in clause 2.1 was intended to mark a separate concept, and was a significant addition to the word "repair". "Good condition" did not mean only general structural care. Severe black spot and mould growth could not be recognised merely as matters of amenity dissociated from the physical condition of the flat, even though they had caused no damage to the structure of the building. Accordingly, the judge was right to conclude that, by failing to provide thermal insulation and allowing excessive condensation and severe black spot to continue, the council had been in breach of their obligations: *Norwich Union Life Insurance Society v British Railways Board [1987] 2 EGLR 137* and *Credit Suisse v Beegas Nominees Ltd [1994] 1 EGLR 76* considered.

Set off - Implied contractual obligation by landlords - Duty of care on the part of the landlords

Westminster (Duke of) and Others v Guild

Court of Appeal [1983] 267 EG 762

Landlord and tenant - Question as to landlords' liability to repair a defective drain running partly under demised premises and partly under property retained by the landlords - Appeal from judge's decision in favour of tenant on preliminary issue - Tenant in landlords' action for alleged arrears of rent claimed by way of defence and set-off that landlords were liable for loss due to failure to repair – Tenant put case as to landlords' liability on alternative grounds of (a) an implied contractual obligation by landlords (there being no express obligation) to keep landlords' part of drain in repair and unobstructed, and (b) a duty of care on the part of the landlords to the same effect - Both grounds rejected by Court of Appeal - Cases on implied obligations discussed and special category situations, as in *Liverpool City Council v Irwin*, distinguished - Normal test of necessity to give business efficacy not satisfied in present case - Suggested duty of care based on Landlords' retention of part of the drain subjacent to their own premises rejected on the ground that there was no duty on the landlords' part to repair a drain through which the tenant had an easement to discharge noxious water from his own premises - Apart from express contract or local custom the owner of a servient tenement is not under any obligation to the owner of the dominant tenement to execute repairs required for the enjoyment of the easement -- Likewise, there were no grounds for

holding Landlords liable on the basis of breach of covenant for quiet enjoyment or of derogation from grant.
Appeal allowed.

Licence - Implied term - Fitness for purpose

Wettern Electric Ltd. v. Welsh Development Agency

Queen's Bench Division [1983] QB 796

Contract - Implied term - Fitness for purpose - Licence to occupy premises for business purposes - Building defective - Whether term to be implied that building fit for purposes of licence

The defendants granted the plaintiff manufacturers a lease of a factory, and, when the plaintiffs' business began to expand, they agreed to extend the factory. While the extension was being built, the defendants offered to grant the plaintiffs a licence to occupy a new unit for 12 months on terms set out in a letter of June 21, 1979, similar to those found in a lease. The plaintiffs went into occupation on June 25, but because of inadequate foundations defects appeared in the building and the unit soon became unsuitable for the plaintiffs' use. By December 21, the building had become dangerous and they had to move to other accommodation. A few days earlier, on December 19, the plaintiffs had returned the draft licence to the defendants, duly approved but undated, stating that it was in order. The plaintiffs claimed damages against the defendants for breach of an implied warranty in the licence that the unit was of sound construction and reasonably suitable for the purposes required by the plaintiffs.

On the preliminary issue of liability:-

Wettern Electric Ltd. v. Welsh Development Agency

Held:

Giving judgment for the plaintiffs, that although the plaintiffs had not communicated their acceptance of the licence until December 19, the parties had by their conduct (by the plaintiffs going into occupation and by the defendants permitting it) made a contract for a licence that took effect forthwith - that, although a term that premises were suitable for their purpose was not an implied term of a lease, a term that the premises were fit for the purposes of the licensee could be implied into the terms of a contractual licence if such a term was necessary to give business efficacy to the agreement or to complete an incomplete agreement that, since the grant of the licence was to enable the plaintiffs to carry on and expand their business while their existing factory was being enlarged, a warranty of soundness and suitability for that purpose was to be included in the terms of the licence and, accordingly, the defendants were in breach of that implied term.

Damages for Waste

Whitham v Kershaw

Court of Appeal 16 QBD 613

Damages - Measure of - Landlord and Tenant - Action for Waste by Reversioner against Tenant.

A covenant by a tenant not to commit waste on the demised property is not with regard to the measure of damages for the breach of it the same thing as a covenant to deliver up the property at the end of the term in the same state as that in which the tenant received it.

Therefore, in an action by the reversioner against the tenant for waste, the measure of damages is not necessarily the sum which it would cost to restore the property to its condition before the waste; the true measure of damages is the diminution in the value of the reversion, less a discount for immediate payment.

Tenants improvements - Consent withheld

F. W. Woolworth and Company, Limited v Lambert

Court of Appeal 1937 Ch 37
27 – 29 July 1936

Landlord and Tenant - Lease of self-contained shop - Covenant not to make alterations without lessors' consent - Proposed alterations - Extension to adjoining premises – "Improvements" – "Damage to or diminution in value of premises" - Consent refused - Whether unreasonable refusal - Onus of proof - Landlord and Tenant Act, 1927), s. 19, sub-s2.

The Landlord and Tenant Act, 1927, s. 19, sub-s.2, provides: *"In all leases whether made before or after the commencement of this Act containing a covenant, condition, or agreement against the making of improvements without licence or consent, such covenant, condition, or agreement shall be deemed, notwithstanding any express provision to the contrary, to be subject to a proviso that such licence or consent is not to be unreasonably withheld, but this proviso does not preclude the right to require as a condition of such licence or consent the payment of a reasonable sum in respect of any damage to or diminution in the value of the premises or any neighbouring premises belonging to the landlord and of any legal or other expenses properly incurred in connexion with such licence or consent nor, in the case of an improvement which does not add to the letting value of the holding, does it preclude the right to require as a condition of such licence or consent, where such a requirement would be reasonable, an undertaking on the part of the tenant to reinstate the premises in the condition in which they were before the improvement was executed."*

The plaintiffs held a lease of a shop at 18 and 20 Commercial Road, Bournemouth, from the defendants for an unexpired term of forty-two years at a rent of £3,500 a year rising after 1945 to £3,750 a year. The lease contained a covenant by the plaintiffs not without the previous consent in writing of the lessors to erect or suffer to be erected or made on the demised premises any structural alterations or additions, and provided that if with such consent such structural alterations or additions were made no fine or increase of rent should be demanded for the lessors' approval.

The plaintiffs proposed to enlarge the shop by pulling down the wall at the back and connecting it with other adjoining land of which they held a lease from another lessor, and by erecting over the whole combined property one large shop, in which the main staircase, staff accommodation, etc. would be removed from the demised premises to the extension. The defendants refused their consent to the proposed alterations except on the payment by the plaintiffs to them of £7000 in respect of damage to or diminution in the value of the demised premises. The plaintiffs offered to reinstate the demised premises in their former condition before the determination of the term, and to take out a policy of insurance to secure the performance of this obligation, but they refused to pay the £7000. The plaintiffs therefore commenced this action, asking for declarations that the defendants were not entitled to withhold their consent to the proposed alterations, and that if they did so the plaintiffs were to be at liberty to proceed with the alterations without such consent-

Held: by a majority (Greene L.J. dissenting) that the proposed alterations were *"improvements"* within the meaning of s. 19, sub-s. 2, of the Landlord and Tenant Act, 1927.

Decision of Clauson J. [1936] Ch. 415 reversed on this point.

F. W. Woolworth and Company, Limited v Lambert

But held: by the whole Court, dismissing the appeal, that the plaintiffs had failed to discharge the onus which lay on them of proving that the defendants had unreasonably withheld their consent to the proposed alterations.

Decision of Clauson J. affirmed on this point.

Tenant's Improvements - Consent unreasonably withheld

Lambert and Another v F. W. Woolworth and Company, Limited

Same v Same

Court of Appeal [1938] Ch 883

1938 April 26, 27, 28; May 11.

Landlord and tenant - Lease of self-contained shop - Covenant not to make alterations without lessors' consent - Proposed alterations - Extension of shop over adjoining land held on lease from separate landlord – "Improvements" - Damage to or diminution in the value of the premises - Consent unconditionally refused - Refusal whether unreasonable - Landlord and Tenant Act, 1927 s. 19, sub-s. 2.

The Landlord and Tenant Act, 1927, s. 19, sub-s. 2, provides: *"In all leases whether made before or after the commencement of this Act containing a covenant condition or agreement against the making of improvements without licence or consent, such covenant condition or agreement shall be deemed, notwithstanding any express provision to the contrary, to be subject to a proviso that such licence or consent is not to be unreasonably withheld; but this proviso does not preclude the right to require as a condition of such licence or consent the payment of a reasonable sum in respect of any damage to or diminution in the value of the premises or any neighbouring premises belonging to the landlord, and of any legal or other expenses properly incurred in connection with such licence or consent nor, in the case of an improvement which does not add to the letting value of the holding, does it preclude the right to require as a condition of such licence or consent, where such a requirement would be reasonable, an undertaking on the part of the tenant to reinstate the premises in the condition in which they were before the improvement was executed."*

By a lease made in 1931 the plaintiffs let to the defendants a shop in Bournemouth for a term of forty-two years at a rent of 35001. a year to be increased in 1945 to a higher figure. The lease contained a covenant by the defendants *"not without the previous consent of the lessors to erect or suffer to be erected any other building upon the said demised premises nor to make or suffer to be made any structural alterations in or additions to the demised premises."*

The defendants proposed to enlarge the shop by taking down the greater part of its back wall and connecting it with premises to be erected on adjoining land held by them on lease from a different owner, to which additional premises the staircases and lavatories would be removed. The defendants applied to the plaintiffs for their consent to the proposed alterations, offering to reinstate the premises in the condition in which they were before the alterations were executed, to give satisfactory security for doing so, and to pay expenses properly incurred in connection with the consent. The plaintiffs declined to give their consent to the alterations.

In February, 1937, the plaintiffs brought the present action against the defendants claiming declarations that the alterations would not be *"improvements"* within the meaning of the above sub-section, and that if the plaintiffs withheld their consent it would not be "unreasonably withheld" within the meaning of that sub-section. The defendants counterclaimed declarations to the contrary effect respectively:

Held, by the Court of Appeal (Slesser and MacKinnon UL, Greer L.J. dissenting), That the proposed alterations would be *"improvements"* within the meaning of the sub-section, and (2.) that the consent of the plaintiffs to the proposed alterations was "unreasonably withheld" within the meaning of the sub-section.

Limitation of the meaning of the word *"improvement"* discussed.

**Dangerous structure notice - Impossible to replace bay
window without providing columns for support**

Wright v Lawson

[1903] WN 108

A house and shop in King's Road, Fulham was let on a
lease dated 24th February 1888 and contained the covenant
by the tenant.... *"will during the said term when, where and
as often as occasion shall require and to the satisfaction of
the lessor or her Surveyor for the time being substantially
and effectually repair, uphold, maintain, drain, paint,
whitewash and cleanse the premises for the time being held
under this demise"*.

There was a further clause to deliver up in repair in
accordance with that repairing covenant.

A Dangerous Structure Notice was served on the tenant on
30th June 1900 requiring a bay window at first floor level
to be taken down or otherwise secured because it was
cracked, bulged, loose, sunk and overhanging. The tenant
instructed builders to carry out a repair, but the builder
could not do so without erecting columns to support the
new window; otherwise it would also be declared a
dangerous structure. The alternative was to set back the
window into the wall of the house and this is what was
done.

Held:

Because it was impossible to replace the bay window as it
had been, the tenant was not liable to do so. Erecting a bay
with columns would not be regarded as a repair of the old
bay window.

Duty to act in Tenant-like manner

Wycombe Health Authority v Barnett

Court of Appeal [1982] 264 EG 619

Landlord and tenant - Extent of tenant's duty to act in a tenant-like manner as formulated in Warren v Keen - Extent of landlord's duty under section 32 of the Housing Act 1961 to keep in repair and proper working order installations within the demised premises for the supply, inter alia[71], of water Appeal by tenant against county court judge's decision holding tenant liable to landlords for damage to house caused by bursting of rising mains water pipe - Tenant in freezing weather left house to stay with a friend for one night, but in fact stayed for two nights during which temperature dropped to 6 or 7 degrees below freezing - Rising main which passed through kitchen to attic and was controlled by stop-cock in kitchen was not lagged and no heating was left on in the house during the two nights - Mains pipe burst causing substantial damage - Landlords contended that the duty of tenant-like user required tenant to take precautions when leaving the house in freezing weather, such as turning off the water and draining the system, having regard to the unlagged mains pipe and the absence of heating - Tenant contended that it was the landlords' duty under section 32 of the 1961 Act to have the mains pipe lagged –

---

[71] among other things.

Held:

(1) that the landlords' duty under section 32 was to keep the pipe in good mechanical condition but that an unlagged pipe which, in freezing conditions, became cracked when the water in it turned to ice was not a breach of this condition;

(2) that a tenant could not reasonably be expected, under the doctrine of tenant-like user, necessarily to lag an internal water pipe or always to keep the house heated as a precaution against freezing Extent of tenant's duty must depend on circumstances, including the length of absence from the house and the severity of the weather - In the present case the judge was wrong in holding that the tenant acted unreasonably

Tenant's appeal allowed.

Repair distinguished from improvement - Neither landlord nor tenant liable

Yanover v Romford Finance and Development Co. Ltd.

(29 March 1983) Page 98 A Casebook on Repairs by D W Williams

A Lease of flat 2 Redbridge Court, Ilford, dated 17 May 1963 was assigned to the plaintiffs by a deed dated 26th May 1972.

Prior to the assignment, the flat had been occupied for ten years by the previous tenant without any complaint of dampness. The flat had been found by the plaintiffs to be in good decorative order before they purchased and by their building society surveyor who did not report damp.

The landlords covenanted to keep in repair the exterior of the buildings and the tenants obligations were to keep clean and in good and substantial repair the interior of the demised premises, including the walls, floors and partitions.

During the winters of 1972 and 1973 dampness appeared which seemed to dry out in the summer and the managing agent's surveyor diagnosed it as condensation. The plaintiffs expert declared the problem to be one of rising damp requiring major works to insert a damp proof course in internal and external walls linked to a damp proof membrane in the floor.

Yanover v Romford Finance and Development Co. Ltd.

Held:

The work of installing damp proof courses was a major building operation to improve the building and to enable it to comply with the relevant building regulations, which could not fairly be termed a repair which either the landlords or the tenants should be required to undertake under the terms of the lease.

STATUTES

We are grateful to Her Majesty's Stationery Office for permission to reproduce Crown Copyrights.

Warning

These extracts are for quick reference purposes but you are advised to consult the full statute in each case. They have been checked and are believed to be free from error but their accuracy is not guaranteed.

Defective Premises Act 1972

1972 CHAPTER 35

An Act to impose duties in connection with the provision of dwellings and otherwise to amend the law of England and Wales as to liability for injury or damage caused to persons through defects in the state of premises.

[29th June 1972]

Be it enacted by the Queen's most Excellent Majesty, by and with the advice and consent of the Lords Spiritual and Temporal, and Commons, in this present Parliament assembled, and by the authority of the same, as follows-

Duty to build dwellings properly.

1.-(1) A person taking on work for or in connection with the provision of a dwelling (whether the dwelling is provided by the erection or by the conversion or enlargement of a building) owes a duty-

(a) if the dwelling is provided to the order of any person, to that person; and

(b) without prejudice to paragraph (a) above, to every person who acquires an interest (whether legal or equitable) in the dwelling; to see that the work which he takes on is done in a workmanlike or, as the case may be professional manner, with proper materials and so that as regards that work the dwelling will be fit for habitation when completed.

(2) A person who takes on any such work for another on terms that he is to do it in accordance with instructions given by or on behalf of that other shall, to the extent to which he does it properly in accordance with those instructions, be treated for the purposes of this section as discharging the duty imposed on him by subsection (1) above except where he owes a duty to that other to warn him of any defects in the instructions and fails to discharge that duty.

(3) A person shall not be treated for the purposes of subsection (2) above as having given instructions for the doing of work merely because he has agreed to the work being done in a specified manner, with specified materials or to a specified design.

(4) A person who-

    (a) in the course of a business which consists of or includes providing or arranging for the provision of dwellings or installations in dwellings; or

    (b) in the exercise of a power of making such provision or arrangements conferred by or by virtue of any enactment;

arranges for another to take on work for or in connection with the provision of a dwelling shall be treated for the purposes of this section as included among the persons who have taken on the work.

(5) Any cause of action in respect of a breach of the duty imposed by this section shall be deemed, for the purposes of the Limitation Act 1939, the Law Reform (Limitation of Actions, &c.) Act 1954 and the Limitation Act 1963, to have accrued at the time when the dwelling was completed, but if after that time a person who has done work for or in connection with the provision of the dwelling does further work to rectify the work he has already done any such cause of action in respect of that further work shall be deemed for those purposes to have accrued at the time when the further work was finished.

Cases
excluded
from
the remedy
under
section 1.

2.-(1) Where-

(a) in connection with the provision of a dwelling or its first sale or letting for habitation any rights in respect of defects in the state of the dwelling are conferred by an approved scheme to which this section applies on a person having or acquiring an interest in the dwelling; and

(b) it is stated in a document of a type approved for the purposes of this section that the requirements as to design or construction imposed by or under the scheme have, or appear to have, been substantially complied with in relation to the dwelling;

no action shall be brought by any person having or acquiring an interest in the dwelling for breach of the duty imposed by section 1 above in relation to the dwelling.

(2) A scheme to which this section applies-

(a) may consist of any number of documents and any number of agreements or other transactions between any number of persons; but

(b) must confer, by virtue of agreements entered into with persons having or acquiring an interest in the dwellings to which the scheme applies, rights on such persons in respect of defects in the state of the dwellings.

(3) In this section "approved" means approved by the Secretary of State and the power of the Secretary of State to approve a scheme or document for the purposes of this section shall be exercisable by order, except that any requirements as to construction or design imposed under a scheme to which this section applies may be approved by him without making any order or, if he thinks fit, by order.

(4) The Secretary of State-

    (a) may approve a scheme or document for the purposes of this section with or without limiting the duration of his approval; and

    (b) may by order revoke or vary a previous order under this section or, without such an order, revoke or vary a previous approval under this section given otherwise than by order.

(5) The production of a document purporting to be a copy of an approval given by the Secretary of State otherwise than by order and certified by an officer of the

Secretary of State to be a true copy of the approval shall be conclusive evidence of the approval, and without proof of the handwriting or official position of the person purporting to sign the certificate.

(6) The power to make an order under this section shall be exercisable by statutory instrument which shall be subject to annulment in pursuance of a resolution by either House of Parliament.

(7) Where an interest in a dwelling is compulsorily acquired-

   (a) no action shall be brought by the acquiring authority for breach of the duty imposed by section 1 above in respect of the dwelling; and

   (b) if any work for or in connection with the provision of the dwelling was done otherwise than in the course of a business by the person in occupation of the dwelling at the time of the compulsory acquisition, the acquiring authority and not that person shall be treated as the person who took on the work and accordingly as owing that duty.

Duty of care with respect to work done on premises not abated by disposal of premises.

3.-(1) Where work of construction, repair, maintenance or demolition or any other work is done on or in relation to premises, any duty of care owed, because of the doing of the work, to persons who might reasonably be expected to be affected by defects in the state of the premises created by the doing of the work shall not be abated by the subsequent disposal of the premises by the person who owed the duty.

(2) This section does not apply-

(a) in the case of premises which are let, where the relevant tenancy of the premises commenced, or the relevant tenancy agreement of the premises was entered into, before the commencement of this Act;

(b) in the case of premises disposed of in any other way, when the disposal of the premises was completed, or a contract for their disposal was entered into, before the commencement of this Act; or

(c) in either case, where the relevant transaction disposing of the premises is entered into in pursuance of an enforceable option by which the consideration for the disposal was fixed before the commencement of this Act.

Landlord's
duty of care
in virtue of
obligation or
right to repair
premises
demised.

4.-(1) Where premises are let under a tenancy which puts on the landlord an obligation to the tenant for the maintenance or repair of the premises, the landlord owes to all persons who might reasonably be expected to be affected by defects in the state of the premises a duty to take such care as is reasonable in all the circumstances to see that they are reasonably safe from personal injury or from damage to their property caused by a relevant defect.

(2) The said duty is owed if the landlord knows (whether as the result of being notified by the tenant or otherwise) or if he ought in all the circumstances to have known of the relevant defect.

(3) In this section "relevant defect" means a defect in the state of the premises existing at or after the material time and arising from, or continuing because of, an act or omission by the landlord which constitutes or would if he had had notice of the defect, have constituted a failure by him to carry out his obligation to the tenant for the maintenance or repair of the premises; and for the purposes of the foregoing provision "the material time" means-

(a) where the tenancy commenced before this Act, the commencement of this Act; and

(b) in all other cases, the earliest of the following times, that is to say-

(i) the time when the tenancy commences;
(ii) the time when the tenancy agreement is entered into;
(iii) the time when possession is taken of the premises in contemplation of the letting.

(4) Where premises are let under a tenancy which expressly or impliedly gives the landlord the right to enter the premises to carry out any description of maintenance or repair of the premises, then, as from the time when he first is, or by notice or otherwise can put himself, in a position to exercise the right and so long as he is or can put himself in that position, he shall be treated for the purposes of subsections (1) to (3) above (but for no other purpose) as if he were under an obligation to the tenant for that description of maintenance or repair of the premises; but the landlord shall not owe the tenant any duty by virtue of this subsection in respect of any defect in the state of the premises arising from or

continuing because of, a failure to carry out an obligation expressly imposed on the tenant by the tenancy.

(5) For the purposes of this section obligations imposed or rights given by any enactment in virtue of a tenancy shall be treated as imposed or given by the tenancy.

(6) This section applies to a right of occupation given by contract or any enactment and not amounting to a tenancy as if the right were a tenancy, and "tenancy" and cognate expressions shall be construed accordingly.

Application to the Crown.

5. This Act shall bind the Crown, but as regards the Crown's liability in tort shall not bind the Crown further than the Crown is made liable in tort by the Crown Proceedings Act 1947.

Supplemental

6.-(1) In this Act-
"disposal" in relation to premises, includes a letting, and an assignment or surrender of a tenancy, of the premises and the creation by contract of any other right to occupy the premises, and "dispose" shall be construed accordingly;

"personal injury" includes any disease and any impairment of a person's physical or mental condition;

"tenancy" means-

(a) a tenancy created either immediately or derivatively out of the freehold, whether by a lease or underlease, by an agreement for a lease or under- lease or by a tenancy agreement, but not, including a mortgage term or any interest arising in favour of a mortgagor by his attorning tenant to his mortgagee; or

(b) a tenancy at will or a tenancy on sufferance; or

(c) a tenancy, whether or not constituting a tenancy at common law, created by or in pursuance of any enactment;

and cognate expressions shall be construed accordingly.

(2)   Any duty imposed by or enforceable by virtue of any provision of this Act is in addition to any duty a person may owe apart from that provision.

(3)   Any term of an agreement which purports to exclude or restrict, or has the effect of excluding or restricting, the operation of any of the provisions of this Act, or any liability arising by virtue of any such provision, shall be void.

(4)   Section 4 of the Occupiers' Liability Act 1957 (repairing landlords' duty to visitors to premises) is hereby repealed.

Short title, commencement and extent.

7.-(1) This Act may be cited as the Defective Premises Act 1972.

(2)   This Act shall come into force on 1st January 1974.

(3)   This Act does not extend to Scotland or Northern Ireland.

Housing Act 1985

Part IV   *Repairs and improvements*

Right to
carry out
repairs.

96.-(1) The Secretary of State may by regulations make a scheme for entitling secure tenants, subject to and in accordance with the provisions of the scheme-

> (a) to carry out to the dwelling-houses of which they are secure tenants repairs which their landlords are obliged by repairing covenants to carry out, and

> (b) after carrying out the repairs, to recover from their landlords such sums as may be determined by or under the scheme.

(2) The regulations may make such procedural, incidental, supplementary and transitional provision as may appear to the Secretary of State to be necessary or expedient, and may in particular-

> (a) provide for questions arising under the scheme to be referred to and determined by the county court;

    (b) provide that where a secure tenant makes application under the scheme his landlord's obligation under the repairing covenants shall cease to apply for such period and to such extent as may be determined by or under the scheme.

(3) The regulations may make different provision with respect to different cases or descriptions of case, including different provision for different areas.

(4) Regulations under this section shall be made by statutory instrument which shall be subject to annulment in pursuance of a resolution of either House of Parliament.

(5) In this section "repairing covenant", in relation to a dwelling-house, means a covenant, whether express or implied, obliging the landlord to keep in repair the dwelling-house or any part of the dwelling-house.

Landlord & Tenant Act 1927

Tenant's
right to
compen-
sation for
improve-
ments.

1.-(1) Subject to the provisions of this Part of this Act, a tenant of a holding to which this Part of this Act applies shall, if   claim for the purpose is made in the prescribed manner-

(a)   in the case of a tenancy terminated by notice, within one month after the notice was served on or by the tenant; and

(b)   in any other case, not more than thirty-six nor less than twelve months before the termination of the tenancy; be entitled, at the termination of the tenancy, on quitting his holding, to be paid by his landlord compensation in respect   of   any   improvement (including   the   erection   of   any building) on his holding made by him or his predecessors in title, not being a trade or other fixture which the tenant is by law entitled to remove, which at the termination of the tenancy adds to the letting value of the holding:

Provided   that   the   sum   to   be   paid   as compensation   for   any   improvement   shall   not exceed –

(a) the net addition to the value of the holding as a whole which may be determined to be the direct result of the improvement; or

(b) the reasonable cost of carrying out the improvement at the termination of the tenancy, subject to a deduction of an amount equal to the cost (if any) of putting the works constituting the improvement into a reasonable state of repair, except so far as such cost is covered by the liability of the tenant under any covenant or agreement as to the repair of the premises.

(2) In determining the amount of such net addition as aforesaid, regard shall be had to the purpose for which it is intended that the premises shall be used after the termination of the tenancy, and if it is shown that it is intended to demolish or to make structural alterations in the premises or any part thereof or to use the premises for a different purpose, regard shall be had to the effect of such demolition, alteration or change of user on the additional value attributable to the improvement, and to the length of time likely to elapse between the termination of the tenancy and the demolition, alteration or change of user.

(3) In the absence of agreement between the parties, all questions as to the right to compensation under this section, or as to the amount thereof, shall be determined by the tribunal hereinafter mentioned, and if the tribunal determines that, on account of the intention to demolish or alter or to change the user of the premises, no compensation or a reduced amount of compensation shall be paid, the tribunal may authorise a further application for compensation to be made by the tenant if effect is not given to the intention within such time as may be fixed by the tribunal.

Limitation on tenant's right to compensation in certain cases.

2.-(1) A tenant shall not be entitled to compensation under this Part of the Act-

(a) in respect of any improvement made before the commencement of this Act; or

(b) in respect of any improvement made in pursuance of a statutory obligation, or of any improvement which the tenant or his predecessors in title were under an obligation to make in pursuance of a contract entered into, whether before or after the passing of this Act, for valuable consideration, including a building lease, or

(c) in respect of any improvement made less than three years before the termination of the tenancy; or

(d) if within two months after the making of the claim under section one, subsection (1), of this Act the landlord serves on the tenant notice that he is willing and able to grant to the tenant, or obtain the grant to him of, a renewal of the tenancy at such rent and for such term as, failing agreement, the tribunal may consider reasonable; and, where such a notice is so served and the tenant does not within one month from the service of the notice send to the landlord an acceptance in writing of the offer, the tenant shall be deemed to have declined the offer.

(2) Where an offer of the renewal of the tenancy by the landlord under this section is accepted by the tenant, the rent fixed by the tribunal shall be the rent which in the opinion of the tribunal a willing lessee other than the tenant would agree to give and a willing lessor would agree to accept for the premises, having regard to the terms of the lease, but irrespective of the value attributable to the improvement in respect of which compensation would have been payable.

(3) The tribunal in determining the

compensation for an improvement shall in reduction of the tenant's claim take into consideration any benefits which the tenant or his predecessors in title may have received from the landlord or his predecessors in title in consideration expressly or impliedly of the improvement.

Landlord's right to object.

3.-(1) Where a tenant of a holding to which this Part of this Act applies proposes to make an improvement on his holding, he shall serve on his landlord notice of his intention to make such an improvement, together with a specification and plan showing the proposed improvement and the part of the existing premises affected thereby, and if the landlord, within three months after the service of the notice, serves on the tenant notice of objection, the tenant may, in the prescribed manner, apply to the tribunal, and the tribunal may, after ascertaining that notice of such intention has been served upon any superior landlords interested and after giving such persons an opportunity of being heard, if satisfied that the improvement-

(a) is of such a nature as to be calculated to add to the letting value of the holding at the termination of the tenancy; and

(b) is reasonable and suitable to the character thereof; and

(c) will not diminish the value of any other property belonging to the same landlord, or to any superior landlord from whom the intermediate landlord of the tenant directly or indirectly holds;

and after making such modifications (if any) in the specification or plan as the tribunal thinks fit, or imposing such other conditions as the tribunal may think reasonable, certify in the prescribed manner that the improvement is a proper improvement:

Provided that if the landlord proves that he has offered to execute the improvement himself in consideration of a reasonable increase of rent, or of such increase of rent as the tribunal may determine, the tribunal shall not give a certificate under this section unless it is subsequently shown to the satisfaction of the tribunal that the landlord has failed to carry out his undertaking.

(2) In considering whether the improvement is reasonable and suitable to the character of the holding, the tribunal shall have regard to any evidence brought before it by the landlord or any superior landlord (but not any other person) that the improvement is calculated to injure the amenity or convenience of the neighbourhood.

(3) The tenant shall, at the request of any superior landlord or at the request of the tribunal, supply such copies of the plans and specifications of the proposed improvement as may be required.

(4) Where no such notice of objection as aforesaid to a proposed improvement has been served within the time allowed by this section, or where the tribunal has certified an improvement to be a proper improvement, it shall be lawful for the tenant as against the immediate and any superior landlord to execute the improvement according to the plan and specification served on the landlord, or according to such plan and specification as modified by the tribunal or by agreement between the tenant and the landlord or landlords affected, anything in any lease of the premises to the contrary notwithstanding:

Provided that nothing in this subsection shall authorise a tenant to execute an improvement in contravention of any restriction created or imposed-

(a) for naval, military or air force purposes;
(b) for civil aviation purposes under the powers of the Air Navigation Act, 1920;

    (c) for securing any rights of the public over the foreshore or bed of the sea.

(5) A tenant shall not be entitled to claim compensation under this Part of this Act in respect of any improvement unless he has, or his predecessors in title have, served notice of the proposal to make the improvement under this section, and (in case the landlord has served notice of objection thereto) the improvement has been certified by the tribunal to be a proper improvement and the tenant has complied with the conditions, if any, imposed by the tribunal, nor unless the improvement is completed within such time after the service on the landlord of the notice of the proposed improvement as may be agreed between the tenant and the landlord or may be fixed by the tribunal, and where proceedings have been taken before the tribunal, the tribunal may defer making any order as to costs until the expiration of the time so fixed for the completion of the improvement.

(6) Where a tenant has executed an improvement of which he has served notice in accordance with this section and with respect to which either no notice of objection has been served by the landlord or a certificate that it is a proper improvement has been obtained from the

tribunal, the tenant may require the landlord to furnish to him a certificate that the improvement has been duly executed; and if the landlord refuses or fails within one month after the service of the requisition to do so, the tenant may apply to the tribunal who, if satisfied that the improvement has been duly executed, shall give a certificate to that effect.

Where the landlord furnishes such a certificate, the tenant shall be liable to pay any reasonable expenses incurred for the purpose by the landlord, and if any question arises as to the reasonableness of such expenses, it shall be determined by the tribunal.

Holdings to which Part I. applies.

17.-(1) The holdings to which this Part of this Act applies are any premises held under a lease, other than a mining lease, made whether before or after the commencement of this Act, and used wholly or partly for carrying on thereat any trade or business, and not being agricultural holdings within the meaning of the Agricultural Holdings Act, 1923.

(2) This part of this Act shall not apply to any holding let to a tenant as the holder of any office, appointment or employment, from the landlord, and continuing so long and continuing so long as the tenant holds such office, appointment or employment, but in the case of a tenancy created after

the commencement of this Act, only if the contract is in writing and expresses the purpose for which the tenancy is created.

(3) For the purposes of this section, premises shall not be deemed to be premises used for carrying on thereat a trade or business-

    (a) by reason of their being used for the purpose of carrying on thereat any profession;

    (b) by reason that the tenant, thereof carries on the business of subletting the premises as residential flats, whether or not the provision of meals or any other service for the occupants of the flats is undertaken by the tenant:

Provided that, so far as this Part of this Act relates to improvements, premises regularly used for carrying on a profession shall be deemed to be premises used for carrying on a trade or business.

(4) In the case of premises used partly for the purposes of trade or business and partly for other purposes, this Part of this Act shall apply to improvements only if and so far as they are improvements in relation to trade or business.

Part II
GENERAL AMENDMENTS
TO THE LAW OF
LANDLORD AND TENANT

Provisions as to the covenants to repair.

18.-(1) Damages for a breach of a covenant or agreement to keep or put premises in repair during the currency of a lease, or to leave or put premises in repair at the termination of a lease, whether such covenants or agreement is expressed or implied, and whether general or specific, shall in no case exceed the amount (if any) by which the value of the reversion (whether immediate or not) in the premises is diminished owing to the breach of such covenant or agreement as aforesaid; and in particular no damage shall be recovered for a breach of any such covenant or agreement to leave or put premises in repair at the termination of a lease, if it is shown that the premises, in whatever state of repair they might be, would at or shortly after the termination of the tenancy have been or be pulled down, or such structural alterations made therein as would render valueless the repairs covered by the covenant or agreement.

(2) A right of re-entry or forfeiture for a breach of any such covenant or agreement as aforesaid shall not be enforceable, by action or otherwise, unless the lessor proves that the fact that such notice as is required by section one hundred and forty-six of the Law of Property Act, 1925, had been served on the lessee was

known either-

(a) to the lessee; or

(b) to an under-lessee holding under an under-lease which reserved a nominal reversion only to the lessee; or to the person who last paid the rent due under the lease either on his own behalf or as agent for the lessee or under-lessee;

and that a time reasonably sufficient to enable the repairs to be executed had elapsed since the time when the fact of the service of the notice came to the knowledge of any such person.

Where a notice has been sent by registered post addressed to a person at his last known place of abode in the United Kingdom, then, for the purpose of this subsection, that person shall be deemed, unless the contrary is proved, to have had knowledge of the fact that the notice had been served as from the time at which the letter would have been delivered in the ordinary course of post.

This subsection shall be construed as one with section one hundred and forty-six of the Law of Property Act, 1925.

(3) This section applies whether the lease was created before or after the commencement of this Act.

Landlord and Tenant Act, 1954

PART IV
Miscellaneous and Supplementary

Extension of Leasehold Property (Repairs) Act, 1938

51-(1) The Leasehold Property (Repairs) Act, 1938 (which restricts the enforcement of repairing covenants in long leases of small houses) shall extend to every tenancy (whether of a house or of other property, and without regard to rateable value) where the following conditions are fulfilled, that is to say,-

(a) that the tenancy was granted for a term of years certain of not less than seven years ;

(b) that three years or more of the term remain unexpired at the date of the service of the notice of dilapidations or, as the case may be, at the date of commencement of the action for damages ; and

(c) that the property comprised in the tenancy is not an agricultural holding.

(2) In accordance with the last foregoing subsection the said Act of 1938 shall be amended as follows:-

(a) in subsection (1) of section one, for the words "a house of a rateable value of one hundred pounds or less" there shall be substituted the words "all or any of the property comprised in the lease", and for the word "five" there shall be substituted the word "three" ;

(b) (in subsection (2) of section one, for the word "five" there shall be substituted the word "three" ;

(c) in paragraph (b) of subsection (5) of section one, for the word "house" there shall be substituted the word "premises" and for the words from "relating" to the end of the paragraph there shall be substituted the words "or for giving effect to any order of a court or requirement of any authority under any enactment or any such byelaw or other provision as aforesaid" ;

(d) in paragraph (c) of subsection (5) of section one, for the word "house", where it first occurs, there shall be substituted the words "premises as respects which the covenant or agreement is proposed to be enforced", and for the words "the house" in the second place in which they occur there shall be substituted the words "those premises" ;

(e) in section three, for the words "a house" there shall be substituted the word "premises" ;

(f)   section four shall be omitted ;

(g)   in subsection (1) of section seven, in the definition of the expression "lease", for the words "twenty-one years or more" there shall be substituted the words "seven years or more, not being a lease of an agricultural holding within the meaning of the Agricultural Holdings Act. 1948".

(3)   The said Act of 1938 shall apply where there is an interest belonging to Her Majesty in right of the Crown or to a Government department, or held on behalf of Her Majesty for the purposes of a Government department, in like manner as if that interest were an interest not so belonging or held.

(4)   Subsection (2) of section twenty-three of the Landlord and Tenant Act, 1927 (which authorises a tenant to serve documents on the person to whom he has been paying rent) shall apply in relation to any counter-notice to be served under the said Act of 1938.

(5)   This section shall apply to tenancies granted, and to breaches occurring,

before or after the commencement of this Act. except that it shall not apply where the notice of dilapidations was served, or the action for damages begun, before the commencement of this Act.

(6)   In this section the expression "notice of dilapidations" means a notice under subsection (1) of section one hundred and forty-six of the Law of Property Act, 1925.

Landlord and Tenant Act, 1954

Jurisdiction of the court
for purposes of Parts I and II
of Landlord and Tenant Act, 1927.

Jurisdiction
of the court
for purposes
of Parts I
and II
of Landlord
and Tenant
Act, 1927.

63.-(1) Any jurisdiction conferred on the court by any provision of Part I of this Act shall be exercised by the county court.

(2) Any jurisdiction conferred on the court by any provision of Part II of this Act or conferred on the tribunal by Part I of the Landlord and Tenant Act, 1927, shall, subject to the provisions of this section, be exercised,-

(a) where the rateable value of the holding does not exceed five hundred pounds, by the county court;

(b) where it exceeds five hundred pounds, by the High Court.

(3) Any jurisdiction exercisable under the last foregoing subsection may by agreement in writing between the parties be transferred from the county court to the High Court or from the High Court to a county court specified in the agreement.

(4) The following provisions shall have effect

as respects transfer of proceedings from or to the High Court or the county court, that is to say-

(a) where an application is made to the one but by virtue of subsection (2) of this section cannot be entertained except by the other, the application shall not be treated as improperly made but any proceedings thereon shall be transferred to the other court;

(b) any proceedings under the provisions of Part II of this Act or Part I of the Landlord and Tenant Act, 1927, which are pending before one of those courts may by order of that court made on application of any person interested be transferred to the other court, if it appears to the court making the order that it is desirable that the proceedings and any proceedings before the other court should both be entertained by the other court.

(5) In any proceedings where in accordance with the foregoing provisions of this section the county court exercises jurisdiction the powers of the judge of summoning one or more assessors under subsection (1) of section eighty-eight of the County Courts Act, 1934, may be exercised notwithstanding that no application is made in that behalf by any party to the proceedings.

(6) Where in any such proceedings an assessor is summoned by a judge under the said subsection (1),-

    (a) he may, if so directed by the judge, inspect the land to which the proceedings relate without the judge and report to the judge in writing thereon;

    (b) the judge may on consideration of the report and any observations of the parties thereon give such judgement or make such order in the proceedings as it may be just;

    (c) the remuneration of the assessor shall be at such rate as may be determined by the Lord Chancellor with the approval of the Treasury and shall be defrayed out of the moneys provided by Parliament.

(7) In this section the expression "the holding"-

    (a) in relation to proceedings under Part II of this Act, has the meaning assigned to it by subsection (3) of section twenty-three of this Act

    (b) in relation to proceedings under Part I of the Landlord and Tenant Act, 1927, has the same meaning as in the said Part I.

(8) Subsections (5) to (7) of section thirty-seven of this Act shall apply for

determining the rateable value of the holding for the purposes of this section as they apply for the purposes of subsection (2) of the said section thirty-seven, but with the substitution in paragraph (a) of the said subsection (5) of a reference to the time at which application is made to the court for the reference to the date mentioned in that subsection.

(9) Nothing in this section shall prejudice the operation of section one hundred and eleven of the County Courts Act, 1934, (which relates to the removal into the High Court of Proceedings commenced in a county court).

(10) In accordance with the foregoing provisions of this section, for section twenty-one of the Landlord and Tenant Act, 1927, there shall be substituted the following section-

"The tribunal.

21. The tribunal for the purpose of Part I of this Act shall be the court exercising jurisdiction in accordance with the provisions of section sixty-three of the Landlord and Tenant Act 1954."

Landlord & Tenant Act 1985

Implied terms as to fitness for human habitation

Implied terms as to fitness for human habitation

8.-(1) In a contract to which this section applies for the letting of a house for human habitation there is implied, notwithstanding any stipulation to the contrary –

    (a) a condition that the house is fit for human habitation at the commencement of the tenancy, and

    (b) an undertaking that the house will be kept by the landlord fit for human habitation during the tenancy.

(2) The landlord, or a person authorised by him in writing, may at reasonable times of the day, on giving 24 hours' notice in writing to the tenant or occupier, enter premises to which this section applies for the purpose of viewing their state and condition.

(3) This section applies to a contract if-

    (a) the rent does not exceed the figure applicable in accordance with subsection (4), and

(b) the letting is not on such terms as to the tenant's responsibility as are mentioned in subsection (5).

(4) The rent limit for the application of this section is shown by the following Table, by reference to the date of making of the contract and the situation of the premises:

Date of making contract
- Rent Limit

Before 31st July 1923.

- In London: £40.
- Elsewhere: £26 or £16 (see Note 1).

On or after 31st July 1923 and before 6th July 1957.

- In London: £40.
- Elsewhere: £26.

On or after 6th July 1957.

- In London: £80.
- Elsewhere: £52.

NOTES

1.   The applicable figure for contacts made before 31st July 1923 is £26 in the case of premises situated in a borough or urban distract which at the date of the contact had according to the last published census a population of 50,000 or more. In the case of a house situated elsewhere, the figure is £16.

2.   The references to "London" are, in relation to contracts made before 1st April 1965, to the administrative county of London and, in relation to contracts made on or after that date, to Greater London exclusive or the outer London boroughs.

(5) This section does not apply where a house is let for a term of three years or more (the lease not being determinable at the option of either party before the expiration of three years) upon terms that the tenant puts the premises into a condition reasonably fit for human habitation.

(6) In this section "house" includes –
     (a)   a part of a house, and

(b) any yard , garden, outhouses and appurtenances belonging to the house or usually enjoyed with it.

Repairing Obligations

11.-(1) In a lease to which this section applies (as to which, see sections 13 and 14) there is implied a covenant by the lessor-

(a) to keep in repair the structure and exterior of the dwelling-house (including drains, gutters, and external pipes),

(b) to keep in repair and proper working order the installations in the dwelling-house for the supply of water, gas and electricity and for sanitation (including basins, sinks, baths and sanitary conveniences, but not other fixtures, fitting and appliances for making use of the supply of water, gas or electricity), and

(c) to keep in repair and proper working order the installations in the dwelling-house for space heating and heating water.

(2) The covenant implied by subsection (1) ("the lessor's repairing covenant") shall not be construed as requiring the lessor –

    (a) to carry out works or repairs for which the lessee is liable by virtue of his duty to use the premises in a tenant-like manner, or would be so liable but for an express covenant on his part,

    (b) to rebuild or reinstate the premises in the case of destruction or damage by fire, or by tempest, flood or other inevitable accident, or

    (c) to keep in repair or maintain anything which the lessee is entitled to remove from the dwelling-house.

(3) In determining the standard of repair required by the lessor's repairing covenant, regard shall be had to the age, character and prospective life of the dwelling-house and the locality in which it is situated.

(4) A covenant by the lessee for the repair of the premises is of no effect so far as it relates to the matters mentioned in subsection (1)(a) to (c), except so far as it imposes on the lessee any of the requirements mentioned in subsection (2)(a) or (c).

(5) The reference in subsection (4) to a covenant by the lessee for the repair of the premises includes a covenant-

      (a) to put in repair or deliver up in repair,

      (b) to paint, point or render,

      (c) to pay money in lieu of repairs by the lessee, or

      (d) to pay money on account of repairs by the lessor.

(6) In a lease in which the lessor's repairing covenant is implied there is also implied a covenant by the lessee that the lessor, or any persons authorised by him in writing, may at reasonable times of the day and on giving 24 hours' notice in writing to the occupier, enter the premises comprised in the lease for the purpose of viewing their condition and state of repair.

12.-(1) A covenant or agreement, whether contained in a lease to which section 11 applies or in an agreement collateral to such a lease, is void in so far as it purports-

    (a) to exclude or limit the obligations of the lessor or the immunities of the lessee under that section, or

    (b) to authorise any forfeiture or impose on the lessee any penalty, disability or obligation in the event of his enforcing or relying upon those obligations or immunities,

unless the inclusion of the provision was authorised by the county court.

(2) The county court may, by order made with the consent of the parties, authorise the inclusion in a lease, or in an agreement collateral to a lease, of provisions excluding or modifying in relation to the lease, the provisions of section 11 with respect to the repairing obligations of the parties if it appears to the court that it is reasonable to do so, having regard to all the circumstances of the case, including the other terms and conditions of the lease.

Leases to
which s. 11
applies:
general rule

13.-(1) Section 11 (repairing obligations) applies to a lease of a dwelling-house granted on or after 24th October 1961 for a term of less than seven years.

(2) In determining whether a lease is one to which section 11 applies-

    (a) any part of the term which falls before the grant shall be left out of account and the lease shall be treated as a lease for a term commencing with the grant,

    (b) a lease which is determinable at the option of the lessor before the expiration of seven years from the commencement of the term shall be treated as a lease for a term of less than seven years, and

    (c) a lease (other than a lease to which paragraph (b) applies) shall not be treated as a lease for term of less then seven years if it confers on the lessee an option for renewal for a term which, together with the original term, amounts to seven years or more.

(3) This section has effect subject to-

section 14 (leases to which section 11 applies: exceptions),

and

section 32(2) (provisions not applying to tenancies within

1954 c. 56. Part II of the Landlord and Tenant Act 1954).

Leases to which s. 11 applies: exceptions. **14.**-(1) Section 11 (repairing obligations) does not apply to a new lease granted to an existing tenant, or to a former tenant still in possession, if the previous lease was not a lease to which section 11 applied (and, in the case of a lease granted before 24th October 1961, would not have been if it had been granted on or after that date).

(2) In subsection (1)-

"existing tenant" means a person who is when, or immediately before, the new lease is granted, the lessee under another lease of the dwelling-house;

"former tenant still in possession" means a person who-

(a) was the lessee under another lease of the dwelling-house which terminated as some time before the new lease was granted, and

(b) between the termination of that other lease and the grant of the new lease was continuously in possession of the dwelling-house or of the rents and profits of the dwelling-house; and

"the previous lease" means the other lease referred to in the above definitions.

(3) Section 11 does not apply to a lease of a dwelling-house which is a tenancy of an agricultural holding within the meaning of the Agricultural Holdings Act 1948.

1948 c. 63.

(4) Section 11 does not apply to a lease granted on or after 3rd October 1980 to-

a local authority,
a new town corporation,
an urban development corporation,
the Development Board for Rural Wales,
a registered housing association,
a co-operative housing association,

or

1977 c. 42.

an educational institution or other body specified, or of a class specified, by regulations under section 8 of the Rent Act 1977 (bodies making student lettings).

(5) Section 11 does not apply to a lease granted on or after 3rd October 1980 to-

    (a) Her Majesty in right of the Crown (unless the lease is under the management of the Crown Estate Commissioners), or

    (b) A government department or a person holding in trust for Her Majesty for the purposes of a government department.

Specific performance of landlord's repairing obligations.

17.-(1) In proceedings in which a tenant of a dwelling alleges a breach on the party of his landlord of a repairing covenant relating to any part of the premises in which the dwelling is comprised, the court may order specific performance of the covenant whether or not the breach relates to a part of the premises let to the tenant and notwithstanding any equitable rule restricting the scope of the remedy, whether on the basis of a lack of mutuality or otherwise.

(2) In this section-

    (a) "tenant" includes a statutory tenant,

    (b) in relation to a statutory tenant the reference to the premises let to him is to the premises of which he is a statutory tenant,

    (c) "landlord", in relation to a tenant, includes any person against whom the tenant has a right to enforce a repairing covenant, and

    (d) "repairing covenant" means a covenant to repair, maintain, renew, construct or replace any property.

The Law of Property Act 1925

Part 1

General Principles as to Legal Estates, Equitable Interests and Powers.

Legal estates and equitable interests.

1.-(1) The only estates in land which are capable of subsisting or of being conveyed or created at law are-

    (a) An estate in fee simple absolute in possession;

    (b) A term of years absolute.

(2) The only interests or charges in or over land which are capable of subsisting or of being conveyed or created at law are-

    (a) An easement, right or privilege in or over land for an interest equivalent to an estate in fee simple absolute in possession or a term of years absolute;

    (b) A rentcharge in possession issuing out of or charged on land being either perpetual or for a term of years absolute;

    (c) A charge by way of legal mortgage;

      (a) Land tax, tithe rentcharge, and any other similar charge on land which is not created by an instrument;

      (b) Rights of entry exercisable over or in respect of a legal term of years absolute, or annexed, for any purpose, to a legal rentcharge.

(3) All other estates, interests, and charges in or over land take effect as equitable interests.

(4) The estates, interests, and charges which under this section are authorised to subsist or to be conveyed or created at law are (when subsisting or conveyed or created at law) in this Act referred to as "legal estates," and have the same incidents as legal estates subsisting at the commencement of this Act; and the owner of a legal estate is referred to as "an estate owner" and his legal estate is referred to as his estate.

(5) A legal estate may subsist concurrently with or subject to any other legal estate in the same land in like manner as it could have done before the commencement of the Act.

(6) A legal estate is not capable of subsisting

or of being created in an undivided share in land or of being held by an infant.

(7) Every power of appointment over, or power to convey or charge land or any interest therein, whether created by a statute or other instrument or implied by law, and whether created before or after the commencement of the Act (not being a power vested in a legal mortgagee or an estate owner in right of his estate and exercisable by him or by another person in his name and on his behalf), operates only in equity.

(8) Estates, interests, and charges in or over land which are not legal estates are in this Act referred to as "equitable interests," and powers which by this Act are to operate in equity only are in this Act referred to as "equitable powers."

(9) The provisions in any statue or other instrument requiring land to be conveyed to uses shall take effect as directions that the land shall (subject to creating or reserving thereout any legal estate authorised by this Act which many be required) be conveyed to a person of full age upon the requisite trusts.

(10)The repeal of the Statute of Uses (as amended) does not affect the operation thereof in regard to dealings taking effect before the commencement of this Act.

Restrictions
on and relief
against
forfeiture of
leases and
underleases.

146.-(1) A right of re-entry or forfeiture under any proviso or stipulation in a lease for a breach of any covenant or condition in the lease shall not be enforceable, by action or otherwise, unless and until the lessor serves on the lessee a notice-

(a) specifying the particular breach complained of ; and

(b) if the breach is capable of remedy, requiring the lessee to remedy the breach ; and

(c) in any case requiring the lessee to make compensation in money for the breach ;

and the lessee fails within a reasonable time thereafter, to remedy the breach, if it is capable of remedy, and to make reasonable compensation in money, to the satisfaction of the lessor, for the breach.

(2) Where a lessor is proceeding, by action, or otherwise, to enforce such a right of re-entry or forfeiture, the lessee may, in the lessor's action, if any, or in any action brought by himself, apply to the court for relief; and the court may grant or refuse relief, as the court, having regard to the proceedings and conduct of the parties under the foregoing provisions of this

section, and to all other circumstances, thinks fit; and in case of relief may grant it on such terms, if any, as to costs, expenses, damages, compensation, penalty or otherwise, including the granting of an injunction to restrain any like breach in the future, as the court, in the circumstances of each case, thinks fit.

(3) A lessor shall be entitled to recover as a debt due to him from a lessee, and in addition to damages (if any), all reasonable costs and expenses properly incurred by the lessor in the employment of a solicitor and surveyor or valuer, or otherwise, in reference to any breach giving rise to a right of re-entry or forfeiture, which, at the request of the lessee, is waived by the lessor, or from which the lessee is relieved, under the provisions of this Act.

(4) Where a lessor is proceeding by action or otherwise to enforce a right of re-entry or forfeiture under any covenant, proviso, or stipulation in a lease, or for non payment of rent, the court may, on application by any person claiming as under-lessee any estate or interest in the property comprised in the lease or any part thereof, either in the lessor's action (if any) or in any action brought by such person for that purpose, make an order vesting, for the whole term of the lease or any less term, the property

comprised in the lease or any part thereof in any person entitled as an under-lessee to any estate or interest in such property

upon such conditions as to execution of any deed or other document, payment of rent, costs, expenses, damages, compensation, giving security, or otherwise, as the court in the circumstances of each case may think fit, but in no case shall such under-lessee be entitled to require a lease to be granted to him for any longer term than he had under his original sub-lease.

(5) For the purposes of this section –

    (a) "Lease" includes an original or derivative under-lease ; also an agreement for a lease where the lessee "as become entitled to have his lease granted ; also a grant at a fee farm rent, or securing a rent by condition;

    (b) "Lessee" includes an original or derivative under-lessee, and the persons deriving tile under a lessee; also a grantee under any such grant as aforesaid and the persons deriving title under him;

    (c) "Lessor" includes an original or derivative under-lessor, and the persons deriving title under a lessor; also a person making such grant as aforesaid and the persons deriving title under him;

(a) "Under-lease" includes an agreement for an under-lease where the under-lessee has become entitled to have his underlease granted;

(b) "Under-lessee" includes any person deriving title under an under-lessee.

(6) This section applies although the proviso or stipulation under which the right of re-entry or forfeiture accrues is inserted in the lease in pursuance of the directions of any Act of Parliament.

(7) For the purpose of this section a lease limited to continue as long only as the lessee abstains from committing a breach of covenant shall be and take effect as a lease to continue for any longer term for which it could subsist, but determinable by a proviso for re-entry on such a breach.

(8) This section does not extend –

(i) To a covenant or condition against assigning, underletting, parting with the possession, or disposing of the land leased where the breach occurred before the commencement of this Act; or

(ii) In the case of a mining lease, to a

covenant or condition allowing the lessor to have access or to inspect books, accounts, records, weighing machines or other things, or to enter or inspect the mine or the workings thereof.

(9) This section does not apply to a condition for forfeiture on the bankruptcy of the lessee on taking in execution of the lessee's interest if contained in a lease of –

(a) Agricultural or pastoral land;

(b) Mines or minerals;

(c) A house used or intended to be used as a public-house or beershop;

(d) A house let as a dwelling-house, with the use of any furniture, books, works of art, or other chattels not being in the nature of fixtures;

(e) Any property in respect of which the personal qualification of the tenant are of importance for the preservation of the value or character of the property, or on the ground of neighbourhood to the lessor, or to any person holding under him.

(10)Where a condition of forfeiture on the bankruptcy of the lessee or on taking in execution of the lessee's interest is contained in any lease, other than a lease of any of the classes mentioned in the last subsection, then-

    (a) if the lessee's interest is sold within one year form the bankruptcy or taking in execution, this section applies to forfeiture condition aforesaid;

    (b) if the lessee's interest is not sold before the expiration of that year, this section only applies to the forfeiture condition aforesaid during the first year from the date of bankruptcy or taking in execution.

(11)This section does not, save as otherwise mentioned, affect the law relating to re-entry or forfeiture or relief in the case of non-payment of rent.

(12)This section has effect notwithstanding any stipulation to the contrary.

Editor's note This section was amended by the Law of Property (Amendment) Act 1929 so that nothing in section 146, sub-section (8), (9) or (10) shall affect the provisions of sub-section (4).

Relief
against
notice to
effect
decorative
repairs.

147.-(1) After a notice is served on a lessee relating to the internal decorative repairs to a house or other building, he may apply to the court for relief, and if, having regard to all the circumstances of the case (including in particular the length of the lessee's term or interest remaining unexpired), the court is satisfied that the notice is unreasonable, it may, by order, wholly or partially relieve the lessee from liability for such repairs.

(2) This section does not apply:-

(i)   where the liability arises under an express covenant or agreement to put the property in a decorative state of repair and the covenant or agreement has never been performed;

(ii)   to any matter necessary or proper-

(a) for putting or keeping the property in a sanitary condition, or

(b) for the maintenance or preservation of the structure;

(i) to any statutory liability to keep a house in all respects reasonably fit for human habitation;

(ii) to any covenant or stipulation to yield up the house or other building in a specified state of repair at the end of the term.

(3) In this section "lease" includes an underlease and an agreement for a lease, and "lessee" has a corresponding meaning and includes any person liable to effect the repairs.

(4) This section applies whether the notice is served before or after the commencement of this Act, and has effect notwithstanding any stipulation to the contrary.

The Leasehold Property (Repairs) Act 1938

PLEASE SEE END NOTE

Restriction on enforcement of repairing covenants in long leases of small houses.

1.-(1) Where a lessor serves on a lessee under subsection (1) of section one hundred and forty-six of the Law of Property Act, 1925 a notice that relates to a breach of a covenant or agreement to keep or put in repair during the currency of the lease a house of a rateable value of one hundred pounds or less, and at the date of the service of the notice five years or more of the term of the lease remain unexpired, the lessee may within twenty-eight days from that date serve on the lessor a counter-notice to the effect that he claims the benefit of this Act.

(2) A right to damages for a breach of such a covenants as aforesaid shall not be enforceable by action commenced at any time at which five years or more of the term of the lease remain unexpired unless the lessor has served on the lessee not less than one month before the commencement of the action such a notice as is specified in subsection (1) of section one hundred and forty-six of the Law of Property Act, 1925, and where a notice is served under this subsection, the lessee may, within twenty-eight days from the date of the service thereof, serve

on the lessor a counter-notice to the effect that he claims the benefit of this Act.

(3) Where a counter-notice is served by a lessee under this section, then notwithstanding anything in any enactment or rule of law, no proceedings, by action or otherwise, shall be taken by the lessor for the enforcement of any right of re-entry or forfeiture under any proviso or stipulation in the lease for breach of the covenant or agreement in question, or for damages for breach thereof, otherwise than with the leave of the court.

(4) A notice served under subsection (1) of section one hundred and forty-six of the Law of Property Act 1925, in the circumstances specified in subsection (1) of this section, and a notice served under subsection (2) of this section shall not be valid unless it contains a statement in characters not less conspicuous than those used in any other part of the notice, to the effect that the lessee is entitled under this Act to serve on the lessor a counter-notice claiming the benefit of this Act, and a statement in the like characters specifying the time within which, and the manner in which, under this Act a counter-notice may be served and specifying the name and address for service of the lessor.

(5) Leave for the purpose of this section shall not be given unless the lessor proves-

(a)   that the immediate remedying of the breach in question is requisite for preventing substantial diminution in the value of his reversion, or that the value thereof has been substantially diminished by the breach;

(b)   that the immediate remedying of the breach is required for giving effect in relation to the house to the purposes of any enactment, or of any byelaw or other provision having effect under an enactment, relating to the safety, repair, maintenance, or sanitary condition of houses, or for giving effect to any order of a court or requirement of a local authority under any such enactment, byelaw, or other provision as aforesaid;

(c)   in a case in which the lessee is not in occupation of the whole of the house, that the immediate remedying of the breach is required in the interests of the occupier of the house or of part thereof;

(d)   that the breach can be immediately remedied at an expense that is relatively small in comparison with the much greater expense that would probably be occasioned by postponement of the necessary work; or

(e) special circumstances which in the opinion of the court, render it just and equitable that leave should be given.

(6) The court may, in granting or in refusing leave for the purposes of this section, impose such terms and conditions on the lessor or on the lessee as it may think fit.

Restriction on right to recover expenses of survey, &c.

2. A lessor on whom a counter-notice is served under the preceding section shall not be entitled to the benefit of subsection (3) of section one hundred and forty-six of the Law of Property Act, 1925 (which relates to costs and expenses incurred by a lessor in reference to breaches of covenant) so far as regards any costs or expenses incurred in reference to the breach in question, unless he makes an application for leave for the purposes of the preceding section, and on such an application the court shall have the power to direct whether and to what extent the lessor is to be entitled to the benefit thereof.

Saving for obligation to repair on taking possession.

3. This Act shall not apply to a breach of a covenant or agreement in so far as it imposes on the lessee an obligation to put a house in repair that is to be performed upon the lessee taking possession of the premises or within a reasonable time thereafter.

Application to house used partly as shop, &c.

4. The application of this Act to a house shall not be excluded by reason only that part thereof is used as a shop or office, or for business, trade, or professional purposes.

Application to past breaches.

5. This Act applies to leases created, and to breaches occurring, before or after the commencement of this Act.

Court having jurisdiction under this Act.

6.-(1) In this Act the expression "the court" means the county court, except in a case in which any proceedings by action for which leave may be given would have to be taken in a court other than the county court, and means in the said excepted case that other court.

(2) The County Courts Act, 1934, shall have effect as if this Act had been one of the enactments referred to in subsection (3) of section fifty-two of that Act, and set out in the first column of the Second Schedule to that Act, and as if all cases other than the said excepted case had been mentioned in the second column of that schedule.

Application of certain provisions of 15 & 16 Geo. 5. c. 20.

7.-(1) In this Act the expressions "lessor," "lessee" and "lease" have the meanings assigned to them respectively by sections one hundred and forty-six and one hundred and fifty-four of the Law of Property Act, 1925, except that they do not include any reference to such a grant as is mentioned in the said section one hundred and forty-six, or to the person making, or to the grantee under such a grant, or to the persons deriving title under such a person; and "lease" means a lease for a term of twenty-one years or more.

(2) The provisions of section one hundred and ninety-six of the said Act (which relate to the service of notices) shall extend to notices and counter-notices required or authorised by this Act.

Short title and extent.

8.-(1) This Act may be cited as the Leasehold Property (Repairs) Act, 1938.

(2) This Act shall not extend to Scotland or to Northern Ireland.

This Act was amended by S 51 of the Landlord and Tenant Act 1954 as follows:-

The Act now applies to every tenancy, whatever the property or rateable value, provided –

○ The tenancy was for a term of not less than seven years certain.

○ That three years or more of the term remain unexpired at the date of service of the schedule of dilapidations under section 146 of the Law of Property Act, 1925; or the commencement of the action.

○ That the property is not an agricultural holding within the Agricultural Holdings Act, 1986.

See S 51 of the Landlord and Tenant Act 1954 supra.

Occupiers' Liability Act 1957

Liability in tort

Preliminary **1.**-(1)The rules enacted by the two next following sections shall have effect, in place of the rules of the common law, to regulate the duty which an occupier of premises owes to his visitors in respect of the dangers due to the state of the premises or to things done or omitted to be done on them.

(2) The rules so enacted shall regulate the nature of the duty imposed by law in consequence of a person's occupation or control of premises and of any invitation or permission he gives (or is to be treated as giving) to another to enter or use the premises, but they shall not alter the rules of the common law as to the persons on whom a duty is so imposed or to whom it is owed; and accordingly for the purpose of the rules so enacted the persons who are to be treated as an occupier and as his visitors are the same (subject to subsection (4) of this section) as the persons who would at common law be treated as an occupier and as his invitees or licensees.

(3) The rules so enacted in relation to an occupier of premises and his visitors

shall also apply, in like manner and to the like extent as the principles applicable at common law to an occupier of premises and his invitees or licensees would apply, to regulate-

(a) the obligations of a person occupying or having control over any fixed or moveable structure, including any vessel, vehicle or aircraft; and

(b) the obligations of a person occupying or having control over any premises or structure in respect of damages to property, including the property of persons who are not themselves his visitors.

(4) A person entering any premises in exercise of rights conferred by virtue of an access agreement or order under the National Parks and Access to the Countryside Act, 1949, is not, for the purposes of this Act, a visitor of the occupier of those premises.

12,13 & 14 Geo. 6. c. 97.

Extent of occupier's ordinary duty.

2.-(1) An occupier of premises owes the same duty, the "common duty of care", to all his visitors, except in so far as he is free to and does extend, restrict, modify or exclude his duty to any visitor or visitors by agreement or otherwise.

(2) The common duty of care is a duty to take such care as in all the circumstances of the case is reasonable to see that the visitor will be reasonably safe in using the premises for the purposes fore which he is invited or permitted by the occupier to be there.

(3) The circumstances relevant for the present purpose include the degree of care, and of want of care, which would ordinarily be looked for in such a visitor, so that (for example) in proper cases-

    (a) an occupier must be prepared for children to be less careful than adults; and

    (b) an occupier may expect that a person, in the exercise of his calling, will appreciate and guard against any special risks ordinarily incident to it, so far as the occupier leaves him free to do so.

(4) In determining whether the occupier of premises has discharged the common duty of care to a visitor, regard is to be had to all the circumstances, so that (for example)-

(a) where damage is caused to a visitor by a danger of which he had been warned by the occupier, the warning is not to be treated without more as absolving the occupier from liability, unless in all the circumstances it was enough to enable the visitor to be reasonably safe; and

(b) where damage is caused to a visitor by a danger due to the faulty execution of any work of construction, maintenance or repair by an independent contractor employed by the occupier, the occupier is not to be treated without more as answerable for the danger if in all the circumstances he had acted reasonably in entrusting the work to an independent contract and had taken such steps (if any) as he reasonably ought in order to satisfy himself that the contractor was competent and that the work had been properly done.

(5) The common duty of care does not impose on an occupier any obligation to a visitor in respect of risks willingly accepted as his by the visitor (the question whether a risk was so accepted to be decided on the same principles as in other cases in which one person owes a duty of care to another).

(6) For the purpose of this section, persons who enter premises for any purpose in the exercise of a right conferred by law are to be treated as permitted by the occupier to be there for that purpose, whether they in fact have his permission or not.

Effect of contract on occupier's liability to third party.

3.-(1)Where an occupier of premises is bound by contract to permit persons who are strangers to the contract to enter or use the premises, the duty of care which he owes to them as his visitors cannot be restricted or excluded by that contract, but (subject to any provision of the contract to the contrary) shall include the duty to perform his obligations under the contract, whether undertaken for their protection or not, in so far as those obligations go beyond the obligations otherwise involved in that duty.

(2) A contract shall not by virtue of this section have the effect, unless it expressly so provides, of making an occupier who has taken all reasonable care answerable to strangers to the contract for dangers due to the faulty execution of any work of construction, maintenance or repair or other like operation by persons other than himself, his servants and persons acting under this direction and control.

(3) In this section "stranger to the contract" means a person not for the time being entitled to the benefit of the contract as a party to it or as the successor by assignment or otherwise of a party to it, and accordingly includes a party to the contract who has ceased to be so entitled.

(4) Where by the terms or conditions governing any tenancy (including a statutory tenancy which does not in law amount to a tenancy) either the landlord or the tenant is bound, though not by contract, to permit persons to enter or use premises of which he is the occupier, this section shall apply as if the tenancy were a contract between the landlord and the tenant.

(5) This section, in so far as it prevents the common duty of care from being restricted or excluded, applies to contracts entered into and tenancies created before the commencement of this Act, as well as to those entered into or created after its commencement; but, in so far as it enlarges the duty owed by an occupier beyond the common duty of care, it shall have effect only in relation to obligations which are undertaken after that commencement or which are renewed by agreement (whether express or implied) after that commencement.

Public Health Act, 1936

Nuisances which may be dealt with summarily.

92.-(1) Without prejudice to the exercise by a local authority of any other powers vested in them by or under this Act, the following matters may, subject to the provisions of this Part of this Act, be dealt with summarily, and are in the Part of this Act referred to as "statutory nuisances," that is to say:-

    (a) any premises in such a state as to be prejudicial to health or a nuisance;

    (b) any animal kept in such a place or manner as to be prejudicial to health or a nuisance;

    (c) any accumulation or deposit which is prejudicial to health or a nuisance;

    (d) any dust or effluvia caused by any trade, business, manufacture or process and being prejudicial to the health of, or a nuisance to, the inhabitants of the neighbourhood;

(a) any factory (not being a factory to which section one of the Factory and Workshop Act, 1901, applies) workshop, or workplace, which is not provided with sufficient means of ventilation, or in which sufficient ventilation is not maintained, or which is not kept clean or not kept free from noxious effluvia, or which is so overcrowded while work is carried on as to be prejudicial to the health of those employed therein;

(b) any other matter declared by any provision of this Act to be a statutory nuisance.

(2) A local authority shall not without the consent of the Minister institute summary proceedings under this Part of this Act in respect of any such nuisance as is mentioned in paragraph (c) or (d) of the preceding subsection if proceedings in respect thereof might be instituted under the Alkali, &c. Works Regulation Act, 1906.

6 Edw. 7 c. 14.

(3) So much of paragraph (e) of subsection (1) of this section as relates to the provision of means of ventilation and the maintenance of ventilation shall not apply to a shop to which the Shops Act, 1934, applies.

(4) In determining for the purposes of the said paragraph (e) whether any factory or workshop is provided with sufficient means of ventilation or whether sufficient ventilation is maintained therein, or whether any factory or workshop is so overcrowded as to be prejudicial to health, regards shall be had to the requirements of the Factory and Workshop Act, 1901, and of any order made by the Secretary of State thereunder, with respect to ventilation of overcrowding in factories and workshops.

Service of abatement notice.

93. Where a local authority are satisfied of the existence of a statutory nuisance, they shall serve a notice (hereafter in this Act referred to as "an abatement notice") on the person by whose act, default or sufferance the nuisance arises or continues, or, if that person cannot be found, on the owner or occupier of the premises on which the nuisance arises, requiring him to abate the nuisance and to execute such works and take such steps as may be necessary for that purpose:

Provided that:-

(a) where the nuisance arises from any defect of a structural character, the notice shall be served on the owner of the premises;

(b) where the person causing the nuisance cannot be found and it is clear that the nuisance does not arise or continue by the act, default or sufferance of the owner or the occupier of the premises, the local authority may themselves do forthwith what they consider necessary to abate the nuisance and to prevent a recurrence thereof.

Power of court to make nuisance order if abatement notice disregarded.

94.-(1) If the person on whom an abatement notice has been served makes default in complying with any of the requirements of the notice, or if the nuisance, although abated since the service of the notice, is, in the opinion of the local authority, likely to recur on the same premises, the authority shall cause a complaint to be made to a justice of the peace, and the justice shall thereupon issue a summons requiring the person on whom the notice was served to appear before a court of summary jurisdiction.

(2) If on hearing of the complaint it is proved that the alleged nuisance exists, or that although abated it is likely to recur on the same premises, then, subject to the provision of subsections (4) and (5) of this section the court shall make an order (hereafter in this Act referred to as "a nuisance order") for either, or both, of the following purposes-

(a) requiring the defendant to comply with all or any of the requirements of the abatement notice, or otherwise to abate the nuisance, within a time specified in the order, and to execute any works necessary for that purpose;

(b) prohibiting a recurrence of the nuisance, and requiring the defendant, within a time specified in the order, to execute any works necessary to prevent a recurrence;

and may also impose on the defendant a fine not exceeding five pounds.

Where a nuisance proved to exist is such as to render a building, in the opinion of the court, unfit for human habitation, the nuisance order may prohibit the use of the building for that purpose until a court of summary jurisdiction, being satisfied that it has been rendered fit for human habitation, withdraws the prohibition.

(3) Where on the hearing of a complaint under this section it is proved that the alleged nuisance existed at the date of the service of the abatement notice and that at the date of the making of the complaint it either still existed or was likely to recur, then, whether or not at the date of the hearing it still exists or is likely to recur, the court shall order the defendant to pay the local authority such reasonable sum as the court may determine in respect of the expenses incurred by the authority in, or in connection with, the making of the complaint and the proceedings before the court.

(4) Where proceedings are brought under this section in respect of a nuisance under paragraph (c) of subsection (1) of section ninety-two of this Act (which relates to certain accumulations or deposits) it shall be a defence for the defendant to prove that the accumulation or deposit complained of was necessary for the effectual carrying on of a business or manufacture and has not been kept longer than is necessary for the purposes

Public Health Act 1936

of the business or manufacture, and that the best practicable means have been taken for preventing it from being prejudicial to the health of, or a nuisance to, the inhabitants of the neighbourhood.

(5) Where proceedings are brought under this section in respect of a nuisance under paragraph (d) of subjection (1) of section ninety-two of this Act (which relates to dust or effluvia caused by any trade, business, manufacture or process), it shall be a defence for the defendant to prove that the best practicable means have been taken for preventing, or counteracting the effect of, the dust or effluvia.

(6) If it appears to the court that the person by whose act or default the nuisance arises, or the owner or occupier of the premises, cannot be found, the nuisance order may be addressed to, and executed by, the local authority.

Penalty for contravention of nuisance order, and abatement of nuisance by local authority.

95.-(1) Any person who fails without reasonable excuse to comply with, or knowingly contravenes, a nuisance order shall be liable to a fine not exceeding five pounds and to a further fine not exceeding forty shillings for each day on which the offence continues after conviction therefore.

(2) Without prejudice to the foregoing provisions of this section, where a nuisance

order has not been complied with, the local authority may abate the nuisance, and do whatever may be necessary in the execution of the order.

Power of individual to make complaint as to statutory nuisance.

99. Complaint of the existence of a statutory nuisance under this Act may be made to a justice of the peace by any person aggrieved by the nuisance and thereupon the like proceedings shall be had, with the like incidents and consequences as to the making or orders, penalties for disobedience of orders and otherwise, as in the case of a complaint by the local authority, but any order made in such proceedings may, if the court after giving the local authority an opportunity of being heard thinks fit, direct the authority to abate the nuisance.

We are grateful to Her Majesty's Stationery Office for permission to reproduce Crown Copyrights.

**We are grateful to the
Property Litigation Association
for their kind permission to
reproduce their
DRAFT PRE-ACTION PROTOCOL**

DRAFT PRE-ACTION PROTOCOL
TERMINAL DILAPIDATIONS
CLAIMS FOR DAMAGES
Property Litigation Association

24 July 2000

Dear Member

Draft pre-action protocol for dilapidations

Over the last year or so, our Law Reform Sub-Committee, chaired by Michael Madden of Ashurst Morris Crisp, has been working on a draft pre-action protocol for claims for damages for breach of a tenant's covenant to repair. The sub-committee has completed the task that was given to it, namely the preparation of a draft protocol, and the main committee has agreed that the project should move to the next stage. What is now proposed is that:-

1. Members should be encouraged to consider whether or not, when advising their clients on dilapidations matters generally, regard should be had to the procedures set out in the draft protocol. Although it is for individual members to decide on the appropriateness of the draft protocol, either generally or in relation to particular circumstances, the draft protocol has been prepared on the basis that it is a worthwhile objective. If the procedure set out in the draft protocol becomes generally accepted and implemented, the Association will have achieved its objective.

2. Members should be encouraged to provide feed-back on the draft protocol over the next three months. This should be sent to **pla@collyer-bristow.co.uk**.

3. The draft protocol will be distributed to other interested organisations and individuals, including the Royal Institutions of Chartered Surveyors, the Laws Society, the heads of certain leading sets of chambers specialising in property law, the Lord Chancellor's Department, the Civil Justice Reform Committee, the British Property Federation, The British Retail Consortium, the Technology and Construction Court and our President. Those organisations and individuals will be invited to provide the Association with their comments on the draft protocol.

4. The draft protocol will be available on the Association's website (shortly to be set up). The address of the website is www.pla.org.uk.

Draft Pre-Action Protocol

5. A seminar, with a panel of speakers similar to that organised in 1999 by the Association for the Woolf Reforms, will be organised, hopefully for 14 November 2000, in the evening. A venue has not yet been arranged. The purpose of the seminar is to give members an opportunity to raise any points of concern on the draft protocol, hopefully in the light of having used the draft protocol in practice, and to provide a forum for an open discussion. The make up of the panel is yet to be determined. It is hoped that the audience will include individuals from the organisations to which the draft protocol has been distributed.

6. Following the seminar, the Association hope that a protocol can then be published which will have received the seal of approval of members and other parties who are involved in the resolution of dilapidations disputes.

There is one issue that the draft protocol does not address, on which feedback from members is specifically invited. It is established law that the cost of investigating what works are required in order to remedy a tenant's failure to comply with an obligation to repair is not recoverable as part of a claim for damages for breach of a repairing covenant. Of course, many leases contain a provision whereby the cost of preparation of a schedule of dilapidations is recoverable from a tenant. In addition, the Court would have, it is submitted, a discretion in relation to such costs (in circumstances where proceedings have been commenced) and might exercise that discretion in favour of the landlord if the Court took the view that the landlord had acted reasonably by, for example, following the steps set out in the pre-action protocol.

The next four months is a time for consultation, at the end of which the Association will have played an important part in furthering the aims of the Civil Procedure Rules and in providing the property industry with the means of resolving dilapidations disputes in a manner more suited to the modern era.

IAIN TRAVERS
Chairman
Property Litigation Association
C/o Lacon House
Theobald's Road
London WC1X 8RW
DX77 London/Chancery Lane
Tel:020 7524 6283
Fax: 020 7524 6524

Email: i.travers@nabarro.com

DRAFT PRE-ACTION PROTOCOL
TERMINAL DILAPIDATIONS CLAIMS FOR DAMAGES
Property Litigation Association

1   Introduction

1.1   This draft pre-action protocol has been drafted by the Law Reform Sub Committee (the **"Committee"**) of the Property Litigation Association and following appropriate consultation it is intended to become part of the programme of Civil Justice Reforms now taking place. This protocol sets out the Committee's views on effective and enforceable standards for the efficient conduct of pre-action litigation relating to claims for damages for breach by tenants or repair obligations in leases following the expiry of the lease.

1.2   This protocol is not intended to be an exhaustive or mandatory list of steps or procedures to be followed. Those will be determined by the facts of each case. In deciding the exact steps and procedures to be adopted regard should also be had to the Overriding Objective as set out in CPR Part 1.

1.3   This protocol is intended to improve the pre-action communication between landlord and tenant by establishing a timetable for the exchange of information relevant to the dilapidations dispute and by setting standards for the content of claims and correspondence and the conduct of pre-action negotiations.

1.4   Compliance with the protocol should enable both landlords and tenants to make an informed judgment on the merits of their cases earlier than tends to happen today. The aim is to increase the number of pre-action settlements. If proceedings are commenced, the Court should be encouraged to treat the standards set out in this protocol as the normal reasonable approach to pre-action conduct. If the Court has to consider the question of compliance after proceedings have begun, it should be concerned with substantial compliance and not minor departures, eg failure by a short period to provide relevant information. In addition, minor departures should not exempt the "innocent" party from following the protocol. The Court should be encouraged to look at the effect of non-compliance on the other party when deciding whether to impose sanctions. For sanctions generally, see paragraph 2 of the Practice Direction – Protocols "Compliance with Protocols".

2   Overview of Protocol – General Aim

The General aim of this Protocol is to ensure that before Court proceedings commence:

(a) the landlord and tenant have provided sufficient information for each party to know the nature of the other's case;

(b) each party has had an opportunity to consider the other's case, and to accept or reject all or any part of the case made against him at the earliest possible stage;

(c) there is more pre-action contact between the parties;

(d) better and earlier exchange of information occurs;

(e) there is better pre-action investigation by the parties;

(f) the parties (or representatives with authority to settle) have met formally on at least one occasion with a view to: (a) defining and agreeing the issues between them; and (b) exploring possible ways by which the claim may be resolved;

(g) the parties are in a position where they may be able to settle cases early and fairly without recourse to litigation; and

(h) proceedings will be conducted efficiently if litigation does become necessary.

THE PROTOCOL

3   The Claim

3.1 The landlord shall serve within a reasonable time (which in the usual case should not be more than two months) following the determination of the tenancy a schedule which indicates the breaches of the tenant's repairing obligations which have not been cured prior to the determination of the tenancy and states what in the opinion of the landlord or his surveyor is necessary to put the premises right. Care should be taken in preparing the schedule to avoid including breaches of reinstatement obligations. If it is intended to claim for breaches of reinstatement obligations these should be listed separately and should (where appropriate) identify any notices served by the landlord requiring the reinstatement works to be undertaken.

Generally   therefore   a   schedule   ought   to   contain:

(a) in the first column – the specific clause under which the repairing obligation arises;

(b) in the second column – the breach complained of;

(c) in the third column – the remedial work suggested by the landlord's surveyor as suitable for remedying the breach complained of;

(d) a column indicating the landlord's view on the cost of the works.

3.2 The schedule should also give space for the tenant's comments on the breaches alleged, the extent of works required and likely cost.

3.3 A specimen schedule of dilapidations is attached at Annex A.

3.4 If possible the schedule should also be provided by way of computer disk or similar form to enable the tenant's comments to be incorporated on the one document.

3.5 The claim should be quantified indicating clearly how the claim is made up;

3.5.1   if the claim is based on the cost of works, it should be fully quantified and substantiated. For example, each item of expenditure should be supported by either an invoice or estimate or a certificate from a surveyor that the sums claimed are fair and reasonable;

3.5.2   if the landlord restricts if the landlord restricts its claim by reference to Section 18(1) Landlord & Tenant Act 1927 (Section 18(1)) a valuation should be provided and sufficient costing of the works provided to demonstrate that the cost of the works would exceed the section 18(1) valuation.

3.6 All aspects of the claim including the VAT status of the landlord should be set out.

3.7 If the claim includes any other losses such as: projected surveyor's fees for negotiating the claim; for lost profits; preliminaries; overheads and loss of rent/service charges; surveyor's fees in preparing the schedule; the schedule must include a section setting these out in detail, fully quantified and substantiated.

3.8 A covering letter ought to be sent with the schedule stating that it is a claim for damages for tenant dilapidations and that it is sent in accordance with this pre-action protocol. The letter ought to specify what in the landlord's view would be a reasonable time to respond to the claim. A specimen letter is attached at Annex B.

3.9 Where the landlord relies on costs already incurred copies of receipted invoices or other evidence of such costs should be enclosed with the schedule.

4   The Response

4.1 The tenant must respond to the landlord's letter in a reasonable time. In the usual case 6 weeks should be adopted as a reasonable time.

4.2 The tenant should respond using the schedule provided by the landlord in sufficient detail to enable the landlord to understand clearly the tenant's views on each item of claim.

4.3 If the tenant relies upon Section 18(1), a valuation should be provided by the tenant.

4.4 If the tenant does not rely on Section 18(1) for all or part of the landlord's claim, a response should be given to each aspect of the landlord's claim.

5 Documents

5.1 In the event that the proposed tenant disputes the claim and the landlord decides that disclosure is appropriate, he should notify the proposed tenant that both parties should disclose the relevant documents in their possession. Relevant documents are those which are material to the issues between the parties and which are likely to be disclosed in Court proceedings.

5.2 If the landlord decides that disclosure is not appropriate he may be required to justify the decision before the Court.

5.3 If the tenant intends to rely on a defence relying on Section 18(1) he should indicate this as soon as reasonably practicable and should request the landlord to provide proportionate and reasonable disclosure of documents relevant to the landlord's intention to carry out works to the premises.

6 Negotiations

6.1 The landlord and tenant and/or their respective surveyors/agents should meet within 1 month of service of the schedule of dilapidations, without prejudice and preferably on site, to review the schedule to ensure that the tenant fully understands all aspects of the landlord's claim and seek to agree as many of the items in dispute as possible.

6.2 In a complex matter it may be necessary for more than one site visit or without prejudice meeting between surveyors to take place. These ought to be conducted according to a strict timetable.

7   Experts

7.1 Experts in like disciplines are required to meet on a without prejudice basis in order to agree facts and limit issues in dispute. This meeting should take place within one month of the service by the tenant of its response. All experts who contributed to the landlord's claim or the tenant's response should attend the meeting which may be in one meeting or series of meetings.

7.2 For so long as the parties are complying with this protocol, proceedings should not be issued less than one month after the meeting of experts nor three months after the service of the schedule (whichever is the earlier).

7.3 In the event that expert evidence is required particularly in relation to valuation issues the landlord and tenant will give serious consideration to instructing a joint expert.

8   Mediation

Both parties' legal representatives are to explore the possibilities of mediation or other alternative dispute resolution process with their own clients and with the other party or, if represented, their legal representatives.

ANNEX A

SCHEDULE OF DILAPIDATIONS

This schedule has been prepared by [name, individual and firm], upon the instructions of [name the landlord]. It was prepared by [   ]   following [name ie. same name as above]'s inspection of the premises known as [property] on [date].

It records the works required to be done to the premises in order that they are put into the condition the premises should have been if the tenant [name] had complied with its covenants contained within its lease of the premises dated [   ].

The covenants of the said lease with which the tenant should have complied are as follows:

[Set out clause number of the lease and quote the clause verbatim].

The following schedule contains:

1.   reference to the specific clause (quoted above) under which the repairing obligation arises;

2.   the breach complained of;

3.   the remedial works suggested by the landlord's surveyor [name ie. same name as above] as suitable for remedying the breach complained of;

4.   the landlord's view on the cost of the works.

The schedule contains the true and independent views of [name, ie. the same name as above] being the surveyor appointed by the landlord to prepare the schedule.

Upon receipt of the schedule the tenant should respond using this schedule in the relevant column below to enable the landlord to understand clearly the tenant's views on each item of claim.

Draft Pre-Action Protocol

1 Clause No	2 Breach complained of	3 Remedial works required	4 Landlord's comments upon breach	5 Tenant's comments upon breach	6 Landlord's comments on work required	7 Tenant's comments on work required	8 Landlord's view on cost of works	9 Tenant's view on cost of works	10 Other comments

DATED

[.................................]

SIGNED

[.................................]

[Name and address of surveyor appointed by landlord]

DATED

[.................................]

SIGNED

[.................................]

[Name and address of surveyor appointed by tenant]

564

[The Company Secretary   [date]

Name of Company   [Our reference]

Registered office address of company]   [Your reference]

[Name of tenant

Last known place of abode]

By recorded delivery

Dear Sirs

Property   **[address of property]**
Our client   **[Name of landlord]**
Lease   **Dated [date] and made between [name of parties]**

We refer to the above Lease under you which you [are] or [were] the Tenant of the Property:

1. We enclose by way of service upon you our client's schedule of dilapidations in respect of the Property prepared by [name of surveyors] and dated [date]. We also enclose a version of the schedule on computer disk.

2. In accordance with the protocol for terminal dilapidations claims please can we have your response to this claim by [a reasonable time] and, in any event, within 6 weeks of this letter. We confirm that we will attend a meeting with you and/or your agents within one month of this letter. Please could you contact [   ] of this office to arrange a mutually convenient date.

3. We also enclose [copies of any documents relied upon].

4. We have instructed the following surveyors/experts on compiling this schedule [name] [description].

Please acknowledge safe receipt of this letter and its enclosures.

Yours faithfully

Table of Statutes

Table of Statutes

WARNING 475

Defective Premises Act 1972

Housing Act, 1985 – Part IV

Landlord & Tenant Act, 1927

Part II

Landlord & Tenant Act, 1954

Landlord & Tenant Act, 1985

The Law of Property Act 1925 – continued

The Leasehold Property (Repairs) Act 1938

Occupiers' Liability Act 1957

Occupiers' Liability Act 1957 – Continued

Public Health Act, 1936

Index of Cases
By Subject

Index of Cases by Subject

The Dilapidations Handbook

"at all times during the said term well and substantially to repair, decorate, cleanse, maintain, amend and keep the interior of the demised premises and the windows thereof and all additions made thereto and the fixtures and fittings therein and all interior walls and appurtenances thereof and the sewers, drains and services serving only the demised premises with all necessary reparations cleansings and amendments whatsoever (damage by fire only excepted)".

Index of Cases by Subject

The Dilapidations Handbook

Index of Cases by Subject

The Dilapidations Handbook

Index of Cases by Subject

The Dilapidations Handbook

Index of Cases by Subject

The Dilapidations Handbook

Index of Cases by Subject

The Dilapidations Handbook

Index of Cases by Subject

The Dilapidations Handbook

Index of Cases by Subject

The Dilapidations Handbook

Index of Cases by Subject

The Dilapidations Handbook

Index of Cases by Subject

The Dilapidations Handbook

Index of Cases by Subject

The Dilapidations Handbook

Index of Cases by Subject

The Dilapidations Handbook

Index of Cases by Subject

The Dilapidations Handbook

Index of Cases by Subject

The Dilapidations Handbook

Index of Cases by Subject

Law of Property Act 1925 Section 146 - continued
Section 146 (4)

The Dilapidations Handbook

Index of Cases by Subject

The Dilapidations Handbook

Index of Cases by Subject

The Dilapidations Handbook

Index of Cases by Subject

The Dilapidations Handbook

Index of Cases by Subject

The Dilapidations Handbook

Index of Cases by Subject

The Dilapidations Handbook

"keep in thorough repair and good condition"

Lurcott v Wakelv and Wheeler [1911] 1 KB 905   307

"keep the cottage dry and the outside in repair".

Hewitt v Rowlands [1924] All ER 344 Court of Appeal   254

"keep the exterior of the said dwelling house and building in repair".

Howe v Botwood [1913] 2 KB 387   265

"making good all damage thereby occasioned"

Greg v Planque [1936] 1 KB 669   231

"not to repair without Landlord's consent in writing"

Sleafer v Lambeth Metropolitan Borough Council
[1959] 3 All ER 378   412

"pay the council the cost (as certified by The Borough Architects for the time being) of painting in a workmanlike manner every third year of the term all outside wood and metalwork and other external parts of the demised premises and any addition thereto heretofore or usually painted."

Edmonton Borough Council v W.H. Knowles and Son Limited
[1962] 60 LGR 124   179

"repair maintain and keep the inside of the premises in good and tenantable repair and condition and deliver them up at the end of the term damage by fire storm or tempest or other inevitable accident and reasonable wear and tear only accepted".

Manchester Bonded Warehouse Company Limited v Carr
[1880] 5 CPD 507   317

"Repair uphold and maintain"

Lister v Lane and Nesham [1893] 2 QB 212   303

"....repair, uphold support amend and keep the premises when, where and as often as required"

Baylis v LeGros [1858] 4 CB (NS) 537   119

613

Index of Cases by Subject

"so often as need should require well and sufficiently to repair uphold sustain paint glaze cleanse scour the premises (with all needful reparations and cleansings) and to leave the premises in such repair, reasonable wear and tear excepted."

"well and substantially repair uphold support maintain and reinstate where necessary the foundations and party walls of the said messuage or tenement buildings and premises hereby demised (damage by fire excepted) but the lessee shall not be responsible for structural repairs to foundations roof main walls and drains. And also will well and effectually repair lead paint paper cleanse amend and keep the demised premises with their appurtenances and all fixtures, additions and improvements which shall during the said term be erected or made in or upon the said premises with all necessary reparations and amendments whatsoever when where and as often as occasion shall require except structural repairs to the foundations roof main walls and drains".

"well and sufficiently repair"

"when and where and as often as occasion shall require well and sufficiently and substantially repair uphold sustain maintain amend and keep"

...."will during the said term when, where and as often as occasion shall require and to the satisfaction of the lessor or her Surveyor for the time being substantially and effectually repair, uphold, maintain, drain, paint, whitewash and cleanse the premises for the time being held   under this demise".

"wind and watertight"

The Dilapidations Handbook

"whole of the demised premises modern and up to date and in good repair and operating condition"

"repair maintain and keep the inside of the premises in good and tenantable repair and condition and deliver them up at the end of the term damage by fire storm or tempest or other inevitable accident and reasonable wear and tear only accepted".

"repair and maintain and in all respects keep in good and substantial repair and condition the interior of the premises and every part thereof including ..... the pipes and all electrical heating mechanical and ventilation installations therein which exclusively serve the premises"

"Repair uphold and maintain"

"....repair, uphold support amend and keep the premises when, where and as often as required"

"repair, uphold, support, maintain....." the premises "with all necessary reparations and amendments whatsoever".

ROMALPA Clause

Roof

Roof terrace

Index of Cases by Subject

The Dilapidations Handbook

Index of Cases by Subject

The Dilapidations Handbook

Index of Cases by Subject

The Dilapidations Handbook

Index of Cases by Subject

The Dilapidations Handbook

Tenant liable

Damp basement – tenant liable for repairs to tanking which form part of wall. Not liable for damage to expedient damp limiting measures.

Fincar SRL v 109 to 113 Mount Street Management Ltd.
[1998] EGCS 173 9Contract Administrator)   199

"well and substantially repair uphold support maintain and reinstate where necessary the foundations and party walls of the said messuage or tenement buildings and premises hereby demised (damage by fire excepted) but the lessee shall not be responsible for structural repairs to foundations roof main walls and drains. And also will well and effectually repair lead paint paper cleanse amend and keep the demised premises with their appurtenances and all fixtures, additions and improvements which shall during the said term be erected or made in or upon the said premises with all necessary reparations and amendments whatsoever when where and as often as occasion shall require except structural repairs to the foundations roof main walls and drains".

Blundell v Obsdale Limited [1958] EGD 144   132

"Well and sufficiently repair"

Anstruther-Gough-Calthorpe v Mcoscar And Another
In The Court Of Appeal [1924] 1 KB 716   106

**"When and where and as often as occasion
shall require well, sufficiently and substantially
repair, uphold, sustain, maintain, amend and keep"**

Lister v Lane and Nesham [1893] 2 QB 212   303

**"Whole of the demised premises, modern and up
to date and in good repair and operating condition"**

Gooderham & Worts Ltd v Canadian Broadcasting Corporation
[1947] AC 66   218

"Wind and watertight"

Calthorpe v McOscar [1924] 1 KB 716   146

Warren v Keen [1954] 1 QB 15   454

Index of Cases by Subject

Alphabetical
Table of Cases

Index of Cases - Alphabetical

The Dilapidations Handbook

---

[1] I had to include this case, because I instituted these proceedings. It is my claim to fame.

Index of Cases - Alphabetical

The Dilapidations Handbook

Index of Cases - Alphabetical

The Dilapidations Handbook

Index of Cases - Alphabetical

The Dilapidations Handbook

Index of Cases - Alphabetical

The Dilapidations Handbook

Index of Cases - Alphabetical

The Dilapidations Handbook

Index of Cases - Alphabetical

Index

Index

Index

The Dilapidations Handbook

Index

The Dilapidations Handbook

Index

The Dilapidations Handbook